1939: THE LAST SEASON OF PEACE

1939

THE LAST SEASON OF PEACE

Angela Lambert

ISIS
LARGE PRINT

Oxford, England
Santa Barbara, California

First published in Great Britain 1989 by George Weidenfeld & Nicolson Ltd, 91 Clapham High Street, London SW4 7TA

Published in Large Print 1989 by Clio Press, 55 St. Thomas' Street, Oxford OX1 1JG, by arrangement with George Weidenfeld & Nicolson Ltd.

British Library Cataloguing in Publication Data

Lambert, Angela
 1939: the last season of peace.
 1. Great Britain. Debutantes, history
 I. Title
 305.5'2'0941

ISBN 1-85089-370-5
Printed and bound by Hartnolls Ltd., Bodmin, Cornwall
Cover designed by CGS Studios, Cheltenham

to my parents

CONTENTS

ACKNOWLEDGEMENTS

This book wouldn't have been worth writing without the first-hand evidence and reminiscences of those who were young in the Season of 1939. I contacted over a hundred of the debutantes of that year, and more than twenty of their escorts. To all those who answered my letters, a long questionnaire, telephone calls and what seemed — to some of them, at least — a number of impertinent enquiries: my very grateful thanks. My views about the purpose and merit of the Season differ, in most respects, from theirs; and although I have tried to suppress my own opinions and record their testimony, I should like to stress that my views are solely my responsibility.

The first breakthrough in my research came when Mrs Patrick Sandilands (née Madeleine Turnbull) answered a personal column advertisement in *The Times,* in which I had asked debutantes of 1939 to get in touch with me. Her generous, encouraging, amusing letter, filled with breezy anecdotes about her young life half a century ago, was the start of a long correspondence. For all those letters, and for her warmth and hospitality when I visited her in Scotland, my special thanks.

The other person whose prompt and lively reply launched me into my research was Mrs Aidan Long (née Helen Vlasto); and for her insights into the manners and mores of that world, and the contacts she gave me with contemporaries who have remained her friends to this day; and for bringing with her to our meeting her Prince of Wales feathers and two jewelled evening bags, "to give you a whiff of those times"; and for her letters and the permission to quote from her book — for all this, I am most grateful.

I cannot spell out my gratitude one by one to more than a hundred people. My thanks are equally due, however, to all those listed below: they know that I owe this book to their kindness.

For welcoming me into their homes, talking to me at great length and showing me photographs, letters, invitations and other mementoes, I am very grateful to the Hon. Mrs Forbes Adam (née the Hon. Vivien Mosley); Mrs Christopher Bridge (née Dinah Brand); the Hon. Basil Kenworthy; Lady Diana Milles-Lade; the Hon. Lady Beckett (née the Hon. Priscilla Brett); Lady Roderic Pratt (née Ursula Wyndham-Quin); Mrs Marigold Charrington; Lady Mary Dunn; the Hon. Mrs Baring (née the Hon. Sarah Norton); Mrs John Miller (née Christian Grant); Mrs Tony Sheppard (née Rosamund Neave); Tom Vickers; Viscount Hood; Mr Charles Fuller; the Hon. Lady Chichester (née the Hon. Anne Douglas-Scott-Montagu); Mr Ronnie Kershaw; Miss Elizabeth Lowry-Corry; the Countess of Sutherland (née Elizabeth Leveson-Gower); Mrs Archie Mackenzie (née Ann Schuster); Lady Sarah Churchill; Mr Alexander Ballingal; Mr Paul Tanqueray.

For giving me tape-recorded interviews and allowing me to use all material, I am also very grateful to: Mrs

Roderick Heathcoat-Amory (née Sonia Denison); Earl Haig; Lady Cathleen Hudson (née Lady Cathleen Eliot); Mrs Denzil Sebag-Montefiore (née Ruth Magnus); the Earl of Cromer; Lady Anne Mackenzie (née Lady Anne Fitzroy).

I sent questionnaires to a further sixty people whose current names and addresses I had managed to track down, usually with the unstinting help of Mr Peter Townend. Of those who replied, two wrote such wonderfully detailed letters (the rare quality of their recall will be obvious from many quotations in the book) that I must mention them individually. They were Mrs Peter Tabor (née Juliet "Mollie" Acland) and Mrs William Tait Campbell (née Rhoda Walker-Heneage-Vivian). But I am enormously grateful to all the following, who answered my questionnaire, and/or my letters and phone calls, and gave me useful and often very detailed information: the Marquess of Abergavenny; the Hon. Mrs Callinicos (née the Hon. Aedgyth Acton); Countess Raben (née Noreen Bailey); Mrs Charles Morton (née Betty Blake); Mrs John Shaw (née Eve Buxton); Earl Cathcart; Lady Caroline Waterhouse (née Lady Caroline Spencer-Churchill); Margaret, Lady Amherst of Hackney (née Margaret Clifton-Brown); the Hon. Mrs Moore (née the Hon. Sheila Digby); Lady Foley (née Ghislaine Dresselhuys); Lady Gillian Anderson (née Lady Gillian Drummond); Lady Bridget Miller Mundy (née Lady Bridget Elliot); Mrs Carrick-Smith (née Lindsey Furneaux); Lord Glendevon; Mrs Michael Gordon-Watson (née Thalia Gordon); Mrs Millard (née Lola Grixoni); Lady Brigid Ness (née Lady Brigid

Guinness); Lady Gibson-Watt (née Diana Hambro); Lady Elizabeth Bonsor (née Elizabeth Hambro); the Countess of Cromer (née the Hon. Esmé Harmsworth); Lady Desmond Chichester (née Felicity Harrison); Miss Helen Hoare; Mrs M. O. Pease (née Virginia Hughes Onslow); Mrs Peter Dean (née Cynthia Joseph); the Hon. Lady Hood (née the Hon. Ferelith Kenworthy); Mr Anthony Loch; Lady Jean Leslie Melville; Mrs Peter Green (née Susan Meyrick); the Duchess of Northumberland (née Lady Elizabeth Montagu Douglas Scott); Miss Barbara Murray; Mrs Daphne Seidler (née Daphne Pearson); Lady Killearn (née Nadine Pilcher); Mrs Charles D'Oyly (née Mary Pollock); Mrs Jack Harrison-Cripps (née Margaret Proby); Mrs R. M. Chaplin (née Susan Ridley); Lord Savile; Mrs Diana Collins (née Diana Trafford); Mr George Turnbull; Lady Aldenham (née Mary Tyser); Mrs Rhona Peyton-Jones (née Rhona Wood).

I am also indebted to Mr John Titman, the Secretary to the Lord Chamberlain's Office, for his help in identifying debutantes who were presented in 1939.

Two particular debts remain. The first is to Mr Peter Townend, editor of Burke's *Peerage* and Social Editor of the *Tatler*. His encyclopaedic knowledge of the British upper classes, not merely over the last fifty years, but stretching back two or three centuries, never ceased to amaze me. He was extraordinarily generous in placing this expertise at my disposal. He allowed me to come to his flat and consult his personal archives of the *Bystander*. He took dozens of telephone calls from me, answering questions which ranged from the most ignorant to the most obscure. He checked my manuscript for correct nomenclature, and saved me from several howlers. The howlers that remain are all my own. The specialized knowledge is all his.

In addition, Mrs Peter Green (née Susan Meyrick) sent me a treasure through the post, in the form of her wonderful scrapbook for the decade 1936-46, which kept me and my family enthralled for hours. It gave me the atmosphere of the period, by way of the ephemera that she had carefully preserved, which was invaluable. I am most grateful to her for entrusting her precious album to me.

Finally, for the spadework in getting together the evidence for this book and then presenting it in an orderly form, my thanks go to Miss Isobel Beney, for her help with transcription of tapes, and to my daughter, Carolyn Butler, who typed the manuscript immaculately . . . and twice.

ANGELA LAMBERT
London, January-August 1988

CHAPTER
ONE

Becoming a Deb is a Difficult Matter: Who Did the Season, and Why?

They were called Guinevere and Georgina and Ghislaine and June, the debutantes of 1939; Patty and Betty and Dorothy and Nan. One of them, an unfortunate girl for reasons quite apart from her name, was called Doreen. There were, as the *Daily Mail*'s gossip column pointed out on 19 May in its account of Queen Charlotte's Ball, a number of unusual names that year: Osla, Lilita, Quenelda, Yolanda, Merelina, Isalina, Freydis, Magdalen and Colin were just a few of them — names that might have featured in a debutante parody of T. S. Eliot's *The Naming of Cats,* if debs read poetry, or wrote parodies. There were names redolent of the thirties, like Pearl and Susan (which they pronounced "Syoosan") and Anthea and Jean, Rhoda and Joan and Audrey and Muriel. There were, as always among the English upper classes, names like Elizabeth,

Mary, Diana, Sarah. They had double-barrelled surnames like Bowes-Lyon, Leveson-Gower (pronounced "Looson-Gore", and woe betide anyone who did not know it), Spencer-Churchill and Windsor-Clive: names that, to the initiated, immediately conjured up titles, country seats and many thousands of acres. Ten of them bore titles, and so did about a third of their mothers, especially if one includes Hons.

So who were they, the debutantes of 1939?

All of them were born in the years immediately after the end of the First World War. Seventeen was the earliest age at which a girl might be presented, eighteen was more usual, so this was the generation of the early 1920s. They had grown up never knowing anything but peace, although their parents were deeply scarred by war.

They nearly all shared the same background: that of the English upper classes. They were aristocrats, or landed gentry, or at the very least they came from families who had been wealthy and established for a couple of generations. Few of them were Roman Catholic, almost none was Jewish. The girls who did not share this background of wealth, land or title (preferably all three) were the unfortunates.

The word "snob" has changed its meaning in the last fifty years. It used to mean someone looking *up*; it has come to mean someone looking *down,* defined in the OED Supplement (1986) as "One who despises those who are considered inferior in rank, attainment or taste"[1] — particularly in the English class system, rank. In the older meaning of the word, the English upper classes had no need for snobbery. They constituted an elite which believed itself to be uniquely fitted to rule, whether as builders of the Empire, members of both Houses of Parliament or landowners. The class war which raged in the 1930s scarcely troubled them. Born to superiority, possessed of the looks that they believed resulted from many generations of breeding (they always cited racehorses to prove their point) and the taste that came from living with beautiful things bequeathed by their forebears, they were not snobbish. It hardly ever occurred to them that anyone else could matter. They valued beautiful manners among their own kind. To everyone else they were polite — because "a gentleman is never rude unintentionally".

In time, however, it became possible for a socially ambitious mother and a very rich father to buy their daughter's way into the Season. They could pay a lady to sponsor their child, present her at Court and hold a dance for her. It was well known that the Countess of Clancarty and Lady St John of Bletso, for instance, charged around £2,000 to bring a girl out. Discreet advertisements would appear in *The Times*: "Peeress would chaperone debutante — every advantage", followed by a box number. Here is how one deb of that era remembers these two:

Old Lady Clancarty was a bit of a mystery. She was rather a battle-axe, and rumour had it that she had been the Earl's cook before he married her. Her face was set in those hardened lines that develop on women's faces if they have to work all their lives, so perhaps it was true that she had been his housekeeper, or something of the sort. She wasn't unpleasant, just very uncommunicative. She had a hatchet jaw and always looked tense. However, despite all this, Alma Le Poer Trench [Lady

3

Clancarty's daughter] and her two brothers were all tall, charming and good-looking, so I suspect they may have been the offspring of the first marriage. It was very hard luck on the girls who had to resort to paid presenters: not that people were unkind to them, I think, but just that they must have felt so out of place. I remember one afternoon in 1939 we ran into Lady Clancarty at Hurlingham, and as we walked along a path with her and Alma, one of her poor, unattractive, clumsy-looking protégées, a girl with a north-country accent, trailed along behind. I remember trying to chat her up, but it was such hard going that I soon gave up.

Lady St John of Bletso was quite the opposite, except that she too was enigmatic. I remember sitting next to her round her fireside at Ennismore Gardens after dinner one night, trying to read what was behind that self-satisfied face and wondering what it was like to be brought out by her. She was small and doll-like. Her blonded hair and enamelled skin gave her an impenetrable appearance, and she hardly bothered to speak to any of us.

One of Lady St Johns protégées that Season (they were known disparagingly as "the Bletsoes" or "one of the Blets") was a girl called Doreen Davison. Twenty years later — even though presentation at Court had ended in 1958 — Lady St John was still sponsoring debutantes, parents still subjecting daughters to social humiliation (for of course everyone *knew*) in the hope that they might encounter an impoverished peer whose family fortunes had dwindled to the point where he was prepared to marry a girl whose parents were recently rich. It had worked, after all, for several generations of American heiresses. Occasionally it still worked. One ex-deb said,

There were perhaps half a dozen mamas each Season who were rich (very rich!), *nouveaux riches*, and were on the prowl to find very eligible but perhaps impecunious husbands for their daughters. One very aggressive one had two daughters and a son for whom she, triumphantly, found members of the aristocracy. One is now a countess, another married a baronet of long lineage, and one of her granddaughters is married to a duke!

Parents paid £2,000, not simply so that their daughter could curtsey to the King and Queen, but in the hope that she would be one of the lucky few who married well. Some of these daughters of *nouveaux riches*, social-climbing parents rose to the challenge and even enjoyed it; for others, as Vivien Mosley (now Mrs Forbes Adams) recalls, it was a dreadful experience:

I think it was complete and unadulterated hell for a great many of them and it was wicked and cruel of their parents to do it. But I do think there was another lot who simply revelled in it, and were actually only too delighted to be pushed. But I was aware that there was a nucleus of girls who obviously had an absolutely beastly time, didn't want to be in that position and were just being forced to, for what even in those days seemed to me to be absolutely ludicrous motives. I remember one or two who actually wept; but besides them there were a lot who spent time in the Ladies. Though even there, some of them were having an awfully jolly time — they just thought, well, fish my mother, if she's making me do this and I'm not being frightfully successful, then I'll go and have a good time in the Ladies' loo with my chum! And they did: and Mum or the chaperone was left sitting on her gold chair looking agonized about where her daughter was because she wasn't being swept round the floor.

The parents' motives weren't just the hope that their daughter would get a good husband — although some *did* — but to move into a world that they, the parents, couldn't have got their girl in amongst. The girls for whom it didn't work were the ones who didn't want that. But they knew there was an awful lot on their back — it was costing a fortune — they were disappointing their parents' high hopes — absolute torture.

Marrying well was the *raison d'être* of the Season. One of the escorts said bluntly: "The Season was invented by the match-making mothers to put their daughters into the marriage market, and to get the biggest catch possible, preferably a millionaire duke. It was the mothers who invented and perpetuated the Season." Many of the debs of 1939 disagree, preferring not to define it so blatantly. Nicholas Mosley (now Lord Ravensdale) put it thus: "The run-up to war during 1939 coincided with what was known as the "coming out" of my sister Vivien: this was the complex of rituals by which eighteen-year-old girls were initiated into membership of the upper-class tribe."[2]

"Ritual", "initiate", "tribe" — the English upper classes, like any other closed social system, preserved their exclusivity by means of customs, codes and language which few outsiders could emulate. These social rituals began long before a girl was presented at Court. From cradle to christening, from nursery to schoolroom, from holidays to finishing school, the fledgling debutante of 1939 had already taken part in a series of rigidly prescribed social conventions that had changed little over the last hundred years. It was because, in a sense, the *parvenues* were entering this world eighteen years after the other debs — who had inhabited it since birth — that they faced such an ordeal. Lady Cathleen Eliot said: "Family was *essential;* and to debs from good families the rest simply didn't count. — They would be ignored. You know: somebody looks at you and you just look at them expressionless and your eyes move on. Like that."

The Times used to be called the noticeboard of the upper classes and in its columns, preferably listed under the Court Circular, births and christenings were announced in an unvarying formula. "The Hon. Mrs So-and-so has given birth to a daughter at Queen Charlotte's Hospital" (or some exclusive nursing home) would be followed a few weeks later by "Princess Helena Victoria [or some other exalted personage] stood sponsor to Major and the Hon. Mrs So-and-so's infant daughter, who was christened at —— church. The Bishop of x officiated and the child was named Elizabeth Frances Laetitia. In addition to Princess Helena Victoria the godparents were ..." Details of the christening robe would follow, mentioning that it was of Brussels or Honiton lace and perhaps referring to previous occasions when it had been used. These announcements launched the baby girl upon her preordained path. Her names would be those of her most important godmother, her mother or one of her grandmothers, and perhaps her wealthiest maiden aunt. Her god-parents would have been selected with an eye to the status they could bestow upon the baby.

After this she retreated into anonymity for some years. Her care was handed over to a nanny, preferably one who had been with the family for a long time, ideally having nursed her mother as well; and one or more nursery maids. Between 1921 and 1939 there were still between a quarter and half a million nannies in England and Wales, and about one and a quarter million domestic servants remained in 1939. Nannies were often rampant snobs, and they instilled an acute awareness of the details of English upper-class behaviour into their young charges:

> It took many years for an outsider to master the complex, subtle distinctions, the nuances of accent, attitude, behaviour and misbehaviour, which went into, indeed go into, that living, changing thing, English upper-class snobbism And Nannies were outsiders. Suddenly they found themselves thrown into a world in which the very air was electric with snobbery. As a result, they had to invent snobbish distinctions ... nice (that is upper-class) children never whisper, have white knicker linings, and Chilprufe next to the skin. Vulgar children (always vulgar, it was common to say common) said Hip, hip, hooray; "we" said Hurrah.[3]

Jessica Mitford, in her autobiography *Hons and Rebels,* conveys exactly the same impression of a closed world:

> Swinbrook [the house built by her father for his family] had many aspects of a fortress or citadel of mediaeval times. From the point of view of its inmates it was self-contained in the sense that it was neither necessary nor, generally, possible to leave the premises for any of the normal human pursuits ... From the point of view of outsiders, entry, in the rather unlikely event that they might seek it, was an impossibility.

According to my father, outsiders included not only Huns, Frogs, Americans, blacks and all other foreigners, but also other people's children ... in fact, the whole teeming population of the earth's surface .... .

Unity, Debo and I were thrown much on our own resources. As a lost tribe, separated from its fellow men, gradually develops distinctive characteristics of language, behaviour, outlook, so we developed idiosyncrasies that would no doubt have made us seem a little eccentric to other children of our age. Even for England, in those far-off days of the middle 'twenties, ours was not exactly a conventional upbringing.[4]

Of course, Jessica Mitford may be exaggerating the foibles of her upbringing, just as her family is an exaggerated version of the English upper class. But the tribal nature of such an upbringing, its narrowness, its ritualistic behaviour, and the codes according to which it lived and spoke and ate and played, were real enough.

This world opened up more for girls when it became normal practice to send daughters to school, sometimes even to boarding school, as had long been the case with their brothers. Girls need not be clever, but they must be "agreeable": that ubiquitous upper-class word that meant, in the case of a child, nicely mannered and not a show-off. Other accomplishments were far more important than cleverness. All country children rode and hunted, and girls as well as boys were expected to be "plucky" on the hunting field. Skiing was not yet a universal pastime, but playing a decent game of tennis was considered essential. Both sexes would have gone to dancing classes from an early age, probably about six or seven years old, while more recently Madame Vacani or

Miss Ballantine would have drilled them in the art of the full Court curtsey. This tricky manoeuvre entailed crooking one knee behind the other and sinking to the floor as low as you could go while keeping your back straight and ensuring that you could get up again in the same graceful movement. It was as difficult as it sounds and everyone dreaded falling over — though there is no record of anyone actually having done so. The last and still the most important attribute of the aspiring debutante was to be pretty. It would be nice if she were witty as well — no, not witty exactly, but amusing: the grown-up equivalent of being agreeable as a child. The fathers would describe a lively, good-humoured girl as amusing; the mothers would call her charming; and her contemporaries would say "she's great fun".

It is extremely difficult to estimate precisely how many girls were presented in 1939, and how many of those "did" the Season thoroughly, going to dances and parties almost every night and attending the major social events. The Lord Chamberlain's Office lists 1,657 "general circle" presentations in 1939, with an additional 175 from the Diplomatic Corps. But of the former number, a high proportion — more than a third — were women being represented upon marriage, or when they changed their style (meaning that they, or their husbands, took a different title). If one assumes that between 900 and 1,000 of the "general circle" presentations were young girls "coming out" — being presented for the first time — this gives a number at least three times higher than the number doing the Season twenty-five or thirty years later. But in 1939, as so many of the debutantes of that year have stressed, it was taken for granted that *everybody* from "the right sort of families" came out. Girls had no choice.

From that total of 900 or a thousand girls, only about one-third wanted, or could afford, to do the Season in the full sense. Many were simply presented, and then went straight back home to the country and carried on their normal lives, attending a few local dances perhaps, but otherwise taking no part in the round of the summer's events. In a few other cases, girls did the Season, but without being presented. Lady Cathleen Eliot, daughter of the sixth Earl of St Germans, was — rather surprisingly — one such. She was never presented at Court ("too expensive", she says); but her name and picture were frequently in Society magazines, and although she did not have a dance of her own, she was invited to most of the Season's parties — her title ensured that.

One hundred and three girls announced their dances in *The Times'* weekly Social column; but here again these were not the only dances given or even the grandest ones. Thus one can only make an informed guess; and on this basis it is probable that between 200 and 400 girls took part in a ceaseless social whirl that can have left them no time for anything else. Among these was an inner circle of about a hundred girls who, in the absence of a single, outstanding "Deb of the Year" (a concept invented by the media), would all have been popular, attractive, well bred and (mostly) rich. Inevitably, it is with that one hundred that this book mainly deals. Most of the rest flared briefly, like fireworks, in one moment of glory, and then vanished again.

There were 228 debutantes at Queen Charlotte's Ball at Grosvenor House on 17 May, and five duchesses: of Marlborough, Buccleuch, Montrose, Grafton and Sutherland. Because of this unusual plethora of duchesses, guests were asked to wear tiaras, white gloves and decorations. "In this way we expect to get people to dress up again and get away from their present gas-mask mood," said the *Daily Mail*'s diarist Neronically. Analysis of nearly half of them — the 103 debs whose names featured in *The Times*' list of the Season's dances — shows that 37 had titled mothers or sponsors. A great many debs were presented not by their own mothers, but by their most well-connected female relative. This was not the same thing as having a paid presenter: far from it. Viscountess Astor, for example, gave a dance for her niece Dinah Brand: in this case because Dinah's mother, the former Phyllis Langhorne, had died in 1937. A girl might be sponsored by her grandmother or, like Lady Mary Pratt, by both her grandmothers: *her* mother, the Countess of Brecknock, was Lady-in-Waiting to the Duchess of Kent, which probably left little time for the rigours of a deb's mother's social round. Of these 103 debs, at least 42 had parents listed in *Who's Who,* while in the case of another 14 the family was listed. All titled people were automatically included in *Who's Who,* while Debrett's *Peerage and Baronetage* made no pretence of valuing merit or achievement. A title was all that was required, or some family connection, however remote, with a title. One of the most anxious chores for girls not born into the "upper crust" must have been the hours spent poring over Burke and Debrett to ensure that they knew by heart the ramifications of the family trees of all dukes, marquesses, earls, viscounts and barons. If they aspired to marry into the peerage they would have to learn by rote what other girls had imbibed at Nanny's knee, or from their parents' gossip.

Another infallible indicator of gentle birth was holding one's coming-out dance at home: be it London house or country seat. More than thirty debutantes on *The Times'* list (not necessarily the ones with titled mothers) gave dances at home. Even in 1939 there was some residual snobbery about entertaining in a public place. Times had changed since the nineteenth century, when every aristocratic family had a mansion in London where they could entertain several hundred guests. Lady Alexandra Metcalfe, Marquess Curzon's youngest daughter, recalls with something like disbelief today that when she was a little girl, in the years just before the First World War, she and her friends would play games in their parents' *ballrooms.* After that war, very many of those great houses were sold; a private ballroom became a rarity; and all except the very richest were forced to hold coming-out dances in hotels, or in one of the remaining large houses, like 16 Bruton Street, that were owned by caterers and hired out for the evening. By far the most popular single venue for debs' dances was 6 Stanhope Gate, a house bordering Park Lane upon whose site the Playboy Club used to stand. In those days it was owned by Searcy's, the large catering company, who ran it as Gunter's Tearooms during the day and a ballroom in the evenings. Of those 103 dances listed in *The Times'* diary for the Season, no fewer than 11 were held at 6 Stanhope Gate. After that, the most

13

fashionable place for one's dance was Claridge's, followed by the Hyde Park Hotel, the Dorchester and the Berkeley.

The cost of these parties was astronomical. The food and drink alone would have cost about 30 shillings a head, or £1.50, to say nothing of the cost of massed banks of flowers, a fashionable dance band, and evening dresses for the debutante, her mother and her sisters. All this meant that a dance which cost under £1,000 was a modest affair: yet in those days £1,000 would have been a very generous annual salary for a professional man, and wealth undreamed of for anyone from the working class.

A dance given at home would have been marginally less expensive and had much more social cachet: "The refinement of private-house entertainment was of a different order. It was much less vulgar than a public place like a hotel, because you couldn't buy your way in." Once a hotel dance was under way, any couple who sported the appropriate clothes and voices could stroll in from the street and gatecrash, as many did. No gatecrashers, however, could have strolled unnoticed into Mary Windsor-Clive's dance at 15 Hyde Park Gardens, or that of Rhoda Walker-Heneage-Vivian a few doors down at Number 8, for the family retainers would have asked them politely to produce an invitation or leave. Therein lay the prestige: giving a dance in one's own house, among one's own furniture and paintings and servants, was the clearest possible proof that the girl was a "real" deb, emerging to take her rightful position in a society which knew her parents and had noticed the social stepping-stones that had brought her to this point.

Since the Season was expensive, exhausting and a social ordeal for all but the most poised, why did anyone — parents or daughters — submit to it? Setting aside for a moment its real purpose, to introduce eligible young people to one another in a safe and enjoyable setting, what other function might it fulfil? Certainly most of the debutantes, and their escorts, claim fifty years later that it was fun. They usually go on to qualify this by saying that it was extremely tiring. During the height of the Season, from late April until the end of July, a debutante would need all her youth and stamina.

Lady Turnbull's daughter Madeleine, who had been a deb a couple of years earlier, remembers:

> There were far more dances than in post-war days; four or five a week at least, and very often one went to more than one dance a night. Then there were countless fork luncheon and drink parties. It was all quite hard work! — especially if one had to go to two or three luncheon parties on the same day — and partook of a course at each!

A girl and her mother, or some other chaperone, would rarely get home before two in the morning; only to rise again by nine or ten o'clock — "because it was inconsiderate to the servants to keep them waiting when one's bed had to be made and the bedroom tidied". However frivolous dancing and making conversation may be considered, they can be quite taxing, particularly to young people who know they are constantly being evaluated, both by their contemporaries and by the older generation. Chaperones —

15

usually mothers — sat around the room and watched like hawks. Rosamund Neave (now Mrs Tony Sheppard) remembers that well:

> There was a lot of snobbery about and people were angling for the best match. You saw the chaperones and the dowagers in their tiaras looking through their lorgnettes to see if somebody was pretty or not and whether they thought she would be a nice person for their son or her cousin's friend or whoever it was. There was always a certain amount of that. It meant that some of the girls were very keen to be asked by Lord So-and-So to dance. My mother always got frightfully excited and would ask, "Who did you meet did you say, darling? Oh, Lord Halifax's son. Oh yes, of course, very nice, yes." So Mummy was slightly snobby but I wasn't interested in all that; I just wanted to have fun.

Faces were scrutinized for everything from family likeness to the presence (or, more likely, absence) of make-up. Clothes were criticized: where from? who made it? how much did it cost? is it new — altered — borrowed — passed down? Girls lived in fear of being caught out in a solecism like having a strap showing or — nightmare — a knicker elastic giving way. Everyone carried a chain of tiny gold safety-pins hidden away in her evening purse, in case energetic dancing called for immediate repairs, and cloakroom ladies had needle and cotton to stitch up snagged hems. Young girls — many of them over-protected and little more than children — were very much aware that they were on show; that "coming out" meant (as it does in quite a different context today) submitting oneself to public scrutiny. It is too crude to liken it to a cattle market; circling the paddock before a race would be more appropriate.

The Season, then, was a forum in which to see and be seen by perhaps two thousand people, of whom several hundred were contemporaries of both sexes, and the remainder were parents, family, friends. It was a forum which gave a girl a chance to prove herself and make her mark in a few short months, knowing that whatever impression she created might remain for the rest of her life. Could such a formidable exposure of oneself possibly be called an *enjoyable* experience?

For those debutantes who were poised, pretty and beautifully turned out, yes, it must have been enjoyable — a game, a nightly parade which would be exhilarating to those who knew they were among the front runners. A young woman recently liberated from school or finishing school could well have revelled in the attention that suddenly focused upon her, after years of Nanny saying primly, "Nobody's going to be looking at *you*, dear!" Suddenly all that had changed. Seamstresses knelt at her feet with pins between their lips, adjusting her hem or smoothing her seams; milliners set wide-brimmed picture hats or witty little confections cleverly askew at just the angle to accentuate her cheekbones: her parents and her sisters frowned and judged and finally approved. Goodness, it must have been intoxicating . . . for some.

But for the girls who knew themselves to be less well endowed with a pretty face, a slender figure, a generous papa and an understanding mother, it must have been like stumbling dazzled into a spotlight. The girl with bad skin; the fat girl; the one who had not outgrown her clumsiness or mastered her shyness; the girl whose mother had no dress sense or whose father was penny-pinching; above all, the girl who knew that she did not fit into the social milieu to which her parents aspired — for these girls it must have been a daily and nightly ordeal, three or four months of it, that they dreaded in advance and loathed when it happened. Interviews with ex-debs (none of whom admits to having been in this position of social ignominy herself) suggest that a number of girls did indeed hate their Season:

> There were always some girls crying in the Ladies; and a few who would spend practically the entire evening there. Some girls were definitely cold-shouldered by the others; mostly because they lacked personality and confidence and just couldn't carry it off. That's why it was such a good training. You had to learn to be snubbed — you had to learn how to cope with not being a big social success, not getting all the gorgeous young men. If you hadn't got the polish, you soon learned. Otherwise you'd spend the evening talking to the cloakroom attendant. There was a lot of cruelty and a lot of competitiveness, and that meant a lot of humiliation. Some girls suffered agonies. Some of the mothers had no idea what they were exposing their girls to. They just wanted them to have a good time. There's a sort of gallantry — almost a heroism — about the upper crust, and these girls didn't want to fail their mothers.

The Season was, and was meant to be, a social testing ground. It taught very young girls — much younger, in terms of worldliness, than today's sophisticated eighteen-year-olds — how to behave gracefully in a crowd of strangers. It taught them how to make conversation, even if much of it was frivolous. It taught them discipline: a discipline that stood some of them in very good stead during the years that followed. "It was an endurance test," said one deb, who nevertheless adored her Season, "a real ordeal." It taught good manners, in the widest sense of the word; not merely how to enter and leave a room unselfconsciously, bestowing your hellos and goodbyes with charm and warmth (which is harder than it may sound), but how to deal with the "difficult customers". Every dance had its quota of awkward young men and lecherous uncles, jealous mothers and crotchety chaperones, unhappy or exhausted young women. At its best, the Season taught a schoolgirl, cosseted and over-protected, how to handle all these situations with tact.

> We were being groomed for a role. It was a tough little world too. The system gave you a little more polish and you emerged with a little more grace, a little more cynicism.
>
> To be frank, it either made you or broke you. If anything was the proper training ground for a lifetime as the wife of an ambassador or some such — role then this was the best there was. You had to be able to remain sure of yourself, keep up conversation with people who bored you, and physically — cope with an unending round of new faces, new situations and learning that other girls and some men aren't always kind — and how to cope with the chilly, ambitious and ruthless real world away from home.[5]

The Season must have been a testing ground for parents, too. How had their girl turned out? How was the son and heir shaping up? How were they doing, as custodians of the family name, the houses, the land? Had they got rid of the Rubens or the Gainsborough to make ends meet? Could they still manage to put on a good show for their daughter's coming-out dance? These questions would have been more discreetly murmured, but everyone was interested to see how well their contemporaries had survived the years of agricultural depresssion and the roller-coaster stock markets of the turn of the decade.

For the British upper classes were changing, and the Season was the perfect opportunity to judge who was most affected by these changes. The upper, upper echelons of the aristocracy remained the same: the Devonshires, the Marlboroughs, the Northumberlands and Westminsters — they were not feeling the pinch. But people a few rungs lower down felt it. Within three years of the ending of the First World War, a quarter of the land in the country — some six million acres — had changed ownership. The slaughter of the sons of the nobility during the war; the agricultural depression which preceded it for several decades; the introduction of death duties — all these had drained capital, not fatally, but perceptibly.

The rich were still rich — extremely rich. In 1938 the top 0.4 per cent of families earned nearly 12 per cent of the income for the entire population: and, inevitably, most of their wealth came from unearned income rather than salary. Or, to put it another way, by 1936 the top 1 per cent of wealth-owners (as distinct from earners) held 56 per cent of the nation's wealth. The remaining 44 per cent was shared out between the other 99 per cent of the population. But the most relevant fact about extreme wealth is that it is determined very largely by inheritance. Most very rich people were born rich, they married rich, and they died rich. Aristocrats did not make money by their own efforts; but they guarded and increased what their forefathers had amassed. This was done by careful deployment of one's assets. Money was surrounded by pallisades of accountants and stock-brokers, trustees and tax experts and financial advisers; property by farm managers who were expert in administering large estates and stockmen who knew about pedigree herds and trainers who knew about racehorses; possessions by picture and furniture dealers who valued and advised in the buying and — more rarely, in those days — selling of works of art. Was a man who took such care of his property likely to leave his *daughter* to the mercies of any glamorous adventurer?

The family was of prime importance, for it preserved the bloodline, to which the upper classes attached an almost mystic significance, and which they believed explained their innate superiority. In its purest sense, it can be seen in the reverence accorded to royal lineage, based on the notion of the divine right of kings. This was perhaps the origin of the belief that the bloodline is an almost sacred inheritance, to be guarded and revered, not tainted by common stock. The blue blood of the nobility was a metaphor that they themselves took very seriously.*

* The expression derives from the *sangre azul* claimed by certain families of Castile, as being uncontaminated by Moorish, Jewish or other admixture; probably founded on the blueness of the veins of people of fair complexion (*Shorter Oxford Dictionary*). Thus racism and anti-Semitism are also inherent in the idea of blue-bloodedness.

The pursuit of wealth was the pursuit of status, not merely for oneself but for one's family. In the last resort the ultimate motivation was a dynastic one: to found a family, to endow them splendidly enough to last for ever, and to enjoy a vicarious eternal life in the seed of one's loins.[6]

Now that wealth was no longer concentrated in the hands of the landed aristocracy, but distributed around a larger — and widening — class of industrialists, financiers and entrepreneurs, it was all the more important that old wealth should control the appropriate setting within which to assess and perhaps ally itself with the young generation of the newly wealthy.

This change in the location of wealth had happened gradually over the previous hundred years. The Industrial Revolution and the rise of technology and communications created a new class of millionaires: families like the Tennants, whose fortune was based originally on a process for making better starch. At a time when laundresses starched acres of table linen, bed linen, cotton petticoats, servants' uniforms and so on, a better starch could be the starting point for a business empire, augmented later on by shrewd investment in mining, railways and banking. Thus Charles Tennant — later Sir Charles Tennant, Bart — made not just himself but all his descendants wealthy, and saw his daughters marry into the aristocracy, while his son entered the peerage and was created Baron Glenconner. Such rich and powerful families simply could not be dismissed for being "in trade". If the first generation was in trade, the second was in Society and the third (if not sooner) was in Debrett.

These new rich families were gradually assimilated by the old aristocracy. After the First World War, yet newer families sprang up whose wealth commanded respect. They too wished to enter the Establishment (a word not used in this sense until the 1960s to describe the class that holds power in government and the City, and also controls social conventions of behaviour and modes of thought); the Establishment needed them. Where better to size up their manners and suitability than during the rigours of the Season?

The English upper classes determined and mono-polized the desirable canons of taste and standards of behaviour and this — class consciousness, in a word, or, more crudely, class snobbery — was the source of their power. No other class ever had the confidence to challenge it, and none created an alternative. If the upper classes pursued a way of life based on country estates and London clubs, on grouse-shooting and hunting during the winter months and dancing and racing during the summer — why then, so would the aspiring upper classes. The new Victorian millionaires moved out of their northern industrial cities, the places which had made them what they were and had made them rich, to settle their families on huge country estates. Their children were schooled in manners and accents that must have been very different from their parents'. They tried to forget, and to persuade others to forget, that they owed all they had to trade.

In the twentieth century this pattern was made easier by the enforced sale of land by the aristocracy and country gentry. The land that the new rich bought was the very same land the old rich had owned. They thus acquired, almost by osmosis, the one thing that money could not buy: ancestry. What they actually bought was merely the appearance (it could not be the reality) of continuity; the illusion of a rooted, continuous bloodline. The hold that the upper classes were able to maintain over people richer (in some cases) and with more energy and newer ideas than themselves was based on tradition and custom, on family trees that could be traced back for generations. The very same attributes in Europe intimidate rich Americans today. For all their money and vigour, they cannot match the history.

The infiltration of this new class was recognized by the honours system, another way of taking on the protective colouring of the aristocracy. Nancy Mitford made the point crisply in *Noblesse Oblige*:

> A lord does not have to be born to his position, and, indeed, can acquire it through political activities, or the sale of such unaristocratic merchandise as beer, but though he may not be a U-speaker* he becomes an aristocrat as soon as he receives his title. The Queen turns him from socialist leader, or middle-class businessman, into a nobleman, and his outlook from now on will be the outlook of an aristocrat.[7]

The desire of the *nouveaux riches* to have their achievements validated by a title ensured that they would conform to the patterns of behaviour laid down by those they wished to join. During the twenty years

---

* U-speaker means a member of the upper class using both words and pronunciation — which — often for no apparent reason — are accepted as correct by the upper classes, and are often used by them to detect aspirants.

between 1918 and 1938, eighty-one new titles were created, including six earls and viscounts. (This excludes the enormous number of knighthoods with which Lloyd George was thought to have debased the currency.) A majority of peerages went to former MPS (ensuring their conformity to the prevailing party line) but industry, finance and commerce accounted for nearly as many. The peerage by now reflected a much wider element in Society than merely its landed interests. As well as helping the new rich to disappear into the ranks of the old after a couple of generations, this form of patronage also made sure that real power stayed concentrated in the hands of a very small number of like-minded people. Thus the grip of the old upper class upon the nation's wealth was not threatened by the influx of a new upper class whose wealth was separate from, and independent of, theirs. The best way to secure this was for the two classes to intermarry. The old family conferred its status and traditions upon the new — or newish — family, receiving in return enough money to ensure that its privileged position would be upheld for future generations.

This, then, was the purpose of the Season. Since arranged marriages could not be foisted upon young members of the upper class — a century before, perhaps, but not any longer — they needed an environment which offered the high probability that within it they would meet the kind of partners whom their parents would have chosen for them; and an environment which excluded all other kinds. "Never marry for money: love where money is" mothers used to tell their daughters. It is a fine distinction; but it preserves the illusion of freedom to make a romantic choice. And so the Season did not merely reflect or display the structure of the English upper classes — it actually controlled and renewed it.

For the time being, those pretty, artless social butterflies, the debs of 1939, might flutter from dance floor to cloakroom, from Ascot to country house, sometimes in tears and sometimes in triumph. But the breeze that wafted them — although they are reluctant even now to admit as much — was a gale far more powerful than their youthful desire to have fun.

Where, in this delicately strung social web, did the established (as opposed to the new) middle classes fit in, if at all? Surprisingly, perhaps, there were a few middle-class girls taking part in the Season, and an impression persists that some of them really did have fun. They were in a sense *hors de combat.* Neither rich nor securely "upper crust", they were usually there because their mothers had been presented and had then married men who took them a notch or two down the social scale. In this way, a daughter of modest background might still have access to rich cousins and their cast-offs. If she were an engaging girl — pretty, unselfconscious, vivacious — her mother's family might decide it was worth the girl doing a Season, "just for the experience, of course". She would not be expected to make a "catch", yet she did, at one remove, belong. A handful, a dozen of such girls could be found each year: "You could do the Season as cheaply or as expensively as you wished. I remember two sisters, poor as church mice, who had enormous fun." Or, in the words of an

American popular song, "Nice people with nice manners, but they've got no money at all."

The Season began "officially" on Friday, 28 April 1939, the day of the Private View of the Royal Academy's Summer Exhibition. *The Times* next day carried a long article describing the fashionable women who thronged the galleries, less to see the paintings (it was a mediocre year in any case) than to be seen to be there. Miss Valerie Cole was dressed in "powder blue, with a very full net veil trimming her large blue hat"; while Miss Sarah Dashwood wore "a raspberry red frock and a white straw hat trimmed with cherries"; and Miss Barbadee Knight was in two shades of brown.

There were other names too in *The Times* that day, also jostling for attention but less likely to get it. They were in the Personal column — German and Austrian Jews, desperate to find a sponsor who might offer them the chance to escape from Hitler: like the German-Jewish couple, "wife good housekeeper, husband perfect motorist, able to do any other work . . . offers to H. Reckerwell, Hamburg"; or the German Jew aged thirty-six, "well educated, best family, asks for opportunity to learn handicrafts . . . H. Knopf, Berlin"; or, most nakedly of all, "Jew, 66, educated, BEGS FOR PERMIT. Singer, Vienna". Under the Domestic Situations Required column there were eleven people wishing to be companions and governesses, six offering themselves as housekeepers and several seeking posts as ladies' maids, like the German-Jewish girl "still in Berlin". Their chances of being noticed were not nearly as good as the smart Society women's whose fashions

27

were described in detail, although for the Jews being noticed was a matter of life and death.

The column headed In Memoriam, On Active Service, contained the names of four men who had died less than twenty-five years before. Douglas Amery Parkes, who died of wounds, remembered by his mother. Roy Bullen, of the King's Royal Rifles, who was killed in France on 29 April 1916. Major Hubert Dunsterville Harvey-Kelly, DSO, ("Baz"), of the Royal Flying Corps. And, finally, Frederick Leycester Barwell, also of the Royal Flying Corps, "killed in aerial combat when attacking five or six enemy aeroplanes single-handed". He had been twenty-two years old. His proud and grieving parents quoted in the memorial notice an extract from the enemy report:

> The combat lasted a full half hour; all the troops in the neighbourhood came out and watched this thrilling fight: the British airman persistently sought combat and half a dozen times appeared to be nose-diving to earth, but each time he flattened out and with admirable daring, attacked again: they were full of admiration for the courage of this pilot.

He was buried by the enemy with full military honours. He was the eldest and dearly loved son of Leycester and Mabel Barwell. The Barwells are not listed in *Who's Who,* so it is impossible to discover whether they had a granddaughter: but, if they had, she would have been just about the right age to be presented in 1939.

CHAPTER
TWO

I've Been to London to Look at the Queen

The Season did not, of course, spring into being with all its events, manners and codes of speech fully formed. It evolved gradually over two or three hundred years, during which royalty, the aristocracy and social behaviour were constantly changing. It was always inspired, however, by the same three motives: the lure of the Court and the great offices of the state, from which honours, preferment and influence derived; the magnetic pull exerted by the entertainments and fashion of London; and the perennial ambition of the nobility to marry off its sons and daughters well.

The boredom and monotony of country life must have weighed especially heavily upon women. Men were preoccupied by the demands of their estates, and found entertainment in country pursuits like hunting and fishing. But, in the days when a household's circle of intimate friends was bounded by the radius of — at most — half a day's journey by horse, carriage or post-chaise (say, fifteen miles), their wives and daughters must have longed for fresh faces to break the tedium and offer a wider choice of marriage partners. The London

Season (although nobody called it that in the seventeenth century) arose naturally out of the isolation of people living in great country houses, albeit in large families served by a huge retinue of servants. For them, London was an opportunity and a diversion. For their men, it might herald promotion, which would make up for the expense and disruption of removing themselves and their families (and servants and livery and plate and linen and books and horses and carriages) up to town for a season — how easily the word leaps to mind: no wonder it came to be called that.

Even those who already lived in London were attracted by Court life — like that engagingly typical social climber, Samuel Pepys. Here he is in December 1662, describing a ball at Court with all the wonder and envy of the *arriviste:*

first to the Duke's* chamber, where I saw him and the Duchess at supper, and thence into the room where the Ball was to be, crammed with fine ladies, the greatest of the Court. By and by comes the King and Queen, the Duke and Duchess, and all the great ones; and after seating themselves, the King takes out the Duchess of York, and the Duke the Duchess of Birmingham, the Duke of Monmouth my Lady Castlemayne, and so other ladies; and they danced the Bransle. After that, the King led a lady a single Coranto; and then the rest of the lords, one after another, other ladies. Very noble it was, and a great pleasure to see .... Having stayed here as long as I thought fit, to my infinite content, it being the greatest pleasure I could wish now to see at Court, I went out, leaving them dancing.[1]

* Of York.

By the following year, Pepys has gone so far as to engage a dancing master, having concluded that it will be a useful accomplishment: for him as well as for his wife:

by and by the Dancing Master came; whom standing by seeing him instructing my wife, when he had done with her he would needs have me try the steps of a Coranto; and what with his desire and my wife's importunity, I did begin, and then was obliged to give him entry money, 10s. — and am become his Scolar. The truth is, I think it is a thing very useful for any gentleman and sometimes I may have occasion of using it; and though it cost me, which I am heartily sorry it should . . . yet I will try it a little while; if I see it comes to any great inconvenience or charge, I will fling it off.[2]

Pepys and his wife never had children, so an advantageous marriage could not have been his reason for wishing to ingratiate himself at Court, and, living in London as they did, its pleasures were all to hand. But for advancement in his career, influential friends were all-important — and Pepys made the most of his.

Three years later, Lord Herbert was writing to his wife, still stuck in the country, about the Queen's birthday ball which he had attended on 15 November 1666: "I never saw greater bravery: a hundred vests [i.e. robes, vestments] that at the least cost a hundred pounds. Some were adorned with jewels above a thousand . . . the ladies much richer than the men."[3] Poor lady — how she must have longed to be there!

The Revolution of 1688 brought William and Mary to the throne, and after them a succession of dull or eccentric Hanoverian Courts. But the Revolution had also imposed limitations on the powers of the monarchy.

The King was no longer the sole source of patronage, office and preferment: these were now dispensed by Parliament as well. Society was beginning to broaden out. Queen Anne and the German Georges reigned over an exciting time. The colonization of America and the opening up of new markets in the East created immense wealth, and led to a new class of successful merchants. The aristocracy, faced with the usual dilemma — could they demean themselves by marrying "trade"? — reached the usual pragmatic conclusion: yes, they could, providing it had enough money.

By the beginning of the eighteenth century, the season was starting to be formalized as a Season. In 1709 Steele used the word in the *Tatler* in its modern sense ("the Company was gone and the Season over") although, heaven knows, the Court of Queen Anne cannot have offered much that was brilliant or vivacious. But by now more than half the great landed families had town houses as well, and their excesses made up for the domestic atmosphere at Court. Here, great hostesses entertained lavishly and the complicated merry-go-round of promotion and favours oscillated up and down. The Season lasted for as long as Parliament sat, from February until the end of July.

In 1711 its first recognizably modern component was established, when Queen Anne's passion for racing prompted her to found a racecourse on the "new heath" at Ascot. She paid for a trophy worth 100 guineas known as Her Majesty's Plate, and another worth 50 guineas. Ascot quickly became a fashionable event, with well-dressed ladies vying with the horses for attention. One of the Queen's Ladies-in-Waiting, a Miss Forester, paraded in male riding costume. Jonathan Swift reported sourly to Stella, "She is a truly silly maid of honour, and I did not like her, although she be a toast."[4]

The role of women was still dictated by the convenience and the commands of men, and even the most spirited rarely defied their fathers or husbands. One who did refuse to submit was Lady Mary Wortley Montagu. She had been famous for her beauty at a young age, ever since her father's friends at the Kit-Kat Club had toasted the length of the little girl's amazing eyelashes. Not only that, she was intelligent, with an observant and questioning mind. She disliked the hypocrisy of London Society, yet conformed for as long as she could. When she could not bear it any more, she became one of the first of the great lady travellers, accompanying her husband to Turkey, and thence into virtual exile in France and Italy. Her letters reflect both her shrewdness and her contempt for the machinations needed to obtain political promotion and influence. Here she is in September 1714, still only twenty-five years old, yet already far wiser than the dim husband whom she is advising:

I need not enlarge upon the advantages of money. Everything we see and everything we hear puts us in remembrance of it ... as the world is and will be, "tis a sort of duty to be rich, that it may be in one's power to do good, riches being another word for power ... The ministry is like a play at court. There's a little door to get in, and a great crowd without, shoving and thrusting who shall be foremost; people that knock others with their elbows, disregard a little kick of the shins, and still thrust heartily forward, are sure of a good place.[5]

In that year, 1714, George I succeeded Queen Anne. He spoke practically no English, had no time for levées and drawing-rooms, and retreated whenever possible to his German palace. George II was not much better. When he succeeded to the throne in 1727, he was besieged by people anxious to get on the right side of him, in case he turned out to play a more active part than his father in disbursing favours. Lord Hervey's *Memoirs* record the scene at Leicester Fields, where the new King had lived while he was heir apparent:

> The King and Queen were already arrived and receiving the compliments of every man of all degrees and all parties in the town. The square was thronged with multitudes of the meaner sort, and resounded with huzzas and acclamations, whilst every room in the house was filled with people of higher rank, crowding to kiss their hands and to make the earliest and warmest professions of zeal for the service . . . . On the 19th [June] the Court removed to Kensington, where the King, by the audiences that were asked and the offers that were made to him by the great men of all denominations, found himself set up at auction and everyone bidding for his favour at the expense of the public.[6]

The following year, the King barred the beautiful and popular Duchess of Queensberry from court for what seems to have been a trifling misdemeanour; the Duchess replied with a spirited letter in which she said she was:

> surprised and well pleased that the King hath given her so agreeable a command as to stay from Court, where she never came for diversion, but to bestow a great civility on the King and Queen; she hopes by such an unprecedented order as this,

that the King will see as few as he wishes at his Court, particularly such as dare to think or speak truth.[7]

It was not long before even the greedy and the sycophantic stayed away, and although the King dutifully held regular levées and even the occasional ball, he was indifferent to England and disagreeable to nearly everyone else. His dullness was enlivened only by his love of practical jokes.

London Society cavorted regardless, generating its own scandals and diversions. It was one of those periods when people went mad for fancy dress. Masques and balls and fireworks became ever more lavish and London burned with the same feverish passion for dressing up as it was to do two centuries later (when, coincidentally, George V's Court was almost as dull as that of his ancestor George II). Horace Walpole wrote with scandalized glee:

> I must tell you how fine the masquerade of last night was. There were five hundred persons of the greatest variety of handsome and rich dresses I ever saw and all the jewels of London. There were to be seen Lady Conway as a charming Mary Stuart, their Graces of Richmond as Henry VIII and Jane Seymour — excessively rich and both so handsome — and all kinds of old pictures stepped from their frames.[8]

Another night, at the opera,

> We had a great scuffle which interrupted it. Lord Lincoln was abused in the most shocking manner by a drunken officer, upon which he kicked him, and was drawing his sword but was prevented. I climbed over the front boxes and stepping

over the shoulders of three ladies before I knew where I was, found that I had lighted in Lord Rockingham's lap.[9]

Yet he must have enjoyed it all, for in 1760 he wrote dolefully, "You cannot figure a duller Season, the weather bitter, no party . . ."[10]

The same year saw the first appearance in Society of an enchanting young woman whose early life epitomized many of the problems of women amid the licence and spectacle of that Hanoverian age. She was Lady Sarah Lennox, orphaned daughter of the late Duke of Richmond, whose elder sister presented her at Court when she was not quite fifteen. Dressed in the height of fashion, all feathers and furbelows, her hair piled high on her head, she found the event an ordeal. "Up I went," she recalled, "through three great staring rooms full of men into the Drawing Room." There, after she had made her curtsey, George II — who had known her as a small child — made her look foolish by trying to cuddle her on his lap as though she were still five years old. She was saved from utter embarrassment by the then Prince of Wales, George II's twenty-year old grandson, "at that time a fine, pleasing-looking young man, of healthy, youthful-looking complexion, a look of happiness and good humour",[11] who came and made conversation with her until she had regained her equilibrium. There were weighty consequences. A few months later the young man succeeded to the throne as George III, and proposed marriage. Actually it was a very good choice. He had fallen much in love with her; she was fond of him; and with her bright, sociable personality and practical nature she might have saved him from some of his own excesses later on. But, naturally, it could not be allowed. His advisers were appalled. The King must make a better match, and lists of eligible if stodgy German princesses were waved before his eyes. Dutifully he chose one, and did his duty over and over again by producing fifteen children and holding two weekly drawing-rooms and two balls a year.

Meanwhile, two years later, Lady Sarah Lennox surprised everyone by marrying a man of her own choice. His name was Charles Bunbury and he turned out to have been a mistake, though Sarah made the best of it for as long as she could. She was bored to tears in the country: "My devil of a horse is as lame as a dog, and Mr B. has been coursing, hunting and doing every pleasant thing upon earth, and poor me sat fretting and fuming at home with Lady Rosse; in short I am patient Grizel to the last degree."[12] Finally, after six glum years, she fell in love with another man, had his child, and was ostracized by society for the next eleven years. The gossips claimed that George III always nurtured tender feelings for her.

London life rolled merrily on without her, and in 1769 the Summer Exhibition at the Royal Academy was held for the first time. It instantly became — and has remained — a must for fashionable society. Founded by Sir Joshua Reynolds, who became its first President, the Royal Academy showed the work of painters like Romney, Lawrence and Reynolds himself.

The social vacuum left by George III and Queen Charlotte was eagerly filled by the great Whig hostesses, who provided political intrigue and intellectual brilliance, and the royal dukes, who provided scandal and debauchery. Walpole disapproved: "The court independent of politics makes a strange figure. The recluse life led at Richmond, which is carried to such an excess of privacy and economy that the Queen's friseur waits on them at dinner and four pounds of beef only are allowed for their soups, disgusts all sorts of people."[13] Yet the Court remained essential for one thing. Before a young girl could mingle in Society as a recognized adult, she had to be presented to the King and Queen. After that, if she were attractive both physically and financially, she would find mercenary suitors drawn to her like vampires to new blood. An observant matchmaker wrote off to a military friend in the country:

> Miss Child comes out this winter . . ., the moment she is fired off, she will be pursued by all the brawny tribe of fortune hunters, so that for her sake and yours I most sincerely wish (provided you like her) that you took the earliest occasion of showing her that sort of attention which she could not but remark. No time to be lost, and I think you should, even now, get away from quarters and take your measures for throwing yourself in her way. Such a prize as that of an amiable girl, with a fortune suited to your rank, is worth any exertion.[14]

Poor Miss Child. Not a thought was given to the girl's happiness. She might have been one victim among thousands: though she, in fact, took charge of her own future by eloping with the tenth Earl of Westmorland. But the majority had less spirit and therefore no choice. Dr Gregory in his book A *Father's Legacy to his Daughters,* published in 1774, warned them realistically: "Without an unusual share of natural sensibility and very peculiar good fortune, a woman in this country has very little probability of marrying for love."

The earliest recorded use of the verb "to come out" in its modern sense occurs at this time, 1782, in Fanny Burney's novel, *Cecilia:* 'She has seen nothing at all of the world, for she has never been presented yet, so is not come out, you know; but she's to come out next year." Fanny Burney was Assistant Keeper of the Wardrobe to Queen Charlotte for five years, but despite her loyalty and affection for the royal family, the tedium of Court eventually became quite unbearable and she asked to be relieved of the privilege. In addition there was the increasing problem of the King's erratic and disconcerting behaviour. Whether he was mad, as his contemporaries believed, or suffered from porphyria, as recent medical research has deduced, made little difference. He was obscene and deluded by turns.

The *beau monde* of London suffered none of this. George III's reign coincided with an era when the art of the political hostess reached its peak: stimulated, no doubt, by the absence of any inspiration at Court. Great Whig hostesses like Lady Melbourne and the Duchess of Devonshire more than made up for it. Then there was Holland House, where the twice-married Lady Holland (who was never received on that account by the more rigid; the loss was theirs, not hers) entertained the most interesting men of her time. The operative word is "men". Young women came out into Society only long enough to find a husband, after which they retired into domesticity and gentle accomplishments like sketching and singing and playing a little upon the pianoforte. Only great ladies of exceptional wealth, intellect and manipulative charm had the chance to do any more in life than be their husband's wife and their children's mother. In the latter role, their skills as matchmakers were crucial; small wonder that the aristocracy was so fascinated by the making of marriages. It offered women a rare opportunity to wield power and exert some influence over the lives of those around them. A marriage for love was a rarity but not an impossibility, provided it were also convenient and suitable for both families; but most daughters had little chance of doing anything other than submit to their parents' wishes.

There were, of course, exceptions — there are always exceptions. At the turn of the century there were three such. They were all related, all remarkable: the Duchess of Devonshire; her sister, the Countess of Bessborough; and *her* daughter, Lady Caroline Ponsonby. Between them these three kicked over most of Society's traces.

Georgiana, Duchess of Devonshire lived in a *ménage à trois* with her husband and her best friend, Lady Elizabeth Foster, who became the Duke's mistress. Between them they bore him a number of children, known collectively as the "Children of the Mist". Legitimate and illegitimate were treated alike — with one significant exception. Lady Elizabeth's son, who was ill-advisedly born before the Duchess had produced an heir, was left with a foster-mother and brought up in France. Nothing could be allowed to threaten the sacred English bloodline.

The Duchess's sister was Lady Bessborough, another great hostess who often shared in the brilliance of Devonshire House and who in her fifties — when most of her contemporaries were regarded as old women —

was still being "courted, followed, flattered and made love to". Young William Lamb was one of her admirers, despite being half her age or less; at least until her daughter, Lady Caroline Ponsonby, was launched into London Society. She had had a crush on good-looking, black-eyed William ever since she was a hoydenish fourteen-year-old. By the time she reached seventeen she was diaphanously thin (could she have been an early anorexic? All the symptoms are there), highly strung, brilliant, moody and tiresome by turns, a towering egoist — and irresistible. And she still loved William. He, however, was but the younger son of a not very rich peer, and only his brother's timely death enabled him — now the future Lord Melbourne — to propose marriage to her. She accepted, and became Lady Caroline Lamb. They had three happy years before everything went wrong.

If such strictures ruled the life of a young woman brought up in the least conventional of families, how they must have limited the freedom and the choices of ordinary young women. Daughters were the chattels of their parents, disposable assets to their fathers, prudish misses to their suitors. Byron has a scathing verse describing the products of such a regime:

> 'Tis true, your budding Miss is very charming,
> But shy and awkward at first coming out,
> So much alarmed, that she is quite alarming,
> All Giggle, Blush; half Pertness and half Pout;
> And glancing at Mamma, for fear there's harm in
> What you, she, it, or they, may be about,

The nursery still leaps out in all they utter —
Besides, they always smell of bread and butter.
(*Beppo*, Stanza 39)

By the beginning of the nineteenth century the
Season was taking on a recognizable shape. A girl was
launched from schoolroom into ballroom or drawing-
room at an early age, somewhere between fifteen and
seventeen, her emergence into Society being marked by
her first presentation at Court. There would be no
formal dance to mark her appearance on the social
scene; that came a good hundred years later. Putting
her hair up signalled her new marriageable status.
Henceforth she might accompany her mother or an
older, married sister when paying formal calls.
Typically, these emergent girls, debutantes in the true
sense of beginners, new arrivals upon the social stage,
were over-protected, mildly accomplished, wildly
romantic, but ultimately passive. How could they be
otherwise? Their sole purpose in life was to be married.
Spinsterhood meant failure. A mother's ambition was to
see her daughters safely married off to men slightly
(better still, greatly) their social superiors, and their
sons to girls who were at least their social equals,
but with more money. Love was not an essential
component.

Social life already had a number of features in
common with the Season of 1939: Ascot, Private View
day at the Royal Academy, Founder's Day at Eton, and
some others, like the parade along Rotten Row and the
spectators it attracted, or the popularity of Vauxhall and
Ranelagh Gardens, which have vanished altogether.

Despite the attractions of Bath and other fashionable country towns, which had their own assembly rooms where people could congregate for balls, cards and concerts and to display the latest in fashions and fiancés, London remained the magnet. It was only in London that the Season took place, and at the end of summer everyone dispersed for the sporting pursuits of autumn and the deep family entrenchment of winter. That tidal rhythm, sweeping everyone of consequence into the metropolis for the summer and out of it again for the rest of the year, had not changed for centuries: it was based on the seasons rather than the Season, and on the fact that wealth was derived from land and land had to be cultivated. But the Court as the glittering centre of Society had apparently become obsolete.

In 1837 the long reign of the Hanoverians ended and Queen Victoria came to the throne aged just eighteen. For the next half-century her dominance was such that the whole country reflected her age and stage in life. When she was an unmarried girl, Society was romantic and excitable, volatile and unpredictable. The young Queen alternated between dashing young men and responsible older ones, like her handsome Prime Minister Lord Melbourne, for whom she felt a more than daughterly devotion, while he in turn was touched by her eagerness and dependence. Yet she was acutely conscious of the formalities of Court life, and insistent that they be observed down to the smallest detail.

At a levée in the first summer of her reign her hand was kissed three thousand times, but this did not prevent her from calling it "the pleasantest summer I EVER passed in *my life*", and she left London — "the *greatest* metropolis in the *world*" — reluctantly at the end of the Season.[15] Then she realized that she took the Court with her; that if she wanted to be gay at Windsor, to dance and go riding and play cards, no one could stop her.

The next Season took place in her Coronation year, and opened with her first State ball in May, followed by two more State balls, two levées and a drawing-room. The young Queen was taking her role as the leader of Society as seriously as she took all the others — not that her responsibilities prevented her from being delightfully irresponsible: "a lovely Ball, so gay, so nice — I felt so happy and merry; I had not danced for so long."[16] But by the following year the novelty of reigning and the freedom from restrictions imposed by her mother were already beginning to pall. In April she told Lord Melbourne that she did not enjoy pleasures so much. "Oh! you will, when they begin," he said, meaning when the Season opened in May.[17] The truth was, though she could not bring herself to admit it, that the Queen needed to be married: for all sorts of reasons. In May she gave a ball for a royal guest, the Tsarevitch Alexander, Grand Duke of Russia, and for the next two weeks entertained him with a theatre, two concerts, a reception and another ball. She was just twenty; ready to fall in love; falling in love, even: "the Grand Duke is so very strong that in running round [in the mazurka] you must follow quickly, and after that you are whisked round like in a Valse, which is very pleasant. . . . I got to bed by a quarter to three but could not sleep till five."[18] Yet her views on marriage were surprisingly modern: "I couldn't understand the wish of getting married

amounting to marrying anyone," she wrote ungram-
matically[19] and when those around her praised Prince
Albert of Saxe-Coburg-Gotha just before his visit, she
wrote anxiously, "I might like him as a friend and as a
cousin and as *a brother,* but not *more. . . .*"[20] Queen
Victoria at twenty was determined to marry for love:
and that included sexual attraction.

She did. She fell in love with Albert on sight, thought
him beautiful, clever and good, and five days after he
had arrived with his brother for a visit to Windsor, she
proposed and was accepted. In February 1840 they were
married: and the Court left mazurkas behind and settled
down to family life and a nursery full of royal infants.

Queen Victoria's courtship and marriage are interesting for the light they shed on the restrictions that
circumscribed young female behaviour throughout the
nineteenth century. Victoria might be Queen, but she
had to obey the same conventions of maidenly decorum
that hemmed in her subjects. Occasionally her own
spirited common sense broke through: as when she
overruled the absurd idea that it would be improper for
Albert to spend the night before their marriage under
the same roof as his bride . . . even though that roof
covered Windsor Castle. True, she fell in love with
Albert: but he was still the carefully selected consort
whose visit to England had been preceded by months of
scheming by her uncle, King Leopold of the Belgians,
and half a host of female matchmakers. She might be
Queen of England; but the youngest son of a minor peer
had more emotional licence than she did.

Once she was married she had to trim her preferences
to those of her husband. Victoria loved London; Albert

preferred Windsor and the country; so they spent increasing time away from London. Victoria loved music and dancing and Albert deplored all frivolity, and especially late nights; so they gave fewer balls and were in bed by midnight. His stern sense of duty began to mould hers; his high-mindedness got the better of her high spirits.

As the century and the Queen moved towards their middle years, Society, like a Victorian family processing publicly to church, also took on an air of whaleboned self-esteem. This ponderousness was reflected in Court manners. No man might sit in the Queen's presence except at dinner, nor any maid of honour in front of Prince Albert. No one spoke until spoken to. Bowing, curtseying, walking backwards and hand-kissing all became rigidly formalized, and so did the precise Court dress permitted in the royal presence. Spontaneity was impossible, with the inevitable consequence. The Court became dull again. Lord Macaulay complained in 1851 that at dinner "a military band covered the talk with a series of sonorous tunes"; Lord Ashley was glad of it, "for the band filled up long pauses in the conversation". "Cant and Puritanism are in the ascendant," wrote Charles Greville in his diary in 1856.[21]

Queen Victoria's domestic life may have been untroubled by jealousy and subterfuge, but Society had its usual share of scandalous liaisons. The Duchess of Manchester and Lord Hartington carried on an affair for years. Lady Arundel lived with an artist, Basil Hodges, and told her friend Mrs Panton that her legal husband "thought he had bought me body and soul with his silly old wedding . . ... Basil is always afraid that

I shall kick over the traces again and make off with someone else and he is always my lover and never the stern, unbending husband."[22] Lady Jersey and Lord Abingdon were publicly accepted as lovers; so were Lady Ailesbury and Lord Wilton, Lady Lincoln and Lord Walpole. But the important thing to remember is that none of these erring couples erred so far as to produce a rival heir. Nor, indeed, would they have been admitted in some of the more high-minded households, let alone at Court. Queen Victoria understood sexual passion, but only within marriage. In 1857 she bore her ninth child, Princess Beatrice, and might well have borne more had not Prince Albert died in 1861, plunging the Queen, the Court and the country into deepest mourning — from which the Queen, at least, never fully emerged.

Away from the Court and away from the scandals, the Season continued to follow its necessary pattern, becoming more like that of 1939 as the century progressed. Debutantes — the word was in common currency by 1837* — were presented to the Queen at an afternoon drawing-room, after their mothers had been carefully vetted by the Lord Chamberlain's Office. Any hint of scandal, let alone a divorce, precluded both mother and daughter from appearing at Court. Divorce at this time was still highly unusual (between 1876 and 1880 there were just 460 divorces) and a divorced

* The context of its first appearance in print is revealing. *Blackwell's Magazine,* issue XLII, observed in 1837: "Gentlemen are apt to dismiss all serious thoughts in addressing a very young debutante."

woman lost not only her property but access to her children as well, no matter who was the guilty party in the case.

Each new debutante embarked, with her first Season, on a voyage into the unknown. She was launched into the great river of Society and, although surrounded by a flotilla of relatives, chaperones and other nervous cygnets like herself, she had to make her own way safely past the rocks of scandal and seduction on the one side and dullness and neglect on the other. If she were too bold, that would be unfavourably remarked upon; if too timid, she would be dismissed as colourless. And yet within a year or two she was expected to find safe harbour as the fiancée of a young man whom decorum prevented her from getting to know properly until after they were engaged. By then it was often too late. The stately Leviathan of trousseau, wedding list, invited guests and marriage date would have been set in motion, and was almost impossible to reverse. Many a girl must have walked up the aisle knowing already that she was making a mistake.

The luckiest debutantes were those who came from a large and united family, for they would keep bumping into aunts, cousins, older sisters — comfortingly familiar faces among the mêlée of strangers; girls like the Hon. Lucy Lyttelton, daughter of the fourth Lord Lyttelton and niece of Mrs Gladstone. She was seventeen and a half when she entered London Society in the early summer of 1859, and her diaries brim with exuberance and with a touching humility. She was so anxious to please, so easily pleased. "I believe it was a dull party," she wrote, having just returned from some official function at the Admiralty, "but we were much amused."[23] London was a merry-go-round of parties and her enthusiasm found new stimulus every day:

London, 24 May. A little past 3 a.m.! Our first ball is over. We danced much more than I expected: M. [her sister Muriel, fourteen months older] 6 times and me 4: twice with Reginald Yorke, Ld. Skelmersdale, and Mr Something Stone. It was fearfully crowded. I saw [here follows a list of names] . . . shall I ever remember them all?

26 May. 'Tis 1 a.m. after a most delightful party here, of which I must at once tell the great event. I was introduced to the Duc d'Aumale, the descendant of the old race of French kings. Low was my curtsey, most gracious was his bow, and oh! he spoke to me, and I said, "Oui, Monsieur!" I thrilled.

28 May. About 1. We've been to the Opera! *Gazza Ladra* at Covent Garden, Lord Ward's box. There being no ballet, Papa let us go. I believe I was slightly disappointed, but it was because I don't know the music well enough, and I must always know it well to be properly worthy.

3 June. ¼4 a.m.! and this is written, ill or well, by the light of dawn: mad and dissipated I feel. We have been to Ly. Derby's ball, which, truth to tell, was very dull: hot crowds of chaperones and old gentlemen, and the dancing a fierce struggle with all-surrounding petticoat.

5 June. My energy is certainly great. I walked to Trinity Ch Vauxhall in the morning with Papa, on the top of yesterday's perpetual tramp, and the night before's dissipation. Ain't a bit tired.

6 June. A little past two, after the pleasantest home ball, that's to say dance, or it was carefully distinguished from a ball by its smallness, absence of champagne, and substitution of modest p.f. [pianoforte] and harp for band . . . . I danced everything but one, valses of course excepted, but I can only remember five partners. I think I must have had more than that.[24]

And so she rattled on, lively and excited despite the restrictions (perpetual chaperonage; valses forbidden to an unmarried girl), until the great day of her formal presentation. In her account of this, her first London Season, a great deal of what Lucy Lyttelton describes would have been the same eighty years later, in 1939. Her emotions, the ceremonial, the graciousness of the Queen: it is all practically interchangeable.

London, 11 June. A very memorable day. ... We were presented at 2 o'clock; and after all the frightful bathing-feel [a Lyttelton family word meaning nervousness] and awestruck anticipation, behold! it was a moment of great happiness to me. The look of interest and kindliness in the dear little Queen's face, her bend forward, and the way she gave her hand to me to be kissed, filled me with pleasure that I can't describe and that I wasn't prepared for. .... I feel as if I could do anything for her![25]

Within a very few weeks she was becoming harder to please, and even a touch waspish:

4 July. We had a prim luncheon at Ly. Windsor's, where nice Victoria Clive sang the tunes that all old cows have died of. For the first time, two balls; duty first, and pleasure afterwards.[26]

But with discrimination came improved descriptive powers. This scene at a ball could have stood for thousands of balls through many decades:

Mrs Hibbert's was the most lovely thing I have ever seen in its way: a tent in the open air for ante-room, from whence you descended by a flight of steps into the ball-room, at the top of which you could stand and see the dancing like a magic picture. A smother of flowers, and cool atmosphere.[27]

The 1860s and 1870s were probably the last years in which the upper class was still to all intents and purposes one large, interrelated tribe. In 1910 Lady Dorothy Nevill wrote in her Memoirs, "Society, in the old sense of the term, may be said, I think, to have come to an end In the eighties of the last century. It is a recurring vanity to believe that one's own time was the best time, the only *real* time; but there is much evidence to suggest that Lady Dorothy was right. By the end of the nineteenth century the invasion of industry and commerce, of Jewish financiers and American millionaires' daughters, had diluted the aristocratic exclusivity of Society.

One consequence of this change was that Society became more demanding, more cynical, even cruel. If its members could win entry by wealth, or on merit or beauty (like Lillie Langtry) or for talent and coruscating wit (like Oscar Wilde) rather than simply attain it by inheritance, then Society would be ruthless to those new members who did not continue to earn their keep. The English novelist Ouida (the pen-name of Marie Louise de la Ramée) spelled it out brutally in her novel *Friendship,* published in 1878:

People must make themselves agreeable to be agreeable to the world; yes, and eat a good deal of dust too, that I concede. If they are high and mighty by birth and all the rest of it, of course they can be as disagreeable as they choose, and make others eat the dust always. But if not, there is nothing for it but to toady. . ... Society is not to be despised. It is pleasant

. . . . We are not brilliant, nor powerful, nor original; but when we are not murderous, we are pleasant, pre-eminently pleasant; we know how to gild things, we know how to gloss them. . ... Now, you see, you people who will live on that rock in the midst of the sea only disturb us. That is the truth. You make us think, and Society dislikes thinking. You call things by their right names, and Society hates that . . .. You shudder at sin, and we have all agreed that there is no such thing as sin. . ... adultery is a liaison, lying is gossip, debt is a momentary embarrassment, immorality is a little slip, and so forth; and when we have arranged this pretty little dictionary of convenient pseudonyms, it is not agreeable to have it sent flying by fierce, dreadful old words. . ... We do not care about anything. Only give us a good dinner and plenty of money and let us outshine our neighbours. There is the Nineteenth Century Gospel.

Elsewhere, Ouida defined it even more unequivocally: "Society always had its fixed demands. It used to exact birth. It used to exact manners. Nowadays it exacts money. Have money and spend it well (that is, let Society live on it, gorge with it, walk ankle deep in it) and you may be anything and do anything."

Something else changed Society radically in the closing years of the nineteenth century: the arrival of the motor-car. It widened people's social circle because it was now possible to drive fifty miles for lunch or an evening party. The train had been the great stimulus to country-house visiting; the car enabled people to visit one another for less than a weekend, and heralded the Edwardians" ceaseless entertaining. Previously, people were visited at home almost entirely by their relatives (hence the necessity for a London Season, to widen one's circle) or by local acquaintances. From the 1890s onwards began an era of frantic party-giving: children's parties, firework parties and above all fancy-dress parties. Hundreds of pounds were spent on fantastically elaborate costumes designed to be worn once only: the French Ambassador's wife at the Court of Catherine the Great; endless Antonys and Cleopatras, mythological gods and goddesses tricked out with breastplates and dubious classical drapery. All this was encouraged by the portly, pleasure-loving figure of the Prince of Wales, soon to become Edward VII.

The last years of Victoria's reign were also the last when strict social precedence was observed, whatever the inconvenience. One debutante from that time recalled, with an exasperation that the years had not dulled,

At these dinner-parties [i.e. those given before a dance] they never kept the older people together as they do now, but all had to go exactly according to rank, so we used to find ourselves going in to dinner with the most dreary old lords, and any young man who happened to be a duke or a marquess was sure to have to take in the hostess, however old and fat she might be, which was very hard luck.[28]

Lady Clodagh Anson was presented by her aunt in 1898, at a ceremony which had altered not at all forty years later, except that fewer royalties would have attended:

Queen Victoria held the Drawing-rooms in St James's Palace in those days in the daytime, so that everyone looked too ridiculous for words sitting all dressed up in evening gowns, veils and feathers at eleven o'clock in the morning in their carriages along the Mall. Crowds came to stare at them, and their comments were very unflattering sometimes. The actual

Drawing-room (it was called a "Court" then) was in quite a small room with a door at each end. The Queen sat on a low chair, and as she was very small indeed, you had to make a deep curtsey to get down low enough. She put out her hand which you took and kissed, and if you were a peeress or a peer's daughter, she kissed your cheek almost at the same time. All the other royalties stood in a close line next to her, which was very convenient, for you really pulled yourself up by their hands, which you shook in turn as you made less and less deep curtsies all along the line; sometimes there were eight or ten of them, and when you got to the last you shot out of the far door.[29]

By the time Queen Victoria died in 1901, a very old lady whom people were beginning to believe must be immortal, the shape and conventions of the London social Season, its events and priorities, were set: and changed little for the next fifty years. Manners changed, yes. The Bright Young Things of the 1920s picked Society up, twirled the old lady around to the sound of jazz, and set her down again breathless, scandalized and secretly thrilled. Customs changed; drugs had become fashionable during the war years, morphine and cocaine being much used as antidotes to the unbearable casualty lists. The practice of swearing came in briefly but had gone again by the thirties. Sex came in with contraception, even though it was largely confined to girls in their twenties, well past the debutante stage, and precautions were of the Marie Stopes variety. But it remained *de rigeur to* pretend to one's family that one was a virgin bride — as indeed the more decorous still were.

Down the generations, one wave of girlhood after another was launched upon the river of Society. In the sixteenth and seventeenth centuries it was a quiet English river, the sweet Thames, running softly, and it led into rural backwaters. By the eighteenth century it was already gathering momentum, becoming more sophisticated and treacherous. In the nineteenth century it began to be fed by the effluvia of factory, brewery and commerce by which, to the many people who shared Lady Dorothy Nevill's old English views, it was polluted. By the beginning of the twentieth century it had become an international waterway, swelled by foreign tributaries, its flow thickened by political undercurrents and checked by the rapids of war. Yet in 1939 Society showed no signs of silting up. It was only in retrospect that people spoke of that year as the last *real* Season. At the time, not only debutantes but also their parents were often serenely unconscious of the imminent turmoil. None would have forecast that, less than twenty years later, the ritual of presenting debutantes to royalty as a signal that they were now marriageable by their peers, would end for ever.

CHAPTER
THREE

The Childhood of the Debs: Preparing to Be a Beautiful Lady*

"There were Masked parties, Savage parties, Victorian parties, Greek parties, Wild West parties, Circus parties, almost naked parties in St John's Wood, parties in flats and studios and houses and ships and hotels and night clubs, in windmills and swimming baths." So wrote Evelyn Waugh in *Vile Bodies* (1930). The decade of the twenties into which the debs of 1939 were born was determined to forget what had happened in the previous decade: for the facts were too terrible to remember. The years between the two world wars were dominated by a sense of guilt: 745,000 young Englishmen died and 1.6 million were wounded between 1914 and 1918; 9 per cent of the male population under forty-five was killed, and the proportion was much higher among the upper classes.

* Pear's soap advertising slogan of 1930s.

The parents of the dead took refuge in a steady, secret grief, comforting one another with memoirs and slim volumes about the sons they had lost and mourning, too, the lost, polished frivolity of the Edwardian era, with its talk of patriotism and Empire.

The guilt of the generation who survived, or had been too young to fight, manifested itself in a decade of almost hysterical hedonism. If one image seems to freeze-frame the jerky cavortings of the twenties, it is that of a nightclub populated by stick-insect people with tendrils of cigarette smoke spiralling up from long slender holders held with scarlet nails between lurid lips — an image of pitiless unreality. These were the years of parties and, above all, nightclubs; the years in which nightclubs were invented. The Embassy was one of the most exclusive:

> To this room right after right for years the fashionable society of London came . . . dukes and earls and princes and their wives and the women they loved, writers, actors, press-lords, politicians, all the self-made men from the war who were trying to break into society, all the riff-raff and the hangers-on . . .. Early in the evening, when the whole room could be seen with a relatively unimpeded vision, it would have been possible for an acute observer to watch the rules of an older society being gradually broken down.[1]

One factor that broke down this old Society was the shortage of upper-class males for its daughters to marry. At least one girl in ten — and in practice more like one in eight — had no corresponding young man because the war had finished him, in one way or another. These girls, who had never envisaged any future for themselves except as wives and mothers, had to lower their standards or stay single. Several things happened in consequence. Chaperones all but disappeared for several years. Young women became far more predatory and overtly sexual than their mothers would have dared to be. They dressed in exaggeratedly revealing fashions; danced well, lived fast and furiously, were "good sports" and good conversationalists and good fun. The tables had turned, and it was now the young women who were pursuing an ever-dwindling pool of young men. They married if they could, often with scant regard for the old standards of eligibility. The first of these marriages produced the debutantes of 1939.

By the late 1930s, the excesses of the twenties were distinctly *démodé"*; indeed they were frowned upon. Robert Fossett, in a letter written in May 1939, spoke disparagingly of the Bright Young Things:

> They were never very bright, and, thank God, they are rapidly ceasing to be very young. Some of them are not so bad and they are perhaps to be pitied rather than abused. But they are a portent and a menace. They are the first generation that was brought up without parental control, without discipline, without the fear of God . . . . They rant and rant about Fascism, but then seem to imagine that you hold up a panzer division with a couple of vermouths, a hang-over, and a dirty joke.[2]

Predictably, once they had paired up and settled down, these Bright Young Couples turned into models of conventional parenthood, bringing up their own children as nearly as possible in exactly the same way as they themselves had been brought up. For the upper classes this meant nannies and nursery-maids and the whole hierarchy of domestic servants which stratified every household: literally as well as figuratively. Helen Vlasto, a debutante of 1939, remembers her childhood home thus:

> The house seemed divided by its different floors into several worlds. We children belonged at the top of the house, though our large, sunny day nursery was one floor down, alongside our parents' bedroom. Right down below the ground floor, with its elegant public rooms, lived the maids, surrounded by kitchen, scullery, pantries, store cupboards, and a massive coal cellar. ... Sometimes, if we could manage it undetected, we would go down the dark twisting stairs to the warm welcome of the servants'' hall, and the sort of sweets we wouldn't have been given upstairs. ... One thing superbly linked the top of the house with the basement, and vice versa, and that was the speaking tube. "Go and whistle down and ask Cook nicely for another plate of bread and butter, there's a good girl," Nurse would say. Having whistled, if you stayed absolutely still, holding your breath, you could hear feet coming along the stone floor towards the speaking-tube in the kitchen, and there was the fun of giving Cook the message and replacing the whistle in the stopper.... After tea was the time for washing sticky fingers and faces, and for a quite painful hair-brushing from Nurse, in her hurry to get us going downstairs. This was the lovely time for doing things with our parents, and often for being polite to visitors in the drawing room.[3]

Warm, safe, cosy memories, the stuff of a protected childhood, more sheltered than the writer could possibly have known. The same stratification could be found on a vaster scale in the most privileged households of all. Describing Cliveden at this time, Michael Astor (whose cousin Dinah Brand and first wife Barbara McNeill were both debutantes in 1939) is describing not just a household but practically a village:

The large English country house and estate has now nearly vanished except as a spectacle for sightseers who today are usually invited to view the corpse now that the spirit has left it. It used to be a community made up of many component parts. There was the life of the house with its many different departments — housemaids, kitchen, pantry, etc; the various offices which attended to the house — carpenters, coachmen, electricians, plumbers, etc., and the life of the gardens, the farm, the dairy and the woods. Cottage and mansion enjoyed a corporate existence. . ..[4]

These upper-class children of the 1920s lived ordered, comfortable lives which they accepted as their birthright. Few of them knew that there was any other way to live, and those who did were not likely to be troubled by the contrast:

It never occurred to any of us that we were privileged children. The poverty and unemployment of the 1920s and 1930s passed over our heads. Even the General Strike hardly impinged beyond the fact that we walked to school instead of going by bus. And to my eternal shame I took for granted the sight of poor children from the surrounding mews walking about in ragged, inadequate clothes and with bare feet. We measured ourselves by our far richer cousins and saw ourselves in the light of poor relations.[5]

The writer, who as Ruth Magnus was a debutante in the 1930s, was unusual in coming from an intellectual Jewish family with a strong social conscience — yet even she had never questioned her privileged position.

Whatever their parents' generation may have endured, these children of the 1920s, the future debutantes of 1939, grew up in an enclosed world. Physically it was enclosed — by higher and thicker walls, bigger houses and larger gardens — and socially, by the battlements of class and wealth. Within this enclave, the children were guarded by literally dozens of people. First, by families whose ramifications often filled pages in *Burke* or *Debrett*. Second, by an array of servants that ranged from Nanny or Nurse, through one or more lesser nursery maids, ladies' maids, valets, butlers and outdoor staff. A modest middle-class family — positively poor in the eyes of its rich cousins — would have had at least half a dozen servants, while at the top end of the aristocratic scale a ducal household might still rule over an almost feudal estate of several dozen servants. In 1931 there were 1.3 million women and over 78,000 men still in domestic service: an increase of 100,000 on the numbers in 1911. The Astors had thirty indoor servants at Cliveden alone in the 1930s, looking after a family of seven, though augmented by dozens of house-guests and family visitors.

To put these figures in perspective, it is worth looking briefly at what was typical at the opposite end of the social scale.

There undoubtedly existed a "culture of poverty" in many of the slum districts of large cities and towns, where thousands . . . eked out a makeshift and precarious existence in which day-to-day survival took precedence over everything else. . . . It was a desperately precarious world, balanced for most on the knife-edge between making-do and complete destitution . . . where doctors on emergency calls disinfected themselves before they left their surgeries, and experienced ones carried a powerful flash-lamp on night calls to the slums, knowing that it was more than likely that their patients would have no money for the gas or electricity meter after darkness fell . . . and dirt, damp and vermin were common accompaniments to everyday life.[6]

In 1938 the great majority of the population — 88 per cent — had incomes of less than £250 a year or £5 a week, and 31 per cent of them — very nearly a third — earned half that, £2 10s a week. The canyon drop from rich to poor can be seen in all its dizzying height from the fact that at the top there were two thousand people whose incomes averaged £43,500 a year. No wonder it gave the rich vertigo to look down upon the poor, and most of them preferred to look away. The social economist Seebohm Rowntree found in a study carried out in York in 1936 that 18 per cent of the population were "in poverty",[7] while a similar study in Bristol in 1937 found that 19.3 per cent of the population had "insufficient income"[8] — meaning not enough money to meet basic needs. They did not eat enough. They were crammed into insanitary houses. Their health was poor. The worst sufferers were children.

These depressing figures might seem irrelevant to the Season of 1939; except that the Season was enjoyed by less than 0.1 per cent of the population while the poverty described above was endured by nearly 20 per cent. The two worlds never touched, but the extreme luxury of the one cannot be seen in context without an awareness of the total wretchedness of the other.

Back to the nurseries and the nannies of the rich.

Every upper-class child had a nanny. A mother who insisted on looking after her own babies and toddlers would have been regarded as eccentric to the point of lunacy. Breast-feeding one's own children was practically unknown, in spite of the fact that the belief still lingered that infants imbibed characteristics from their wet-nurse. (The Tennant family, all dark, believed that their sister Charty was fair because she was the only one to have had a blonde wet-nurse.) A mother's time with her children was regulated by their nanny and often amounted to no more than an hour and a half a day. This tantalizing proximity yet separation must have had something to do with the way in which mothers were idolized. The daily, hourly, ever-present figure in a child's life was Nanny.

Mollie Acland (now Mrs Peter Tabor) lovingly conjured up that first cosy world:

Our childhood was very sheltered and secure. We lived in two rooms, a day nursery and a night nursery, just going downstairs — changed into organdy or velvet — from 5 to 6 p.m. We also went down the back stairs in the mornings to play in the garden and park . . . 'looking after bantams, making bows and arrows, bird-nesting, etc. In the afternoon, Nanny and the Nursery maid changed into grey costumes (the rest of the time Nanny always wore white and the nursery-maids print dresses) and we went for a formal walk. (I remember the awful pinching leather gaiters!) Nan taught me to read when I was four, and then we had a governess when we were about nine as well as a French Mam'selle and a German Fraülein in the holidays.

Nanny brought order, predictability, security — in a word, *routine* — into the lives of her charges. She tamed and disciplined them, taught them manners and, since nannies were tremendous snobs, inculcated a consciousness that they were special; and was rewarded by losing the boys at eight to prep school and the girls to either a school or a governess. But Nanny was overwhelmingly the greatest influence in the life of an upper-class child, and the first thing that they all had in common. It is easy to construct a sort of composite nanny; and, although there were wide variations on the theme, Nanny's rules and maxims were the first unifying code buried deep in the communal memory of the upper classes. "Bread and butter first, *then* jam." "No such word as can't." "If a thing's worth doing, it's worth doing well." "A place for everything and everything in its place." "'*She*' is the cat's mother." "Someone's eyes are bigger than her tummy." And, clamping a handkerchief round the nose of a child with a cold, "*Big* blow!"

It is important to remember that most upper-class English girls were badly taught, because their ignorance was used as a weapon against them. It justified the emphasis on being docile, biddable, amiable — "Be good, sweet child, and let who will be clever" — since poor, helpless, ignorant creatures, they couldn't possibly manage on their own. Education is power; to be uneducated is to be helpless. The women who taught them were ever-present examples of what became of girls who did not marry. They could in due course become maiden aunts, precarious hangers-on at the fringes of the family, or they could become governesses. With the superfluity of women after the First World War, which was particularly marked in the upper classes since three times as many officers were killed as ordinary soldiers, there was no obvious employment for these women except as governesses, or teachers, or — at worst — companions to ladies older and richer than themselves.

Not all girls educated by governesses were badly taught, and there were other sources of knowledge besides the schoolroom. Brothers, and friends of brothers, staying during the school holidays were a great source of information, and one that clever girls had always exploited. There were a few governesses who did their job brilliantly. The Hon. Priscilla Brett (now Lady Beckett) remembers one such:

> I was with a governess who actually became rather famous in our circles. She was called Cuffy, and she was a wonderful teacher. She taught us French and German, when I was in Vienna and then in Paris; and she took us to all the good museums, the opera — we had a wonderful time and I loved it. If you had a governess like that you did terribly well. The Asquiths had this amazing woman called Miss Strachey. So the governesses could be very much better than the schools, but presumably if the governess wasn't much good, you didn't get much of an education.

Yet as late as 1938 there were 365 posts for governesses notified to the Governesses' Benevolent Institution, which means — if we assume a turnover of, say, 20 per cent a year — that there were at least 1,825 working governesses just before the war. (The war more or less finished them off: in 1945 there were only fifty-seven posts registered, ten filled, and, of the applicants, only one was under forty-five.)[9]

Those who had a little capital started schools. By 1910 there were already some twenty-one girls' public schools, teaching about 5,000 pupils. Princess Helena College (the first, originally founded under another name in 1820), Queen's College in Harley Street (attended by several of the 1939 debutantes), Roedean, Cheltenham, Wycombe Abbey, Sherborne — the roll call is well established. They were more concerned to inculcate character — which they tended to call "uplift" or "moral fibre" or something suitably vague so that no girl could ever be quite sure she had it — than an academic education. Here is how a headmistress addressed her pupils at the Godolphin School:

> I believe that, with few exceptions, there is a spirit of earnest work in the school, and a growing realisation as the girls reach higher forms that school life must lead on to definite service in the larger life when school days are over . . . character . . . self control . . . neat smartness . . . good taste . . . school before house . . . the spirit of reverence . . .[10]

and so on, in a rising tide of pseudo-spiritual fervour that smacks disturbingly of Moral Rearmament. It was Nanny's routine and discipline all over again, this time imposed upon dozens, even a couple of hundred girls rather than just a nurseryful. The rules they were taught to obey were those they were assumed to need for adult life: first of all, the mores and conventions of the English class system, and secondly, and confusingly — in a setting where sex was never discussed — those which would render them marriageable.

In my day and for my sex nothing but the class structure could have made possible the educational system. The schools I attended had to be Schools for Young Ladies, the parents had to be subjected to searching enquiries during the first interview, one peer's daughter had to be acquired as a pupil and her father's name retained on a list of patrons. . . . My parents, along with the parents of most of my contemporaries, had only one requirement in return for fees that would have kept their sons at Eton: that we should be turned into marriageable young ladies. . . . . At the ink-stained desks of these schools we sat pinioned by boredom, while there took place around us what can only be described as the tittle-tattle, the merest gossip of education.[11]

Boys meanwhile, the brothers of the debutantes-to-be, were also educated by ordeal, but in their cases their minds were quite well furnished. The ordeals they had to endure were those of bullying or fagging or homosexuality — which seems to have been either wildly indulged or sternly forbidden — or the public schools' worship of prowess at games. Ignorance about sex was not their problem, rather it was ignorance about emotions: how to express them, respond to them in others, or share them with members of the opposite sex. Young English men left their expensive and snobbish public schools as ill-educated in matters of the heart as their female counterparts were in matters of the mind.

It is tedious to keep repeating the obvious: namely, that there were exceptions. Ruth Magnus, for example, who came from an intellectual home, read avidly and was encouraged to discuss what she read and her political ideas with her parents and with her father's erudite friends. She had a girl cousin who went to university and, furthermore, in 1912 a female cousin of her mother's had also gone to university, which was at that time quite exceptional. As a result Ruth suffered the inevitable disillusionment during her Season of finding most of the men "awful — deadly dull — no conversation at all: you talked pattatee pattata."

However, before these two ill-equipped groups of young people were ritually propelled towards one another by the Season, there was one final stage for the girls to pass through. Many, if not most, were sent away for three to six months to a finishing school. Before this, they were young girls; afterwards they were ready to be treated as young women. The finishing schools taught them a foreign language: usually French, surprisingly often German, occasionally Italian; gave them a light dusting of culture ("how to tell a Manet from a Monet", as one wrote), instilled the rudiments of feminine skills like arranging flowers, and, most important of all, introduced them to a selection of well-bred foreign girls.

One of the debutantes of 1939 who was partly "finished off" (to use the curious jargon) in Germany, has written an account of her time there. She did not attend a formal school, but lived with a family:

In Germany I continued to study the piano, but showed no real talent, and just enjoyed being in such an entirely new atmosphere. This was 1937, and the children of the family with whom I was living were fervent members of the Hitler Youth Movement, and did their best to make me feel lazy, unhealthy and decadent. Their meetings and other outdoor activities were strenuous and repetitious, and I was not a little frightened of their much vaunted violence and tendency to bully each other into greater and greater excesses.[12]

In view of the imminence of war, which should have been obvious to the parents, if not to the girls themselves, it is surprising how many debutantes continued to be sent to Germany as part of their education. It was, in one sense, very civilized — the language of Goethe, Heine and Schiller remained unchanged, even if its current users were the Hitler Youth — yet in another sense it seems naive to the point of blindness. Mary Tyser (now Mary, Lady Aldenham) went to Paris first and then to Munich:

I stayed at school till I was nearly sixteen and then spent a year in Paris at Mlle Fauchet's finishing school in Passy. It was *very* schooly, too, which was a great disappointment as I thought I had finished with lessons, but I enjoyed it there, and Mlle Fauchet made old buildings, French history and culture come to life and I learned a lot — including fine sewing: cami-knickers in satin with inset lace, for example! Then for the last three months of 1938 I was in Munich at Gräfin Cucca Harrach's house, where I was dismayed to find that, in spite of School Certificate standard German, I could understand little of what was said to me. However, I did gather a bit about what was going on in Germany. We had watched the tanks coming back from the invasion of Czechoslovakia earlier, but none of this meant very much to me and I had no understanding of its real significance.

The level of cultural education which was nominally supplied is spelled out more clearly in this account, by a debutante of 1938:

They [the finishing schools] were fearfully expensive by today's values — £120 a term [about £2,400 in 1989 money]. I had resisted the whole thing but my mother wanted me to do everything that was socially right and proper. I got caught up with some very snobby girls who were horrified later to find me working in Peter Jones. There were nine of us at the school. We learnt bridge, we did a cathedral a week and a museum a week. Wherever we went we were escorted. If you went to the hairdresser, someone sat there to make sure you weren't assaulted or something. I found it very difficult because I had been fairly free in London. The Russian who taught us bridge had taught the Spanish royal family and constantly went on about *"mes enfants d'Espagne"*. We went to the opera but we had to leave before the last act of *Faust* because the ending was not considered suitable.[13]

Some girls, like Lady Jean Leslie Melville, were taken on a tour of Europe instead of going to a finishing school:

I was taken away from boarding school aged sixteen and sent abroad with a Swiss woman who took young girls to the Continent to learn languages and look at art and picture galleries, etc. I had three terms in Italy and one in France, mostly in Paris. After this I could speak French fairly well and quite a lot of Italian. I studied German at school but never got very far with it.

At the end of this rarefied period of childhood and adolescence, what had the potential debutante to offer? The great majority came from backgrounds that ensured they were well born, well heeled, well mannered and well groomed. Some of them were well read — those from intellectual homes where intelligence was prized and good libraries available — and a few were well educated. Most would have been "accomplished", in the Victorian sense, with a veneer of musical and artistic ability, and most spoke at least one foreign language with tolerable fluency. The greatest difference between them and the eighteen-year-olds of today would have been that, beneath a façade of beautiful manners, they were completely unsophisticated. They had been so over-protected by nannies, governesses and their parents that most were grown-up children. Above all, they were so naive sexually that their ignorance required the protection of chaperones and the censorship of adult conversation. Lady Jean Leslie Melville again:

It has to be remembered that things were not discussed in front of children as they are today, and children did not grow up so fast, nor did they know half of what the children nowadays know. There was no such thing as "teenagers". We were schoolchildren and that was it; we wore and did what we were told and we did not stop to argue . . . it was not worth our while!

An obvious consequence of this was that debutantes had a certain amount of smalltalk but no conversation. They could exchange pleasantries about the last dance, the next dance, the present dance; they could remark how fearfully pretty Miss x was looking (the girl whose dance it was) and how amusing the food/flowers/band leader; they could discuss the last season's hunting. But practically all other subjects were taboo. Each sex complains of the other's dullness. The girls said over and over again how boring the men were. A young man who escorted many of the debutantes in 1939, attended a number of dances with his sister who had come out the previous year. Here he describes the difficulty of finding suitable topics:

The girls were normally seventeen years old and they'd just left school. They had led very sheltered lives, first of all in the nursery and then with their mothers chaperoning them. They were normally extremely shy — there were of course exceptions, but most were shy — and they would blush when spoken to, which I found rather fetching. Nowadays one rarely sees a girl blush. These girls didn't have much experience of life — and found it extremely difficult to make conversation. In fact I remember one girl — who shall be nameless — and I was sitting out with her, and she had an evening bag with little silver bobbles on it, and she said to me, "You know, every time I can't think of something to say, I pull one of these off." And I confess I replied rather brutally, "I'm surprised there are any left, my dear!"

It seldom crossed the minds of these shy, unformed, unconfident young women that they had any choice but to submit themselves to the social ordeal that the Season represented for almost all of them. One did it. One's mother had done it, and one's grandmother had done it. One's older sisters had done it and one's aunts had done it. They might warn against exhaustion, boredom, the embarrassment of having your dance programme unfilled ("Fill up your own and then pretend you're too tired to dance"), yet all accepted its inevitability. Many fathers must have been homesick, bullied and miserable as boys at prep and public school; yet when the time came, they too unquestioningly sent their own sons to face the same ordeal, often at the same schools. So it was with the mothers. They had been through the rite of passage between childhood and adulthood, and now their daughters must endure the same ritual. They were expected, somehow, to find a partner who would offer marriage. Yet, officially, no deb was permitted to be alone with a young man, however suitable. Their participation was closely monitored. In the words of Lady Jean Leslie Melville:

Debs were watched almost the whole time by chaperones and dowagers, who were quite likely to be peering through their lorgnettes and sitting on gilt chairs around the ballrooms. No deb was allowed to go out alone with a man during her first Season, on any account or any excuse whatsoever! Nowadays it is very difficult to make young girls understand this . . . they think it is a joke. The Season was really a method of being officially launched into Society and meeting people and of course young men: presumably with a view to marriage.

"I never envisaged a future for myself other than as a wife and mother," said Ruth Magnus, one of the cleverest girls of that generation; "and looking back, I'm very sorry not to have gone to university. But one conformed much more, and just accepted one's destiny. Lots of girls got engaged to get away from their home and family. I got engaged because it was the thing to do, and then managed to get myself unengaged again before the war started." The war overturned many debs' expectations, sometimes for the better. "The war emancipated these girls. It came as a wonderful release" was the comment of one former deb. She had a "good war"; she travelled widely, met glamorous, suntanned young men and ultimately married one. For other young men of that generation the war was a final release.

When war was declared, most of the young men who had partnered the pretty, blushing young girls through nights and days of extravagant frivolity turned into serving officers immediately. They had grown up deeply conscious of the fact that the generation of young men before them had been decimated. One of the escorts of the debs of 1939 spoke, in a voice full of emotion, of the effect that had: "This — aura — of war; this haunting fear that there would be another one; this haunting nightmare of the last one". Yet he and most of his contemporaries joined up at once, expecting to be "gun-fodder" like the previous generation. Ferelith Kenworthy (now Lady Hood), wrote with the same deep emotion about her escort at the Eton and Harrow match that year:

He was an Old Harrovian, and at the end of the match he disappeared on to the pitch to join in the general scrum which ensued, with top hats, straw boaters and umbrellas flying everywhere through the air. Imagine my dismay, as an eighteen-year-old at being thus deserted by my young male escort! He did come to claim me, but I am afraid the story has a sad sequel, as he was later killed in the war, on 23 April 1943, at the Battle of Longstop Hill, in Tunisia. It was the fate of so many of our dancing partners. His name was Captain Ralph Barrie Erskine, of the Argyll and Sutherland Highlanders. He died that we might live in peace and freedom. At least six of the young men with whom I used to dance regularly were later killed in the war. So it was a very sad time to be young.

CHAPTER
FOUR

Change Your Partner, Dance While You Can*

It is customary today to describe someone female who is no longer at school as a "young woman", in deference to feminism, and in recognition of the worldliness and independence of today's school-leavers. In 1939, the young products of the schoolroom who were about to embark on their debutante year would certainly have been described as "girls": and most members of their society would have called them "gels" and not "gurls". Many of them cling to the same usage today. "I'm having an afternoon of bridge with the gels," they will say, referring to a group of people who are in their late sixties. They are uncomfortable at hearing one of their generation described as a "woman" since to them the word has condescending implications, as in "my cleaning woman" or "the little woman who makes my dresses". In 1939 they never thought of themselves as women, and would have found the term "young ladies" patronizing. Bachelor uncles ingratiated themselves by saying, "Now, young lady ... "

* From "The Dead Echo" by W.H.Auden.

They had the same problem in describing their escorts. The term "young man" was also patronizing: housemaids had a "young man", debutantes never. The generation before them had sometimes referred to "my best young man" to indicate a favoured suitor, but by 1939 the expression had fallen into disuse. "Boyfriend", whatever Sandy Wilson might think, was another word scarcely ever used. Male escorts were sometimes called "debs' delights" in 1939, but the expression was slightly pejorative: the equivalent, perhaps, of "hooray Henry" in present-day speech. "There were certainly "debs' delights","" recalls one debutante of 1939, "but they were not always very nice men. They were called that because they seemed to go to all the dances." Another corroborates that impression:

The young men who never missed a free dinner and went to everything — the "debs' delights" — had, of course, to make themselves agreeable to the hostesses and debs or they would have been dropped from the "List". The young men one so hoped to see, as one struggled up the staircase to the tune of "Smoke Gets in Your Eyes", hardly ever turned up.

The expression must have been quite new, however, for someone who was presented just five years earlier says, "I never heard the expression debs' delight" used in those days. We used to speak of some young men (they were called "chaps" or "men", never, never "boy-friends") as "taxi tigers", and later on we said as

"NSIT", not safe in taxis.' The Americanism "beau" to describe a favoured escort had also fallen into disuse by 1939, although it was common in the 1920s, and can still be heard sitting oddly upon the lips of octogenarians today.

"Gels" and "chaps": these were innocent, friendly, sexless words to describe young people who had as yet no maturity, no separate sense of self. They were the offspring of their parents; pawns in a courtly game of nodding and smiling, backing and advancing, curtseying and holding doors open and at all times deferring to the wishes of the adult world they stood — literally — to inherit. How different, how arbitrarily, unfairly different from the child of parents advertising in the Personal column of *The Times* on 2 May 1939: "Jewish parents in Bohemia ask asylum for their boy; healthy, well-educated, age 11." What did he inherit?

When it comes to describing the parents of the girls and chaps who dined and danced the summer away, there is no shortage of words. Names, titles, honours, initials; they were landowners and aristocrats, politicians and judges, soldiers and administrators, bankers and entrepreneurs. Their names could have been found, sometimes in the identical form, over the previous centuries. They were the English upper class in microcosm.

Taking a random sample* of forty-five debutantes from those presented in 1939, one gets the following breakdown. Seventeen had fathers who were peers — that is to say, dukes, marquesses, earls, viscounts or barons, men who were hereditary noblemen and members of the House of Lords. One girl's mother was a countess and another was a baroness in her own right, though in both cases without the entitlement to a seat in the Lords. A further four girls had fathers who were baronets — a hereditary title, passed down from father to eldest son, but not carrying with it the mark of nobility or the right to sit in the Lords. Finally, there were six girls whose fathers had been knighted; leaving just sixteen whose fathers had no title at all, and even

* The sample consists of the first forty-five debutantes whose present names and addresses I was able to verify. This means that it is not, in any strict sense, a "random" sample. Those people whose addresses were easiest to obtain were either those whose names were passed onto me by a contemporary — therefore they are more likely to fail within a handful of groups of friends — or those whose present whereabouts was easily traceable through a current Debrett, which means that the sample inclines towards the members of the aristocracy listed in its pages. A truly random sample could not have been selected without full knowledge of the present location and childhood origins of *all* debs in 1939, and this proved impossible to compile in the limited time available. Those debutantes who were not themselves of noble birth and those who married "commoners" disappear from view as far as the reference books are concerned. They could only be located through a contemporary who had remained in touch for nearly fifty years. It is a tribute to the success of the Season in forging lifelong friendships that so many have in fact done so.

among these their mothers often came from noble families.

In 1938 there were 750 members of the House of Lords (excluding bishops, archbishops and peers of the blood royal, as Debrett of that year called them reverently). It was not like today's Upper House, swollen to double that number with life peers. Furthermore, in 1939 Roman Catholic peers were still listed in the index to the House of Lords in italics, to distinguish them from members of the Church of England. (This usage was the last vestige of discrimination against Catholics in the nobility. Until 1829, Catholic peers were not even allowed to take their seats in the Upper House.) They were an intimate elite, whose titles dated back centuries, occasionally six or even seven centuries, guarding their precedence jealously according to the date of their creation. If not quite as rigid as the *Almanach de Gotha*, it was none the less an intensely proud and self-conscious community. It would not lightly surrender the rank and lineage of its daughters.

The debutantes fall, then, into three groups. Nineteen girls had at least one parent from the hereditary nobility, with another four whose fathers were baronets. The fathers of six more were members of the knighthood. Only sixteen had fathers who were commoners and some of them were Honourables, the sons of peers. A mere handful were middle class, and they, of course, were rich.

Of the forty-five debutantes making up this sample, ten were Lady So-and-so, meaning that they were the daughters of dukes, marquesses or earls; while another nine were Honourables — the daughters of viscounts or barons. Yet even here there is an anomaly, since there was one more girl, a plain "Miss" in 1939, who was destined to become a countess in her own right. Twenty, therefore, of the girls bore an outward sign of their nobility. (Not that anyone in their circle would have committed the solecism of introducing a girl as "the Honourable So-and-so". Honourable was only for envelopes, just another of those tiny meaningless rules which defined you as coming within or without the magic circle.)

How did these girls' fathers occupy themselves? Six out of the forty-five were — or had been — Members of Parliament. One debutante's mother took over from her husband at his death, and became MP for his constituency in 1927; while another's son eventually went on to become an MP in his turn. This startlingly high percentage — over 13 per cent — confirms the belief that the parents of those who did the Season were not merely upper class, but were in a very real and active sense powerful members of the Establishment. With nineteen fathers sitting in the House of Lords, and six in the House of Commons, twenty-five out of a notional forty-five were actively concerned with the government of the country. (Notional because, of the forty-five fathers, five had already died. So the figure is even more dramatic: twenty-five out of forty, or 62 per cent.) In addition to this, another five were JPS and three more were lords-lieutenant of counties. Of the remainder, most were high-ranking army or naval officers, two were press barons, two were courtiers and one was a banker.

It is much harder to discover information about their mothers. Three or four were divorced (two of those were American) and had remarried; the number being, if anything, surprisingly low, since their first marriages would have been under pressure of the First World War, or in its immediate aftermath. Three were dead, the daughter's dance being given by her aunt, or her two grandmothers or, in one case, her father. The reference books divulge the mothers' parents, where they were of the nobility, but reveal very little else about them. None had a degree. None, it is surely safe to assume, had a job, or ever contemplated working for a living — an attitude they passed on to their daughters. Born to be wives and mothers, their job was to marry well and, in due course, to marry their daughters well. Whatever skills this required, most of them managed it. Only three of the forty-five debutantes in the sample have not married in the last fifty years.

In the four months between the New Year and the beginning of the Season proper, mothers got together for a ceaseless round of meetings (known as "Mums' lunches" or "Mums' teas" or "Mums' cocktail parties") to co-ordinate the coming-out dances. The most fortunate girls were the ones whose mothers already had a wide circle of friends: dating back to their own Season; local neighbours; connected with their husbands'' activities as MP or country squire; or, best of all, other family members. Any of those who had sons or daughters of the right age would be rounded up to form the nucleus of each mother's list. These lists would then be exchanged, so that already in January and February each deb would slot into a group of her contemporaries.

If the girl — who at this stage was probably still at a finishing school abroad — were well connected and seemed likely to prove popular and attractive, other mothers would solicit her company to meet their own daughter; and thus girls' lunches, teas and cocktail parties were arranged for March and April, so that they could get to know one another.

The great arbiter of dances and the "List" was Lady Royds, about whom Madeleine Turnbull wrote in detail:

> She was a very dominant figure in the Seasons from 1937 to 1939. Her husband had been an Admiral, and after he retired he became one of the Assistant Commissioners of the Metropolitan Police Force. (In those days, all the senior police officers in London were amateurs, not professionals as they are now.) She was built on very generous lines, and her face was deeply creased, rather like an English bulldog. But if you gazed carefully through the creases you could discern two kindly, twinkling, and very perceptive eyes. She was very, very nice; but very formidable.

Lady Royds' first task was to gather together the mothers of prospective debs, who might not yet know one another, so that they could plan the Season. Mothers could agree to give a joint dance; they could work out a timetable, so that dances would not coincide with other major evening occasions; and they could pinpoint whose were likely to be the most sought-after dances of the summer, and ensure that their girl was invited. There was much jostling for position. Certain dates were more favoured than others. July was a bit late for all but the grandest dances. Nor would a girl choose, if she could avoid it, to have her dance the night before, or the night after, a very spectacular ball, for fear of comparisons. Lady Royds' tea-parties would begin in January, and within a month or six weeks the shape of the coming Season would be broadly determined.

The *first* Mum's tea-party my Mother went to in January [said Madeleine Turnbull] was at Lady Royds', and there she met Mrs Prescott Sandilands who, eleven years later, became my mother-in-law!

My elder brother was always being rung up by hostesses who literally begged him to come to their dinner-parties. He was rather grand about it all, and refused any but the most exotic or interesting invitations.

By late February the List would have been distributed, and invitations sent out to those debs who were family friends, school friends, or deemed desirable for all the usual reasons, with young men ticked off from the List to act as their partners. This meant that mothers and daughters had to invite dozens, if not hundreds, of young people whom they had never met. People unknown at the beginning of the Season had, however, become quite familiar by the end.

All this involved the mothers in a hectic whirl of activity. Dates would be pencilled in and invitations despatched, each to be listed, answered and ticked off. The protocol for these invitations was rigid and invariable. Invitation cards were always embossed; always white; and the stiffer the better. Replies were always phrased in the same terms: Miss Lucy So-and-so thanks Lady So-and-so very much for her kind invitation to luncheon on such-and-such a date, and has much pleasure in accepting. Nobody would think of deviating from this formula.

The initial flurry of lunches meant that the pattern of the Season emerged very early in the year, as the "best" dates were booked and caterers and dressmakers, florists and wine-merchants secured for the evening. Then the big invitation for the main dance could be ordered, written and sent out, with each deb's mother sending and receiving hundreds.

Young men to partner the girls were the perennial problem. Once brothers and cousins and local friends and brothers' contemporaries from school or university, regiment or City had been roped in, there was still a shortfall. This deficiency was made up, as far as possible, from private lists kept by some of the more experienced mothers who had already put previous daughters through their Season; and also by the two or three self-appointed doyennes of the debutante world, whose knowledge of young eligibles was jealously guarded and sparingly shared.

All this demanded considerable organizational skills from the mothers. Some — like Susan Meyrick's mother, Lady Meyrick — engaged social secretaries to handle the work. Those who did not, or were not good at it themselves, especially if they lived in the country and would not be based in London 'til April or even May, found their daughters very much handicapped as a result. The debs for whom the Season presented the greatest ordeal were those who embarked on it knowing almost no one. For them, the terror of the first few dances, as they entered a ballroom to find a sea of strange faces, must have been paralysing. Lady Mary

Pakenham, a deb from an earlier Season, endured just such an ordeal, chiefly because her parents lived in Ireland, so her contacts before the Season had been limited. First, the dinner-party before the dance:

> off I went to the house of some total stranger whom I would find standing in the middle of a drawing-room full of Italian furniture. A semi-circle of guests stood behind her twiddling their fingers and scraping their feet. There was generally a rather sheepish daughter pretending that the party was nothing to do with her, just a harmless whim of her mother's, and a son who arrived very late with his hair on end, and a father who would have been jovial if he had dared. The men had little tickets given to them in the hall to say who they were going to take down to dinner, but the girls were kept in the dark until the last exciting moment when, after watching more highly prized men giving their arms elsewhere, the spottiest of all advanced unwillingly with the encouraging words, "It seems I've got to take down you."[1]

Worse was to come. That was just dinner, where with luck a deb was in the company of only about twenty people. At the dance she had to brave several hundred.

> Other debutantes may have been as shy as I was, but I don't believe there was ever one who was more so. I used to hear my teeth chatter as I went through the hall and, when I sat out, I had to hold my knees to prevent their knocking together, keeping the other hand up to my face to conceal a muscle that ticked in my cheek.[2]

In every Season there were bound to be some girls who were paralysed by shyness. The trouble is that fifty years later, most of them have forgotten it, or they think they must have exaggerated the extent of their terror. Ann Schuster (now Mrs Archie Mackenzie) has not:

> I was so frightened myself that I felt a great bond with anybody like that. I can remember beginning to smoke then, and my hands shaking — but it did give you something to do. And it was just as bad before going in to each dinner-party. Then, you'd get settled in and perhaps even have a conversation with the men on either side of you, and then suddenly it was about ten o'clock and the whole business would start up again when you went on to the dances. You had two ordeals, if you were shy, to get through. Then when you got to the dance, you had to reorientate because some of the men at the dinner-party — not many, but some — would be fairly shameless in deserting their dinner partners and meeting various girlfriends. Therefore one or two girls would be left without partners, which was very embarrassing for them. When you went to the cloakroom there would be people taking refuge there. I even remember one who had torn her dress deliberately so that she could go to the cloakroom and have it repaired.
>
> I found it an ordeal, meeting a lot of strangers, after having lived in the country with my friends around and my animals, suddenly having to be tidy, having all these evening dresses, and trying to sort of become a personality: a new and quite different sort of person.

All the mothers' machinations in the first few months of the year were designed to avoid, as far as was humanly possible, their daughters having to endure such torments as these. A few girls stood head and shoulders above the fray by reason of their beauty, their zest for it all or their unusually noble birth. The rest needed all the protection their mothers could arrange to ensure that, even if miserable, at least they had allies with whom to be miserable.

By the late 1930s an unofficial "little Season" had grown up, starting early in the New Year with Hunt Balls and other country events. The beginning of May signalled the start of the *London* Season; elsewhere it had already been in full swing ever since Christmas. This was especially so in 1939, because much of that summer was taken up by the royal tour of the United States and Canada. This meant that King George VI and Queen Elizabeth were out of the country from 6 May until 22 June. The presentation of debutantes at Court had thus begun as early as March, when there were three Courts — on 9, 15 and 16 March — followed by another two much later, on 12 and 13 July after the royal couple's return.

Edward VIII, during the brief period between his two roles as Prince of Wales and Duke of Windsor, had scarcely bothered to conceal his boredom with the elaborate formalities of presentation to the monarch. On 21 July 1936, at an afternoon reception in the gardens of Buckingham Palace, he sat looking glum and petulant while rain threatened and a procession of mackintoshed debs made their curtseys before him. When the skies finally opened, he hurried inside and let it be known that all those who had not yet reached the dais could consider themselves presented. Mothers were scandalized; daughters disappointed; but the King was relieved to have been spared the final hour or so of this tedious chore.

After his Abdication on 11 December, the great publicity machine whose job it is to invest the monarch with super-human qualities ground to an abrupt halt, reversed, and set off again purposefully on its task of glamorizing the new King George VI and his Queen. Chips Channon, the diarist and gossip of the thirties, had recorded less than a week earlier, "The Duke of York is miserable, does not want the throne, and is imploring his brother to stay." That much was common knowledge. Chips went on to say, "We must keep our King, until now the most popular man the Empire has ever known; but I wonder whether his selfishness and stupidity over this muddle do not really make him unfit to govern?"[3] So they did: so indeed they did.

At first sight the new King and Queen were unpromising material. While it was true that she had charm and prettiness, a nice smile and a great desire to be liked, her husband was utterly unprepared for his role as head of a still-mighty Empire. Handicapped by a bad stutter, a nervous manner and a facial tic that betrayed tension in public, his only real asset was his sense of duty. Having once accepted that the Crown was a cup that would not pass from him, he embarked on the task of being as good a king and figurehead as his capacities allowed. By the end of his reign of just over fifteen years, he had won the love, and his wife the adoration, of his subjects.

It must have seemed impossibly difficult at the beginning. The King and Queen had been a home-loving, even domesticated couple, with their two delightful little daughters and their small (by royal standards) house in the grounds of Windsor Park, their corgis and labradors. Since their marriage they had not cultivated, or been much taken up by, Society and they lacked a loyal circle of staunch supporters to tide them over the first difficult months. One thing, however, was certain. George VI's accession meant a welcome return to a *British* social circle and the old, upper-class conventions of entertainment and hospitality. Former friends of the exiled Duke (and now Duchess) of Windsor soon found that they were exiled from social favour; whereupon most of them did a rapid Vicar of Bray, forgot their disgraced princeling and turned with the prevailing wind. Society had been dominated for two decades by rich, smart, sometimes vulgarly ostentatious and decidedly *American* hostesses. Now their reign, too, was over. The loosening of mores and morals which had started during the First World War and had continued through the hysterical twenties was now decisively halted. The mood of Society — emphasized by the wholesomeness of the new royal family and underscored by growing fears of war — was one of rectitude. People continued to entertain lavishly; but it was the lavishness of old family houses with old family retainers serving traditional English food on old family silver. Chaperonage was enforced again. The sharp chic of Mainbocher was out; the delicate charm of English dressmaking was back.

The new King and Queen learned their roles fast. George VI took lessons to overcome his stutter. They went on a successful royal tour to France in July 1938 where the Queen was dressed by Norman Hartnell and wore a truly dazzling selection of jewellery. They still made occasional mistakes. On 20 April 1938, the King sent Hitler the customary greetings telegram on the occasion of his forty-ninth birthday. He also wrote a personal letter from Balmoral that August, appealing to the German President "as one ex-serviceman to another" (what touching, and misplaced, humility) to avoid the horrors of another world war. In the event, he was persuaded by Chamberlain to abandon the letter.[4]

On 15 March 1939, Hitler and his armies entered Prague and proclaimed to the world that Czechoslovakia had ceased to exist. On 1 April, Hitler said, in a speech at Wilhelmshaven:

> We do not dream of waging war on other nations, subject, of course, to their leaving us in peace also. . . . But should anyone at any time show any desire to measure his strength against ours by force, then the German people will always be in a position and ready and determined to do the same!

At the end of this speech, most tellingly, Hitler stated: "There is no point in bringing about co-operation among nations, based upon permanent understanding, until this Jewish fission-fungus of peoples has been removed."[5] Three weeks later, on 20 April 1939, the King again sent a congratulatory telegram to Hitler, on his fiftieth birthday. This may have been protocol, but it was also unfortunate.

With Society and the rituals of the Season, the King was on surer ground. In 1937 he decided — or perhaps it was the Queen who decided — that the presentation of debutantes would take place as before at an evening Court.

The ceremony began at 9.30 p.m., and preparing for it took the whole afternoon. Most former debs still speak of the occasion with breathless, rose-tinted awe. They describe queuing in the Mall ("and of course everyone would crowd around your car and peer in at you, sitting there in your Prince of Wales feathers''); they speak deprecatingly of their own dress (''one must have looked absurd'') and admiringly of the dresses of others; they murmur compliments about the King and Queen (''they smiled so kindly at every single girl''). A great beauty of the Season says, ''When I curtseyed, the King looked down the front of my dress!''; while another recalls being shocked to realize that he wore a heavy layer of make-up.

One deb gave a rollicking and wholly convincing account of her presentation, stipulating only that it should be quoted anonymously:

Oh my God, my actual presentation. It really was hilarious because there one was, utterly dolled up, gold lamé train and all. Mother and I sat in our car, in a queue in the Mall, in the pouring rain, looking like that, I ask you. And then one got there and eventually it came to one's turn and one's presenter went in first and there were the King and Queen, sitting on their thrones. We had to curtsey to one, get up, walk one and a half steps, bonk bonk bonk, and then curtsey to the other. Then get up and walk backwards out of the room, doing something with the damned train. You weren't allowed to pick it up and throw it over your arm, of course — you had to go whip, whip [here she mimed kicking the train backwards] and one practised this till one was nearly blue in the face. Anyway, trust me, I was born clumsy. I managed the King, down I went — and when I say down, I mean it was *really* down, it wasn't just a bobbity-boo, you had to sink to your very ankles. Down I went, got up — I managed that and did my bonk bonk bonk, down I went again in front of the Queen. And as I went down, I heard — I knew it — my heel break off! It did, it did; and all my friends said, trust *me*.

Another debutante wrote a very different account of her presentation; equally accurate, but rather more serious. It is worth quoting in full because it conveys so well the atmosphere of half a century ago. . . .

All my life, as far back as I can remember, my Mother had promised me that she would present me at Court when I reached the age of eighteen. I wore white satin, with a white satin court train lined with palest lily-of-the-valley leaf green, and carried a bouquet of white roses and lilies-of-the-valley (my favourite flowers). I had three Prince of Wales ostrich feathers on my head, with a long silk gauze veil hanging down behind. (This dress afterwards became my "best" dress and was worn for many happy occasions — such as the Royal Caledonian Ball — and I still have my Court ostrich feathers, carefully kept in a box and labelled.) My darling Mother wore cream satin and a diamond tiara and Court ostrich feathers, and looked beautiful. Our dresses were specially made for us by BETA of Knightsbridge, which no longer exists, I am afraid. My Father wore full-dress naval uniform, complete with decorations and sword, and looked splendid.

Several friends came in to see us off, and we drove away just at 6.30 p.m. We had to drive round and round the Mall until the gates of the Palace were opened, with huge crowds staring into our cars and commenting loudly on the occupants!

Our car was the second car to pass into the courtyard of Buckingham Palace. It was strangely quiet in there, and we could not hear the traffic at all.

Then came a long wait, but there was plenty to watch — Beefeaters and Kings-Men-at-Arms arriving in horse-drawn carriages. At last it was time to drive up to the door. We left our evening cloaks in the car, so that we could go straight through and get seats in the Throne Room. There we sat and watched everyone arriving, and had time to admire the room itself.

The white walls were picked out in gold, and had tapestries hanging on them. At the far end was a red canopy with the profiles of Queen Victoria and Prince Albert, and in front of that were the two thrones. The middle of the floor was railed off for the Diplomatic Corps and all round the walls were red plush seats. A military band in the gallery played throughout.

It was a wonderful gathering, with the varied full-dress uniforms and decorations of the diplomatic, naval and military men present, and the beautifully dressed women. Never before had I seen so many well-dressed women gathered together, although they were almost outshone by the brilliance of the uniforms.

Suddenly came the roll of drums, and everyone stood up for the National Anthem, as the Royal Procession entered. The King and Queen were preceded by bowing attendants, and followed by Ladies-in-Waiting. They took their places on the thrones, the Princess Royal next to the Queen and the Duchess of Gloucester next to her.

We moved slowly down the long corridor and, at the end, handed in our cards with our names written on, while our trains were taken from over our arms and laid down by the attendants.

Then our names were announced, in clear tones, before we made our curtseys. The Queen smiled graciously at us all. The King wore the red and gold uniform of a field marshal, and the Queen wore a gold dress with a wonderful jewelled train. After making our Court Curtseys we passed on, and lined up in the corridor, where we were joined by my Father. Thus we were able to watch everyone else paying their homage and proceeding down.

When the last Presentation was over, the National Anthem was played, and the King and Queen proceeded slowly down the Throne Room to the Banquet Hall, smiling and inclining between rows of bowing subjects.

Then we went down to supper, where we drank delicious iced coffee out of G.R. IV cups and ate excellent savouries off "Honi Soit Qui Mal y Pense" plates. We met a great many friends, and my Father introduced me to a great many people he knew. We walked about and admired the beautiful State Rooms, the paintings, and the china in cabinets, to say nothing of the wonderful uniforms!

Eventually we went down to take our places and to hear our names called out as our cars arrived. We climbed in and drove straight to Lafayette's to be photographed. Lafayette and other court photographers stayed open all night. We were sustained with hot coffee, but even so, were almost too tired to stand! As we came out, there were crowds of women gathered outside to watch us. I feel very honoured to have seen the most brilliant Court in Europe.

The value of this account is that most of it was written down just a few days after the Presentation had taken place, hence the wealth of detail. Every girl must have performed exactly the same steps, felt the same sense of occasion, and known that henceforth she was officially "out".

Many insist that the Season of 1939 was in some way special, different from other Seasons of that decade and certainly different from any that followed it. Mrs Christopher Bridge, née Dinah Brand and niece of Lady Astor, said:

It was an extraordinary Season I think — other people will tell you this. It was a sort of — as if there was going to be — something was going to happen — there were such huge balls given. It was such a very grand Season and it always had the feeling I suppose of, this is the end of . . . I don't think I was aware of it, but looking back, I think it was an extraordinary Season. Sort of before the deluge. I think the adults may have had a feeling that there were mad days and dark clouds ahead and we were going to have a wonderful time while the Season lasted. It was certainly the last "real" Season.

For over a year, the imminence of war must have been increasingly obvious, even if many young girls were sheltered from realizing it. The former Lady Cathleen Eliot, daughter of the Earl of St Germans, wrote, "Politics were not discussed in my family so it was a complete surprise when war was declared. War was not talked about at home, or within my circle of friends." She was not unusual. Lady Jean Leslie Melville also said, "I don't remember anyone talking about the likelihood of a war. But parents knew; and the unusually large number of presentations at Court that year — 1,657 — must reflect their fear that by the following year there might be no presentations, no Season and no dances.*

Having successfully negotiated the ordeal by etiquette of presentation at Court, the other high point of the Season was the girl's own dance. Not every girl had one. There were about 400 dances in the Season, starting gradually soon after Christmas when they were

* Curiously enough, although there were no presentations at Court in 1940, a number of girls — including Churchill's daughter, Mary — did have a Season. (See Chapter 10.)

interspersed with Hunt Balls and other country events; warming up after the first Presentation on 9 March; and reaching a climax in May and June, when there were usually two or three different balls and dances every night. There are, for instance, thirty-seven dances listed in *The Times* for June, and these would have been only about a third of the total number, for many people preferred not to have their private dance publicly announced. Only the most popular and significant debutantes were asked to every dance; but all those who were spending the Season in London could have expected to receive at least three or four invitations a week.

By the end of June the King and Queen had returned from their tour of Canada and the United States, and the press outdid itself in adulation, hailing the event in tones more appropriate to Hannibal's crossing of the Alps or Alexander the Great's conquest of the known world. Even Harold Nicolson likened the Queen to Cleopatra. Never, it would seem, had two people embarked on a trip so momentous, or met with such resounding success. They evoked feelings — if *The Times* was to be believed — little short of idolatry. Describing the procession from Waterloo Station to Buckingham Palace, an over-excited correspondent wrote:

> It was, one felt, a processional route all too short for so memorable an occasion — but compressed into it were the heartfelt affection and enthusiasm of a whole nation. At the station barriers, and at every accessible spot which the royal carriage would pass, people had been content to wait for hours — and to feel themselves amply rewarded by seeing the

procession for a few fleeting moments. They carried away with them an unforgettable picture — the King, a quiet, happy smile lighting up his face as he raised his hand again and again to the salute in answer to the plaudits of the crowd; the Queen, a gracious, charming figure, smiling too, but undoubtedly profoundly moved.[6]

Country Life matched this in patriotic fervour and outdid *The Times in* conferring not only popularity but a kind of spiritual radiance upon the royal couple:

That their welcome was fanned into triumphant flame is due to the genius of the King and Queen for establishing, in a quite remarkable way, what can only be described as direct psychological contact with millions of individuals — a contact that was at once simple and mystic. Naturally as it comes to the King and Queen to emanate that happiness that is Heaven's gift to them, to do so unremittingly for such a period betokens spiritual resources no less remarkable than the physical stamina required.[7]

The royal publicity machine had done its work. In just two and a half years the inconvenient memory of Edward VIII, described by Harold Nicolson as "a wizened little boy", had been effaced. George VI and Queen Elizabeth were now firmly enthroned. With their country on the verge of war every patriotic symbol was needed: above all, that of the monarchy.

Three weeks after their return, the final Courts were held at Buckingham Palace, closely followed, as usual, by royal garden-parties. By then it was mid-July, and few could fail to realize that the war would happen within a few weeks, at best months. In spite of this, says Anthony Loch,

I do not remember that the impending war was a common topic of conversation with the girls, which tended to be on a frivolous or banal level. In moments of relaxation, people preferred not to think too much about the possibility of war. You might say that it was a case of "regardless of their fate the little victims play".

The end of the Season saw the gulf between the debs and the young men who were their contemporaries widen dramatically. Most of the girls still did not realize the gravity of the situation. But the men knew; and were conscious of the huge areas of unshared experience that were about to open up. One of the young men said,

I was very well aware that war might be just round the corner. I joined the Territorial Army the day after I left school. Most of the young men of my generation were convinced there was going to be a war. We had all been to public schools, we had all been in the Officers' Training Corps for the very reason that we were going to flock to the colours singing patriotic songs when the time came. The girls in general were not so aware. They had had sheltered lives and these matters were not discussed in front of them. During the Season we did not talk about the forthcoming war to our dancing partners. We wanted them to enjoy themselves and we wanted to enjoy ourselves. From the male point of view, it was very much an atmosphere of "eat, drink and be merry, for tomorrow we die". But we never had any doubt that we would win. Never. [Was this propaganda, or was it patriotism?] It was patriotism in the sense of duty. It was natural. Anything else would be unthinkable.

PART TWO

That Unspeakable Summer

Prologue

On 15 March 1939 Germany invaded Czechoslovakia at 6 a.m. It had long been expected, once the Sudetenland had been annexed, and resistance was hopeless. Anthony Eden, the former Foreign Secretary who had resigned the previous year over Chamberlain's attempts at rapprochement with Mussolini, said, "We are heading for a universal tragedy which is going to engulf us all." The British government made no official protest but in the eyes of much of the press and, increasingly, of the public, appeasement was seen to have failed.

Behind the scenes, within the government a radical change of heart was taking place. Many Conservatives were beginning to urge conscription, particularly in view of the growing threat to Poland. Harold Nicolson wrote in his diary on 17 March, "The feeling in the lobbies is that Chamberlain will either have to go or completely reverse his policy." On 31 March, when Chamberlain was to make a statement in the House of Commons, Nicolson recorded the scene:

Chamberlain arrives looking gaunt and ill. The skin above his high cheekbones is parchment yellow. He drops wearily into his place. David Margesson proposes the adjournment and the P.M. rises. He begins by saying that we believe in negotiation and do not trust in rumours. He then gets to the centre of his statement, namely that if Poland is attacked we shall declare war. That is greeted with cheers from every side. He reads his statement very slowly with a bent grey head. It is most impressive.[1]

Chamberlain's words were unequivocal:

I now have to inform the House that ... in the event of any action which clearly threatened Polish independence ... His Majesty's Government would feel themselves bound at once to lend the Polish Government all the support in their power.[2]

A poll in the *News Chronicle* showed that just over 50 per cent of those questioned still supported the policy of appeasement — a testimony to people's unquenchable optimism. But the government had changed course.

On 7 April — Good Friday — Italy invaded Albania. "The terrible inevitability of war has descended upon us," wrote Chips Channon in his diary that night.[3] From that Easter weekend onwards, the only question was when? How soon?

On 27 April the government announced its plans for a Compulsory Military Training Bill, affecting some 200,000 men between the ages of twenty and twenty-one.

On 28 April, Hitler addressed the Reichstag for two and a half hours. His speech was ostensibly a reply to Roosevelt's message calling for assurances that Germany and Italy would not attack independent nations. (He had listed no fewer than thirty-one, including Poland.)

In spite of superficial assurances of Germany's continued friendship towards Britain, Hitler said:

I am now compelled to state that the policy of England is now both unofficially and officially leaving no doubt about the fact that such a conviction [i.e. that a war between England and Germany would never again be possible] is no longer shared in London, and that, on the contrary, the opinion prevails there

101

that no matter in what conflict Germany should some day be entangled Great Britain would always have to take her stand against Germany. Thus a war against Germans is taken for granted in that country ...

Since England today, both by the press and unofficially, upholds the view that Germany should be opposed under all circumstances, and confirms this by the policy of encirclement known to us, the basis for the Naval Treaty has been removed.[4]

In a private conversation with the Rumanian Foreign Minister, Grigore Gafencu, Hitler's real attitude emerged nakedly and characteristically. Their meeting was described to Harold Nicolson and recorded in the latter's diary for 23 April:

[Hitler] had spoken quite calmly at first but when he touched on ideology he began to scream. He had spent the whole time abusing this country. He had complained that there was no British statesman of sufficient magnitude or vision to agree with him to divide the world between them. . . . All that he wanted was that we should not thwart his destiny in Eastern Europe. It was at this stage that he began to scream. He said that it was grotesque to imagine that he wanted to invade Holland or Belgium. The only small countries he wanted to dominate were those of the East. . . . . He said that if war came we might be able to destroy three German towns, but that he would destroy every single British town.[5]

There could no longer be any real hope of avoiding war with Germany: hence that "unspeakable" summer.

CHAPTER
FIVE

The Last Four Months
of Peace: May

There has always been something wonderfully democratic about the Royal Academy's Summer Exhibition. Anyone can submit a painting, and in 1939 10,565 people did so. The selection process is rapid and — apart from the right of Royal Academicians to have up to six works hung — necessarily random. In the few seconds during which each work of art passes before the eyes of the selection panel, many quite good pictures are chosen and some better ones rejected; many bad ones are excluded, and some accepted. The artists range from distressingly mawkish Sunday painters (whose works are usually the first to sell, being cheap and often small) to a few geniuses — though they are rare and their works nearly always remain unsold.

Kenneth Clark, then Director of the National Gallery, had described the Royal Academy in 1935 as "a period piece". He went on, "We must remember that in so far as the future of art depends on popular esteem or approval, the Royal Academy still holds a very much higher place than all the other cliques or fashions of art which a critical minority are prepared to accept. The

Summer Exhibition did not pretend to display the new, the adventurous or even the best of British art. It was — and is — reassuring precisely because it showed what the British like to paint, and what they like to buy: flower studies, green country landscapes, domestic interiors, views from the studio window. That particular year, though, even *Country Life* admitted, "The standard is not very high and the style is not very modern but at any rate there are fewer lapses than usual and fewer fashionable portraits without any artistic merit."[2]

London's other art galleries were providing a catholic selection of modern art. Picasso's *Guernica* had been shown in two different places: at the New Burlington, where it attracted 3,000 visitors, and at the Whitechapel, where — interestingly — four times as many people came to look at it. There was a Cézanne exhibition at the Rosenberg and Helft Gallery, to mark the centenary of his birth, and Monet was on show at Tooth's. Wildenstein had an exhibition of recent French pictures called "Paris 1938", Reid and Lefevre were showing English and French painting under the title "Entente Cordiale"; and the London Gallery had "Living Art in England", a show mounted in aid of Czech, German and Jewish artist refugees. From the early thirties, the rise of National Socialism and, simultaneously, the rise of an art of propaganda that might be called Aryan Brutalism had driven many artists out of their own countries. Some had settled in London, within walking distance of a group of British artists living in Hampstead who called themselves Unit One: artists like Moore, Hepworth, Ben Nicholson and

Paul Nash, whose work tended towards surrealism or abstraction. They were joined in 1934 by Walter Gropius from Germany, the architect who founded the Bauhaus; Moholy-Nagy from Hungary and Naum Gabo from Russia in *1935,* and Piet Mondrian from Holland in 1938.

Private View day was anything but democratic. Traditionally, it took place on the Friday before the first Monday in May; in 1939 this was 28 April. The exhibition then opened to the public the following Monday, 1 May, and remained open until 7 August.

The Times next day listed the names of seventy-three Society visitors, almost all women (men got in under the guise of escorting one of the women), the list being headed by the name of Mrs Neville Chamberlain. She was "an early-morning visitor, wearing a leaf-green ensemble. . . . Pink carnations were fastened to her coat." The costume of each one of the sixty-three women is laboriously described. It seems a pointless exercise, tedious to all but the wearer, and hardly even complimentary to her, since not a word of praise is bestowed. It is simply a recitation: "a cornflower-blue flowered toque with a printed crepe dress"; "black with a silver fox fur and a toque of multi-coloured flowers"; "printed crepe in fuchsia colourings" — a social convention fossilized into unreadability. On every major social occasion that summer, the same catalogue was repeated: for Ascot, Goodwood, Henley, even the Chelsea Flower Show.

On 1 May the International Opera Season at Covent Garden — also opened under the direction of Sir Thomas Beecham, adorned by a glittering selection of opera singers whose very names make mouth-watering reading. The debs, had they wished (and few of them did wish — or had the time), could have heard Richard Tauber in Smetana's *The Bartered Bride,* Eva Turner in Puccini's *Turandot* (in which Jussi Björling made his London debut) or Gigli in *Tosca,* besides a small Wagnerian selection — for in England, unlike Germany, a composer's music was thought to be of universal appeal, even Wagner's.

Also on 1 May, *The Times* announced that over 2,000 men per day had enlisted in the Territorial Army during April, and that the total number of applications for the first three weeks of the month was greater than for the whole of 1936.

Never mind; the Season was now under way — and it started well, with two large dances that must have had the debs and their escorts shuttling between them all night. The first was for Miss Lindsey Furneaux, and was held at 44 Cadogan Place, the town house of Lady Pamela Berry, who, as a relation of Lindsey's parents, gave the dance together with the Countess of Birkenhead. Lindsey, now Mrs Carrick-Smith, recalls that it was "an absolutely marvellous dance", from which a few, isolated incidents stand out in her memory:

For some reason my strongest image from that evening is of my darling aunt Margaret Birkenhead, who was dancing with Neville Ford. He was about 6 foot 5, and as they turned her nose hit the button of his white shirt front and bled all over it!

I wore the most wonderful dress from Victor Stiebel that Pamela and Sheila [the Countess of Birkenhead] had given to me — pink tulle with bumblebees tangled up in it all over the place. And my feet were hurting me so much that I called to our butler — his name was Sheridan — and I said, "Sherry, can you keep these for me?" and I took my shoes off and he put them into the pockets of his tail coat, one in the left and one in the right, and there they remained.

Lindsey's sister, less than two years her senior, was reading Modern Languages at Somerville College, Oxford, and their parents had decided that Lindsey, despite the fact that she was training to be a nurse at Colchester General Hospital, should "do" the Season that year. "I had a very small Morris Ten at the time," she remembers, "and I used to drive down to London or into the country for dances; drive back home to Essex; get up very early in the morning to exercise my horses — riding one and leading the other — and *then* go off and spend the day nursing. I think I was so tired most of the time I hardly knew what I was doing. Luckily I was very strong." Tiredness is a recurring theme in the debs' accounts of that summer. Many of them also point out what very good training it was for the war, when there were to be many sleepless nights.

The *Daily Mail*'s columnist, Charles Graves, wrote approvingly about Lindsey Furneaux's coming-out:

The dance which the Duke and Duchess of Kent attended was first class. The debs this year are at least as well dressed as anyone else, and it seems no longer to be an advantage to be a sophisticated young married woman. Somehow they must have persuaded their mothers and fathers to let them be dressed by Schiaparelli and Molyneux. Altogether I think it's safe to say that the debs are going to have a more attractive Season than any of their predecessors, except those who came out in 1919. For when a chap is Army-minded, he pays real attention to girls at dances. . . . But when he is merely sports-minded he is inclined to lean up against the champagne bar, and talk of his golf handicap or shooting or horses to other chaps.[3]

In fact, there were still plenty of the latter around, the boring, idle chaps up from the country who attended the dances for food and drink and even perhaps an heiress.

The other deb dance that night was given for Guinevere Brodrick by her mother, Viscountess Dunsford. Lady Dunsford was an unconventional figure. She was rumoured to have been a showgirl until she met and married the American multi-millionaire, George J. Gould. They had a son and two daughters (of whom Guinevere was one). Preferring the splendours of an English title, she later married Lord Dunsford. His family name was Brodrick, and the new Lady Dunsford immediately changed all the children's surnames and even had the effrontery to make them "Hons", although as they were not Viscount Dunsford's children they were not entitled to the honour. Then she set out to conquer the London social scene.

Guinevere's dance was held in the lovely house that used to belong to the financier, Clarence Hatry, which had been specially decorated for the occasion with lemon trees in fruit. A deb who was there that night remembers Guinevere as "a sort of moving light — she was absolutely lovely, and everybody sort of rushed round her like bees round a honey pot. And she had an extraordinary pushy Mum. At Guini's coming-out dance, she was in slinky black satin and Lady Dunsford

was in white tulle and baby blue bows. Unforgettable."
At this stage in the Season the male guests were still
wearing white tie rather than uniform; white tie and the
invariable white gloves, lest their hands should leave
stains on the girls' delicate dresses. That night Jack
Harris and his band played all the latest American dance
tunes and it was generally agreed that it was a lovely
dance for a girl who was described by many of her
contemporaries as "very lovely and charming: but she
had such a sad life ...".

The following night Mrs Charles Hambro gave a
dance for her two step-daughters, Cynthia and Diana.
Diana, now Lady Gibson-Watt, was not an altogether
willing debutante:

It meant absolutely nothing to me — it made no impact on my
life whatsoever, and I would have hated my daughters to do
the Season. I wanted to be a concert pianist, so I had my sights
set on higher things. I enjoyed moments of it, of course. The
trouble was, I adored dancing, but being six foot tall I could
never find tall enough partners. That was all I cared about: if
they were taller than me and could dance. There weren't very
many of those, and I certainly didn't meet one single young
man I could possibly have wanted to marry. And of course
nobody slept around in those days ... well, only a very, very
few. It wasn't chiefly because of the fear of pregnancy: you
were brought up to believe it was wrong. And you did believe
it.

Morals, like manners, were different then: and not
only among the upper classes. One of the most startling
details, to a modern eye, comes from the regular
advertisements in *The Times* Personal column
announcing that valuable items of jewellery had been

handed in to the police, and asking their owners to come and claim them. On a single day the Metropolitan Police announced under FOUND: a diamond and pearl bracelet; a ciné camera (a rare and expensive luxury); a diamond and sapphire flexible bracelet; and a diamond ring. One does not know, of course, who handed them in; but at a time when £3 or £4 a week was a normal working wage, and when a modest diamond ring cost £40, such honesty seems quite remarkable. It must also be pointed out, however, that in another day's Personal column the Chancellor of the Exchequer duly acknowledged receipt of £3 4s 9d conscience money, or about £65 at today's values. The fact that it is not a lot is immaterial: how long is it since conscience money insertions appeared in *The Times* at all?

The next night there was another dance — there was always another dance, if not several. On 3 May Lady Meyrick gave what is described in *The Times* as a "small dance" for Miss Susan Meyrick at 6 Stanhope Gate. These premises also housed the famous Gunter's Tearooms, where everyone went for leisurely teas in splendid surroundings. Gunter's was an institution, a favourite meeting place for country godmothers, half-term schoolchildren, bachelor uncles or budding romances. It was owned by Searcy's, the caterers, who also owned 23 Knightsbridge (it is Agriculture House today), and both were popular for deb dances. The Meyrick dance cannot have been very small, since no fewer than twenty-seven hostesses gave dinner parties beforehand. In fact, Susan Meyrick (now Mrs Peter Green) estimates that there were about 300 guests, who would have included, besides her own contemporaries, many friends of her parents' generation, among them the invariable rows of chaperones watching over the girls. (The chaperones were known irreverently by the debs as "the dowagers on the touch line".)

We had dinner at Claridge's first — a party of about twelve of us — and there was one young man whom I was very keen on, called Rodney Wilkinson, though actually being about ten years older than me he seemed very grown up. Later on he became a pilot in the Battle of Britain, and was killed. Then the dance itself. I wore a cream-coloured dress from Jacqmar, made of the most marvellous material. We had those prehistoric dance cards with all the numbers, and the men had to fill in their names — if you were rather shy, as I was, it nearly killed you — wondering if all your numbers would be filled up and hoping you'd get someone you really liked for the supper dance (that was usually number 8 or 9) because then you could stay with them for a good long time while you ate supper, at about midnight or one o'clock. On the invitation it gave the time for the dance, usually about 9 p.m. to 3 a.m.; and after that, if you could give your mother the slip, you'd go on to a nightclub. The dance would end with everyone letting their hair down a bit, probably doing the Conga all round the room, and then you'd go home and pretend to go to bed, but actually you slipped out and went off to, say, the Embassy Club, where Edmundo Ros had this marvellous Latin-American band. That was frightfully daring.

Having one's own dance wasn't a tremendous ordeal — though it probably was for my mother. She loathed and hated the whole thing . . . hated the sitting around.

It does seem another world. The war ended it all. Nothing ever went back to being quite the same again.

The next day, 4 May, Rosamund Neave had her coming-out dance. She was the sister of Airey Neave, who was later to make a sensational escape from Colditz. Rosamund was not quite eighteen, but despite being comparatively young she was in many ways an ideal deb, relaxed, cheerful, excellent company, and she already had hosts of friends. First her mother gave a dinner dance at the Ladies' Carlton Club, and at ten o'clock those fifty guests were joined by another 350 or so from all the other dinners, for the start of the main dance. Marius B.Winter's band played "You Couldn't Be Cuter" and — appropriately, as it turned out — "Love Walked In". (Rosamund married one of the young men at her dinner, Tony Sheppard, just six days after war was declared.) The dance ended with the Palais Glide and the Lambeth Walk — the current craze from the musical *Me and My Girl* by Lupino Lane, which had opened in 1937. (The King and Queen had gone to see it the previous evening.)

My mother had been presented and had had a Season and all the other mothers during my Season were people she'd known then, as a girl, and so that's how it went: from generation to generation. The great thing as far as I was concerned was that you got asked to these weekend house parties all over England, which was frightfully good for one. You played indoor games in the evenings, and tennis — very self-conscious-making if you didn't have good legs — and after a Season you found you could cope with any situation, whatever it might be.

It is easy to give the impression that the Season was simply a round of almost indistinguishable evenings, as one deb after another held the spotlight wearing her best dress, spending between £600 and £1,000 of her father's money (more, for a truly spectacular dance), and then joined the swarm of other butterflies who dipped and swung through banks of hothouse flowers for the brief summer. A few of the more serious debs were studying or working — a tiny proportion, it is true, but there were some art students, music students, even two girls who were studying ballet. For the others there were plenty of hours to be filled during the day.

Most girls, however late they might have come home, would be up again by nine — ten at the latest. Sonia Denison (now Mrs Heathcoat-Amory) remembers that:

Our parents were very strict. I always had to be up for breakfast next morning, if I was in London. That was the discipline. It was bad, slovenly, to lie in bed all morning. We had to get up, even if we'd got home at three or four o'clock the night before, we still had to be up for a nine o'clock breakfast. Then they'd say, if you're tired you can't go out.

This must have meant that popular girls like Sonia got through the Season somehow on five or six hours' sleep a night; while the men — at any rate those who were working, or at Oxford or Cambridge, or in the Army — had even less.

Earl Haig, who was an undergraduate at Christ Church at the time, remembers that a group of men would drive down to London for a ball; dance; often go on to a nightclub; drive back up to Oxford; and only just have time to change out of white tie into undergraduate flannels before heading for a tutorial or lecture. (This may have been the origin of the notorious "45 Club", open to members of Oxford or Cambridge who had driven from Piccadilly Circus back to their college at either university in less than three-quarters of an hour. True, it would have been easier in the dawn hours, and on the relatively traffic-free roads of the late thirties, but it must still have been a hazardous journey.) Such an occasion might explain the story which appeared in *The Times* in May, describing a car accident on the outskirts of Cambridge early one morning. The passengers, Lord Granby (the present Duke of Rutland), Lord Andrew Cavendish (the present Duke of Devonshire) and Mr Mark Howard, were in a car which struck a telegraph pole and overturned, and they were all slightly injured. The telegraph pole was broken. "The car was travelling from London, where", commented the report, dead-pan, "it was understood the men had been attending a party."

The Hon. Sarah Norton, now The Hon. Mrs Baring, was presented in *1938,* but like many debs attended the big social events of 1939 as well:

> It seems to me amazing now that we managed to keep going night after night. And it wasn't just dances — there were lunches as well, almost every day. We weren't ever allowed to dress in a sloppy way. For instance, you always wore white gloves to go out to lunch — always. I was allowed to have lunch without a chaperone as long as the young man had asked my mother first whether he might invite me. After lunch we used to go to Keith Prowse in Bond Street and listen to records — they had these cubicles where you could listen for hours, and nobody seemed to mind if you didn't buy anything, so we all congregated there in the afternoons.

There were dress fittings as well; hats and shoes to be bought; hair appointments; tea-parties — it was a wholly self-indulgent life. Some were aware of it at the time; most, with hindsight, feel guilty. Sarah Norton says, "We were spoilt brats, and when I look back on it I'm ashamed that we had this minute, privileged society and everybody else was either working or suffering. I think that's why I was pleased, in a sense, when the war came: it meant that I could do something useful at last."

Another deb of the 1939 Season remembers a slightly different routine to her days. She was Rhoda Walker-Heneage-Vivian, one of three daughters of Admiral Walker-Heneage-Vivian. The family lived at Clyne Castle in Wales, but also had a town house at 8 Hyde Park Gardens — huge, superb, with a ballroom. There the family would spend the summer months.

My days fell into a pattern. Getting up at about 10 a.m., writing letters (you always thanked the hostess for the previous night's dance) and then doing the flowers. These came three times a week from our home in Wales by train, in huge boxes. Ann [one of her sisters] and I hated this chore and usually ended up by ramming them bad-temperedly into vases and dashing out. We had a lovely butler called Martin who would sometimes help us out. His wife was Cook, aided by a kitchen maid. The mornings were spent window-shopping — usually walking up Oxford Street as far as Bond Street and meeting friends in Selfridges for ice-cream sodas. I had little money — a monthly allowance of £20 to buy accessories — but my father paid for dresses and shoes. I haunted Selfridges' Bargain Basement, Galeries Lafayette and Marks and Spencers. . . . Then came lunch-parties with other debs, then a lot of cinema-going, and the evening dinner and dances. Twice I went to a film premiere with a young man alone (normally this was never allowed). One of these was *Wuthering*

Heights, and the other was *Gone With the Wind*, and my escort was Ronnie Howard, son of the late Leslie Howard. This was allowed ... but straight home afterwards.

As the Season got into its stride and girls began to make friends, they would often arrange to meet for lunch. Ann Schuster remembers these relaxed, light-hearted occasions, which were a relief amid the formality of the rest of the Season's events:

They weren't organized — we didn't have these awful things that our mothers used to do, the mothers' lunches: no, you'd just have said, perhaps the night before, let's get together and talk about this ... some funny thing that had happened ... and you'd get together, six or eight of you, and have a sandwich at somebody's house. It was all very informal and we discussed hairdressers, compared lipstick (Revlon is the name that sort of sticks in my mind) and scent and pinched things from our mothers' dressing tables. It was all part of trying to learn how to be sophisticated — that was what we all wanted to be. Sophistication was the ultimate: knowing how to put on a veneer.

Most girls would end the afternoon at about five and come home to try and get an hour's sleep before starting to get ready. Those who had been to the hairdresser that day would have a quick bath, followed by another pause if it was deodorant day, because "The only anti-perspirant was Odo-ro-no which took twenty minutes to dry and lasted a week. (Shop girls and typists almost invariably smelt of BO.)" If debutantes expected one application of Odo-ro-no to suffice through a week of strenuous dances, some of them must surely have smelt of BO too. There were also a couple of products available for removing what an advertisement delicately calls "unwanted hair". It was called Bellin's Wonderstoen and — according to an advertisement in *Vogue* — all a girl had to do was "just rotate this dainty little disc over the skin and the embarrassment of unwanted hair vanishes like magic, instantly. It never fails. Wonderstoen is sure, harmless and odourless. Facial size 5/6 or de luxe size for arms and legs 13/6." Another product, Veet, was described by the makers as "a dainty white cream that leaves the skin soft and velvety-smooth without a trace of ugly bristly stubble like the razor leaves". This one made no claims to being odourless. One suspects that most young women simply borrowed a razor to achieve the desired daintiness.

The use of cosmetics varied according to the strictness of parents. Some girls wore no make-up at all. There was a wide range of cosmetics for those who chose to use them. Yardleys were famous by the late thirties for their beautiful sculpted boxes whose lids were embossed with a bee on a flower (designed by Reco Capey), and these continued to be the hallmark of Yardley products for the next twenty-five years. They offered eye shadow (mostly in safe English pale blues and greys) at 2s, cream rouge at 2s 6d, loose powder in boxes veiled with fine gauze to stop it flying about, at 3s 6d, lipstick at 3s and 5s 6d. These prices, if multiplied to allow for inflation, are exactly comparable with the cost of the same products today, although young women have become far more skilled in the art of make-up, and most start using it well before the age of seventeen or eighteen. Boots offered a range of skin-care products, including something mysteriously called "muscle oil" for 2s 6d. For the mothers, Harriet Hubbard Ayer offered Luxuria, which is described in the same glowing terms of hyperbole and fantasy that are found advertising anti-ageing products today. Hope springs eternal.

Made up, dressed up, complete with evening bag and evening cape or fur wrap, the girls and their mothers set out. They usually assembled at the dinner hostess's house at about eight o'clock for drinks (sherry or an orange juice for the debs, a cocktail for their mothers) before sitting down to eat. Most dances began at ten, but it was not considered advisable to arrive too punctually (perhaps because the most eager and least sophisticated young men would arrive first, and no deb wanted to find her dance card filled up by *them*) so the flood of guests did not start until some half hour later. By eleven o'clock the dance would be in full swing; between midnight and 1 a.m. supper was served; by 2 a.m. the first guests were starting to leave; and by four or five in the morning the dance would be on its last legs. "When we got back from a dance [says Mollie Acland] Mummy's maid "Rawly" [Christina Blanche Rawlings] would always be waiting up for her, and usually Ellis the butler too. If we were at home in the country, Nan would always be up to see me to bed."

The Season did not consist entirely of entertainments centred around the debutantes. There were very many charity events. In early May alone, the Docklands Ball at the Dorchester raised money for the Dockland Settlements; the Wendy Dance was held in aid of the Wendy Society; the England Ball was organized by the Council for the Preservation of Rural England; there were balls for the Blind, dinners for the English Speaking Union and the Gardeners' Benevolent Institution and the Friends of the Poor, and lots, lots more — all of them worthy, fund-raising events that enabled the wealthy and privileged to don evening dress and spend an agreeable evening among their own kind in the certainty that they were doing good. Few debs would have attended these: at least, not willingly.

Then there were private dinner-parties, which provided more opportunities for those who held the reins of power to meet socially and subtly, imperceptibly to exchange information and exert influence, while at the same time ensuring that power remained within their own charmed circle. These occasions were all but invisible except to those who took part, and their effectiveness was all the greater for it. Nothing need be written down, nothing voted upon, but a discreet conversation before dinner, a word in the right ear while relaxing over a glass of port or brandy before joining the ladies, could have far-reaching consequences.

What, for example, were Ambassador Joe Kennedy's real thoughts when the King and Queen came to dine at the American Embassy two nights before they set sail for their tour of Canada and the United States? The guests included some glittering members of the British aristocracy (among them, significantly, the Duke and Duchess of Devonshire), as well as all nine Kennedy children — gathered around the same dinner table for the first time in two years. Doubtless the Ambassador was anxious to underline his family's meteoric rise through the ranks of British Society, though this was due far more to the charm and vivacity of his elder daughter Kathleen (always known as "Kick") than to his own warm feelings for Britain. Secretly, Joe Kennedy was convinced that Germany would win the coming war. Mollie Acland says robustly, "We *hated* the Kennedys — though Eunice was attractive. But they were all anti-Brit and yet pleased to the point of crawling when they were asked to Windsor." Rose Kennedy was scarcely a prepossessing figure. One deb who knew the whole family well, and liked its younger members, described Rose as "a dreadful simpering idiot". Chips Channon, who met her on another occasion, was equally unimpressed: "She is an uninteresting little body, though pleasant and extraordinarily young-looking to be the mother of nine. She has an unpleasant voice, and says little of interest." But he found in her at least one redeeming feature: "She too keeps a diary, and I always like people who keep diaries; they are not as others; at least not quite."[4]

On 6 May the King and Queen set off on the start of their seven-week tour of Canada and the United States, going by train to Portsmouth with Queen Mary and the two princesses, as well as most of the other immediate members of the royal family, who said their goodbyes aboard the *Empress of Australia.* "I have my handkerchief," the little Princess Margaret was reported to have said, to which her thirteen-year-old sister added stoutly, "To wave, not to cry."

That same weekend, over in Bavaria, Unity Mitford had arrived at Berchtesgarten from her flat in Munich (from which a wealthy Jewish family had been summarily evicted to enable her to occupy it) to spend the weekend with Hitler. A newspaper photograph shows them taking tea together. Hitler, unsmiling, looks overweight and menacing while Unity — also overweight, also unsmiling — seems ill at ease in the presence of her hero. One can read too much into a split-second image. Perhaps when the photographer had gone they relaxed and smiled and went on talking eagerly about Germany's glorious future; but in that split second she looks like a fat intimidated Fräulein and he looks brutish and coarse. They must both have known that Hitler's mistress, Eva Braun, was infuriated by the presence of "that English Valkyrie". She would not pose a threat for very much longer.

The plight of the Jews in Germany was worsening daily. Not for nothing did desperate parents offer their children, through the columns of *The Times*, to any stranger who would give them a safe house. This advertisement for example, taken from *The Times* in early May, is typical of scores that appeared regularly throughout the summer: "Permit desired from Jew or Gentile for my daughter (15, German Jewess) which would enable her to do useful work. Experienced in looking after children; speaks English; well educated. Edith Sigall, Leipzig, Germany." There is poignant appeal in the words "my daughter" rather than just "German Jewess". A mother sending her child into the unknown, fearing never to see her again but hoping that the child, at any rate, might survive and even do "useful work".

That first week in May a new law had been enacted in Germany whereby Jews would not be permitted to occupy flats in a building which also housed Aryan tenants. In addition, Jewish families were not allowed to occupy homes "disproportionately large in relation to their numbers", a useful phrase that meant whatever the authorities wanted it to mean. The authorities could force Jewish houseowners to "modify" their properties, and to sublet the space thus made available to other Jews. The Jewish community was being squeezed and segregated; forced into an easily identifiable ghetto. These facts were reported blandly and with little editorial comment in the British press.

Is it unreasonable to wish that some of the debs — carefree, pampered creatures — had concerned themselves with the persecution of Jews and other minorities in Nazi Germany? Many young people fifty years later care desperately what happens to the starving and the persecuted in other countries. The answer is that so did some of the debs; those in particular whose eyes had been opened by a visit to Germany. Margaret Clifton-Brown (now the Dowager Lady Amherst of Hackney) had been in Vienna during the Anschluss; she had seen Hitler, and understood what he represented. She felt tremendous anxiety about the war which she had no doubt was coming, and soon; and about her own ability to face it. She feared for the Jews. Sarah Norton was another who had no illusions about what the Nazis meant to do to the Jews, though she could not have foreseen the finality of their solution.

I had been sent to Germany to learn German and "be finished". I hated the Germans and everything about their country except the people I lived with. Certainly I was conscious of the political situation: it was all around me, affecting everything. I could see the Stormtroopers on the streets, telling everyone to say Heil Hitler! I was conscious of the persecution of the Jews, and most angered by it. Anti-Nazi families were frightened of their own children, who were being indoctrinated by the Hitler Youth movement and would inform against their parents. The Graf and Gräfin I lived with didn't dare speak freely in front of their own son.

The English families most conscious of Jewish persecution were, of course, those who were Jewish themselves. Ann Schuster remembers a number of Jewish musicians who came to stay on their way to more permanent homes in Switzerland and America, and her father's growing fears about the future:

Two or three years before the war he used to come back from Vienna in a state of terrible apprehension. We had servants in those days and they would stand in the dining-room and he couldn't bear anybody behind his chair. My mother used to have to arrange for the butler to stay out of the room, because he couldn't bear it — anyone. ... He was working for Rothschild then, and he had seen his boss (I forget now which Rothschild it was) forced by the Nazis to scrub the streets. Vienna in fact was worse in those days than Berlin.

The rest of my generation — nearly all the girls I knew here — went to Munich when they were sixteen or seventeen: it was the thing to do then. But my father wouldn't let me. I didn't understand why, really. Eventually he himself had to stop working out there and then he concentrated on trying to make people realize the dangers that were building up. He even went to see Churchill, who agreed with him, but was powerless.

I think there were a lot of quite powerful people in England, the Redesdales being the most obvious, who were really committed to, were admirers of, Hitler and his regime and would go out of their way to meet any Nazi socially because they were rather splendid, to their way of thinking. I think a lot of the English upper class were inclined that way; and the rest — well, they weren't very politically minded. People like my mother, who would just say, oh, it'll be all right in the end; and if we do have a war it'll be over very quickly and, you know, Bob (my father), you're making too much of it all.

And yet, the extraordinary thing is that I, personally, never encountered any anti-Semitism at all. And nor did another friend, Naomi Rothschild, or one or two others. Perhaps it just wasn't among the young. Perhaps I never met it because my mother was fairly choosy about what families she met and what lunches I got involved in. But I was never conscious of this at all. And yet it was definitely there.

Anti-Semitism was, and still is, prevalent among the British upper classes, albeit less overtly today than it was in 1939. To outsiders, people either deny their own anti-Semitism or seem genuinely unaware of it. At most they may accept that they were "condescending" towards the Jews, and add that they felt "a bit sorry for those in Germany". One otherwise delightful man said he would not have dreamed of marrying a girl who was Jewish: "I didn't like their attitude and their manners and, anyway, one always thought of what they would look like in twenty years time. I do know one — a charming man, but an obvious Jew in appearance and oh, what is it about him? — well, he's got mannerisms and he thinks and talks rather a lot about money."

The aristocracy in particular was obsessed with questions about the extent to which its blue blood was permeated by Jewish blood. Loelia, former Duchess of Westminster, recalled her ducal husband's prurient fascination with the subject:

Benny [as she called Bendor, the second Duke] was usually excessively careless about his belongings and left his valuables lying about anywhere, but he used to lock up one book with elaborate secrecy. This was called *The Jews' Who's Who*, and it purported to tell the exact quantity of Jewish blood coursing through the veins of the aristocratic families of England. According to Benny, the Jews themselves, not liking to be revealed in their true colours, had tried to suppress this interesting publication and his copy was the only one that had escaped some great holocaust.[5]

Mollie Acland, now Mrs Peter Tabor, has written a convincing and candid description of how her kind felt about the Jews. It is notable for its lack of malice as much as for the unconscious prejudice it reveals. Yet she did not think of herself as anti-Semitic; nor was she, by upper-class standards.

About the Jews: we knew that Hitler had concentration camps — there was a very good film called *Pimpernel Smith* with Leslie Howard, about an Englishman helping internees to escape — but not the full extent and horror, which actually didn't really get going until the war. We knew Jews were emigrating as fast as they could, and though we weren't anti-Semitic as such, Jewish people were "different". They had funny noses and funny names which they anglicized, but very often became very, very rich. We enjoyed *The House of Rothschild* with George Arliss, but our Divinity lessons had taught us that the Jews weren't good news for Jesus. I can't remember any deb who would have admitted, let alone been proud to admit, her Jewish faith.

Precisely the same tone of voice can be heard in a report by a *Times* correspondent from Shanghai, where in May 2,000 Jewish refugees arrived from Europe, to add to the 8,000 already there. The man from *The Times* had been aboard one of the Jewish refugee ships, and his article describing their plight begins:

"I sell you this camera. Yes? Only eight pounds. Yes?" The would-be salesman is a scrubby little Jew, 22 years old, who needs a shave.... He was summarily put in a concentration camp at the time of what he calls the November Action. This morning he showed me, with a sort of furtive pride, a certificate of dismissal stating that "der Jude Hans Pringheim" served in the S. Concentration Camp till February 3, 1939. "I sell you this camera for seven pounds. Yes?" The little Jew told me that an emigrant is allowed to take exactly 10 marks out of the country, less than a pound.

The writer is not unsympathetic to the refugee. (He buys the camera, at any rate.) But the unconscious language of anti-Semitism, which he takes for granted his readers share, is ingrained in his description; along with a profound unconsciousness of the significance of Sachsenhausen concentration camp from which Hans Pringheim has fortunately been discharged. Nor does his article mention that Sir Victor Sassoon had recently made a desperate plea for help for the Jewish refugees in Shanghai, pointing out that the cost of feeding them had now by the most stringent economies been reduced to 3d per person a day, but that if more homes could not be provided, many new arrivals would have to sleep in the streets. By the end of 1939 there were to be nearly 30,000 Jewish refugees in China. And yet, as one deb wrote, "The plight of European Jews was a topic of casual conversation only."

Anti-Semitism was not entirely universal. Some people were openly prejudiced against Jews (including many writers in the thirties, such as Pound and Eliot); others were appalled by such an attitude. One deb of that year, who came from a family at the very heart of the British Establishment, said vehemently:

People said things then that could never be said now, like, what would you do if your daughter married a Jew? That's something nobody could ever say now — at least, I sincerely hope not. But the upper classes then were anti-Semitic. But in my group we were none of us anti-Semitic. It froze me instantly. It made me so furious: when people used expressions like "Jew-boy". And I must say that when stories percolated through from Germany about Jews being made to scrub the streets — well, I think that horrified everybody. But people don't like facing things, you know, and they didn't face it nearly enough. But everybody wanted to avoid a war, and I think that was the fatal thing. People just, you know, hoped for the best.

Meanwhile, hoping for the best, ignorant of the worst, the Season rushed on, and with it the dances. At weekends people took off for the country. There were sporting events to be enjoyed, fresh air to be breathed, sleep to be caught up on, and for those who still hankered for the society of their peers, there were country-house weekends. By Monday everyone would be back in London.

On Monday, 8 May, Lady Craigmyle gave a dance for her daughter the Hon. Ruth Shaw — and, perhaps because it was held at Claridge's, a relatively public venue, she took the precaution of inserting a notice in the Court Circular of *The Times* (the Court Circular was the senior prefects' noticeboard) warning guests that those who had not received admission cards must bring their invitations: presumably to guard against gatecrashers.

At the same time, a few hundred yards away at 6 Stanhope Gate, Sonia Denison and Rosemary Beale-Browne — best friends then, as now — were sharing their coming-out dance. An unusual feature of this one was that, as Rosemary's mother had died in 1933 and she was the only child, she was brought out by her father. He was very popular among the other debs' mothers, who could rarely persuade their husbands to come with them on the endless round of dinner-parties and dances, so there was always a shortage of older men. The Brigadier-General, who chaperoned his daughter conscientiously, was always greatly in demand to take lone mothers in to dinner.

Sonia Denison (now Mrs Heathcoat-Amory) remembers the relief of coming out after having been cooped up in a boarding school she did not enjoy:

> I think I'd been rather spoiled at home, with a governess, and I disliked going to school. We didn't work very hard — there was no standard at all: we weren't really taught at school. Ridiculous. So my dance — it was lovely. I had a wonderful dress . . . blue with white spots — such lovely clothes. I never wore them again. They were made into cushions, I think, in the end. Whereas my grandsons and granddaughters — they live a different life. They're very capable, very intelligent, and unspoilt.

The main dance that week was given the following evening, 9 May, by Viscountess Astor for her niece,

Dinah Brand. Dinah's mother had been one of the five remarkable Langhorne sisters from Virginia. In 1904, two of them — Nancy and her favourite and nearest sister, Phyllis — travelled to England in search, among other things, of more satisfactory husbands. Americans were popular in Edward VII's time, and the two of them took Society by storm. Phyllis duly married an Englishman, Bob Brand, and Dinah was one of their three children. When Phyllis died of pneumonia in 1937, Lady Astor took on much of the responsibility for these three, and it was under her auspices that Dinah came out in 1939. Her aunt, being a divorced woman, could not present her personally at Court, but she did everything else, bringing Dinah to live with her during the summer weeks in the Astors' splendid London house. It was a generous gesture, for Nancy was by then an active and hard-working MP, and, having abandoned her support for Chamberlain and appeasement, was now implacably opposed to Hitler. But she found time from her political commitments to give a wonderful dance for her niece at 4 St James's Square. Dinah recalls:

Oh, such beauty The rooms, the flowers, the dancing, the music — you were on *air*! I remember all the flurry and excitement beforehand — wonderful flowers brought up from Cliveden — there were gardenia trees in full bloom all round the ballroom, and the smell was unbelievable. And the excitement:
one felt one was *it*. First the excitement of my dress, which was made by Victor Stiebel at Jacqmar; I remember going to a couple of fittings with my aunt Nancy, to Victor Stiebel himself. It was tiers and tiers of silk and chiffon in different

blues, and cost £19. I wore it to all the other big dances that summer, and then the war came, and I never wore it again: except that I found it years later, and it had survived amazingly well, and still fitted me. With it I wore a pearl necklace and tiny diamond earrings ... it was not done for unmarried girls to wear a lot of jewellery, though of course all the mothers sat round in their tiaras keeping an eye out. There was a sort of security in that, even though we used to play them up a bit.

First we had dinner, served by footmen all in livery and white gloves. I sat next to the Duke of Gloucester. Then at about ten the guests started arriving for the dance — I remember them coming up these wonderful shallow stairs and being received by me and my aunt. Ambrose's band played — all the hit tunes — "Cheek to Cheek" — all the favourite tunes of that summer — "Anything Goes". I had a wonderful time, it being my ball, and the house looked so beautiful. I went back to it only the other day, and could hardly believe it possible today that such a huge house was actually *lived* in.

It was an extraordinary summer because of the undercurrents of doom and gloom ahead and all of us having a wild time. The men knew what was coming — they were already beginning to get involved in the Army; they knew that war was on top of us and we had very little time left. It was the last whirl before the storm, though I don't think many debs were aware of that — we were simply out to have the best time possible.

When you're young you don't even want to think about war coming — it's even quite exciting, in a terrible sort of way — but we were very protected. My father knew of course, but he'd only say, "There's going to be trouble." But, as for us, we just sailed along in a cloud — until we were thrown into it hook, line and sinker. We were in it up to the eyes.

It was an extraordinary year — the end of an era. One minute we were all aglow and aglitter and the next we were pitched into the cauldron.

However magical the previous night's dance may have been, there was never time to savour it, for there was almost always another the next day. The dance given for Helen Hoare and Mary Tyser on 10 May must have been in complete contrast to Dinah Brand's. Lady Astor's style of lavish and confident hospitality ran on practised wheels oiled by perfectly trained servants, accustomed to the rich, famous, powerful and beautiful. They had waited upon everyone from Hollywood film, stars to British politicians meeting at Cliveden or St James's Square to plan and influence the course of history. The young people invited for weekends at Cliveden were usually the most vivacious and intelligent of their age group.

By comparison, Helen Hoare and Mary Tyser were unsophisticated country girls. Helen's only contact with a glittering social circle would have been through her aunt, the Marchioness of Londonderry — another great political hostess of the twenties and thirties. Helen had studied in France and also in Germany, where she had been arrested in Munich for photographing a sign outside a greengrocer's shop that said "No Jews allowed". But although she came to her Season with some political awareness, she admits that socially she was very naive:

I hadn't been to many dances before — the Season had only just begun — and I remember being rather frightened before my own got going. I wore my only really smart dress, a white ballgown from Worth that my godmother had given me, and just a little touch of lipstick and powder. No rouge. No eyeshadow. I seem to remember that the dinner-party beforehand was at Londonderry House: not that I knew any of the young men. But people were very kind; I was good at dancing; and in the end I know I enjoyed it. Apart from that the Season made very little impression on me. I just remember seeing lots and lots of other people's beautiful houses.

Mary Tyser (now Lady Aldenham) was only seventeen and started the Season straight from boarding school. She had led a life sheltered even by the standards of her contemporaries, for her father, who was old enough to be her grandfather, had brought her up according to strict Victorian principles of young womanhood. She was never allowed to go anywhere alone and certainly not to a nightclub; she usually wore no make-up; no jewellery; for all these things would have horrified him. But during the Season her father remained at the family's country house in Essex, while Mary and her mother took the Lumleys' house at 39 Eaton Square ("Oh, on the *small* side of the square ..." she remembers a snobbish neighbour at lunch saying to her mother).

I think my mother enjoyed the dances more than I did: she had a wonderful time and couldn't understand why I was so unhappy. But lots of those very grand dances were agony for me — not one familiar face among the rows of boring young men whom I didn't want to dance with and who certainly didn't seem to want to dance with me, tongue-tied as I was with shyness. Not that most of them had a great deal to say for themselves.

Sometimes I just hated every minute of it and longed to get away, and it would be my mother who begged to stay on and I who was trying to persuade her to leave! My own dance was quite an ordeal ... having to stand at the top of the stairs (we'd borrowed Mrs Sassoon's lovely house at 2 Albert Gate, opposite the French Embassy) — standing there for at least an hour, shaking hands with all these arriving guests, none of whom I knew.

Being poor did not matter in the least, as long as you came from a good family. Blood was considered far more important than money. Madeleine Turnbull, who came out in 1937, said emphatically:

It was infinitely more prestigious to come of a family of ancient lineage and be poor as church mice than to be jumped up and enormously rich; so the latter were secretly scorned.

Being a debutante didn't have to be expensive. I think I was given £100 for the whole Season but I had to buy all my clothes with that. But then you could buy the most super evening dress for about £4.50. Quite a lot of people didn't give a dance — we didn't, because my parents couldn't really afford it — but we gave cocktail parties, and it really didn't cost much in the end. You see the whole thing was linked up with this feeling that money wasn't the main thing. It was more — well — either you were accepted or you weren't accepted. So in fact the girls who ostentatiously flaunted the fact that they had a lot of money were doing themselves a grave disservice. Far from making them more popular or more accepted, it did the reverse. People just slightly laughed behind their backs.

I think it was because, during the First World War, there'd been war profiteers who made a lot of money out of the war, and it was still too close for people to change their ideas. New money was a bit suspect, I think, because of that.

On the other hand if the daughters fitted in, weren't brash or difficult and didn't stick their necks out — well then, nobody would have minded them.

Christian Grant (now Mrs John Miller) was a Scottish debutante, whose childhood had been one of the utmost austerity; first because of her father's rigid attitudes about money, and then, after his death when she was ten, because a bungled will left her mother to manage on a pittance. Her father had been Sir Arthur Grant of Monymusk, tenth Baronet; but in spite of an ancestral castle and a retinue of servants, his six children had spent their early years in terror of his displeasure (he beat them all, even the girls): "Once I was thrashed for waiting outside the dining-room door to eat the scraps that came out from a grown-up dinner party; my father saw me and, thinking I had been eavesdropping, beat me instantly, without giving me time to explain that I was there only because I was hungry." The same economy was practised when it came to their clothes, and — apart from one good dress to wear in front of visitors — the younger children never had anything new:

My nearest sister and I, at the tail end of the family, had to wear whatever fitted us. This was all right when the handed-down boy's garment was a kilt, but not so good when it was grey flannel trousers or striped football socks brought back from a boarding school in England. Rough hand-knitted jerseys, their snagged stitches cascading from neck to hem, were gathered around our small waists by large dog collars, the brass labels of which proclaimed our names to be Rover or Thunder or Trust. . . . On our feet, in winter, we wore heavy black boots made by the village shoemaker, their soles almost solid with nails; in summer, unless the weather was particularly bad, we went barefoot. . . . My brothers, who during the day looked more untidy than the village children, came down to dinner in immaculately pressed scarlet kilts, lace-edged shirts and velvet jackets, the silver buttons of which were embossed with our family crest.[6]

This strange combination of thin gruel and double cream — harsh deprivation side-by-side with ancestral pride — was familiar to the upper classes, and certainly no one would have thought any worse of Christian Grant for being a deb on a very small allowance. On the contrary, she was greatly admired by her contemporaries, one of whom said that with her original dress sense and tremendous flair, Christian always looked wonderful. What mattered was the hereditary title and castle; the nannies and cooks and maids and governesses; the formal manners over candle-lit dinner-tables; the knowledge of shooting and fishing.

When it came to bringing out her daughter, Lady Grant looked for another mother with whom she could share, and halve, the cost of a dance. And so Christian joined up with a girl she barely knew — Ann Schuster — and the two held their dance at 6 Stanhope Gate: a setting that must by then have been very familiar to most of their guests. Christian remembers in detail the ritual of getting ready:

Most girls went to the hairdresser before a dance, especially their own, but as I was hard up by the standards of those days — I had £10 a month, which had to cover everything — I just washed my hair in the bath and pinned it up with Kirbigrips. I did wear make-up — Max Factor's pancake base! — and lipstick, and pale pink nail varnish. The dress I wore was the one I'd been presented in: pink brocade with little silver flowers all over it. It didn't take very long to get ready — I was eighteen and I had a healthy bloom. We met for the dinner-party at about eight or eight-thirty. I would have perhaps one sherry before the meal, and then lashings of champagne with it — champagne night after night, yet I never remember anyone getting in the least drunk. I suppose because we all rushed about and danced it off.

My own dance was more fun than any other, mainly because it was such a lovely feeling to know that you were — giving all your friends a nice evening. And I was lucky: I knew just about everybody who came. They were all real friends — from school and so on — and not just people who'd been asked out of duty. I was furious when they played Auld Lang Syne at the end of the dance — I just didn't want it to stop.

Christian summed up rapturously the feelings of a deb at the beginning of the Season:

Being suddenly catapulted into this fairytale world where everything was champagne and flowers, strawberries and cream, it was deliriously marvellous. Having been brought up to believe that one was plain and stupid and uninteresting and everything, suddenly to have admirers and be told that one was fanciable — it was lovely, glorious. I remember going on the bus down Park Lane one wonderful May morning and looking out, and all London was rather like today, absolutely golden, with the sun shining, and I remember thinking — it's marvellous, life is wonderful, and these two wonderful young men are in love with me. It was just lovely.

For all her light-hearted romanticism, Christian became more daring as the Season wore on. Ann Schuster became a great friend, and remembers their con-spiratorial discovery:

Well, Christian said, you miss all the fun if you go to bed at the end of the evening. You tuck your mother up, and then you slip out and you've arranged to meet somebody. So you go, either to a nightclub (and I thought, nightclub? No!). But there were all sorts of things that people did which were fun, like going to Richmond Park at dawn, and wandering through the park in your evening dress; and Covent Garden of course, strolling through the market; and then the odd nightclub. But I mostly did outdoor things, all tremendously innocent . . . .

The following week was marked by two of the highlights of the London Season besides, of course, the dances . . . never forget the dances: there were always at least ten a week, sometimes even more. Ten dances a week for thirteen weeks, up till the beginning of August, as well as the Oxford Commemoration and Cambridge May Balls, and regimental dances, and dances for Hurlingham and Ascot and Goodwood and Henley and charity; yacht-club dances and Cowes Week dances — all summer long, dances and more dances. Next, however, on Tuesday, 16 May, came the start of the Chelsea Flower Show.

The Royal Horticultural Society had held its annual show in the grounds of the Royal Hospital, Chelsea only since 1913, and it did not become an essential element of the Season until after the First World War. Before then, it had been something of a specialists' occasion for learned horticulturalists and enthusiastic amateur gardeners — including, of course, the owners and their head gardeners from the great country estates. In the 1920s it first began to blossom as a social event, and by 1939 a well-established order of precedence had developed over the four days of the Show. It always opened on a Tuesday, inaugurated by a visit from the royal family, most of whom were keen, if theoretical, gardeners. The King and Queen did not attend in 1939 (they were stuck in fog in an ice field somewhere outside Quebec), but Queen Mary was there, and so were the Kents, the Gloucesters and Princess Alice. Lady Sybil Phipps and her daughter Clare made the opening morning, but it was not a great occasion for debutantes: too cold and wet, too early in the day, and over-crowded with the older generation.

Once royalty had been shown round, the Private View occupied the rest of the morning; but although this meant, in principle, that it was reserved for Fellows of the Royal Horticultural Society, in practice the humbler Fellows were unlikely to turn up on the day traditionally attended by the aristocracy and country gentry. On the first afternoon the President's Tea-Party was held in his Tent: another occasion cherished by the social elite, when fertilization and cross-pollination and the merits of newer varieties of upstart flowers could be intricately debated. It was only on the last three days, when admission was cheaper, that ordinary members of the public came.

The days of spreading Edwardian lawns were already receding, those times when special flat leather "horse boots" had been on sale at the Show, so that the huge lawn-mowers and rollers pulled by one or even two horses could create a perfectly smooth surface, not pockmarked by the horses' hooves.

The week of the 1939 Flower Show suffered catastrophic weather. In a mainly dry month of average temperatures, the wettest days by far exactly coincided with the Show, which was buffeted by strong winds and torrential rain. But the displays, protected by two giant marquees, were magnificent and the crowds undeterred. The rock gardens were so realistic that a pair of wild ducks settled on one of the rock pools and feasted on the surrounding vegetation. It was to be the last Show for eight years. Once war had begun, the Royal Horticultural Society devoted most of its resources to instructing people how to grow their own vegetables and aid the war effort.

The following evening, on 17 May, the twelfth annual birthday ball in aid of Queen Charlotte's Maternity Hospital took place at Grosvenor House, attended by nearly 1,400 people. Lady Howard de Walden had arranged the first Queen Charlotte's Ball in 1927, and ran it virtually single-handed until the war, and then again after it until her retirement. "She used to preside over it like a sergeant-major and all those children [i.e. the debs] really jumped to attention when she appeared. Having had six children of her own, she had a great thing about birth and babies." Her lifelong interest in medicine and health also stemmed from the time, during the First World War, when she had run a hospital in Alexandria; but the Ball was always in aid of Queen Charlotte's Maternity Hospital. All those connected with it donated their services free; Jacksons of Piccadilly gave the giant cake, and each year a different cosmetic company would provide presents for all the Maids-in-Waiting (debutantes from previous years) and this year's Maids of Honour. The Guards of Honour were the favoured girls who actually dragged the cake into the ballroom, and as they had to be slim and elegant as well as reasonably strong, this was regarded as a great honour. Their present, in 1939, was a bottle of scent by Schiaparelli, attached to a cyclamen-coloured satin pincushion. (The colour suggests that the scent may have been "Shocking", which came wrapped in bright pink packaging — hence the description "shocking pink" — in which case one hopes the girls did not all wear it at once, since it is a powerfully sweet, heady scent.)

The views of the debs themselves on this ritual varied. "Pretty damned absurd," one called it.

Absolutely idiotic. One just had to giggle one's way through it, because it was absurd. Or at least I did — all my friends did. I think there were some girls who were over-awed and thought it was all rather marvellous. I thought it was idiotic but it wasn't really, looking back, because it did raise an enormous amount of money: so that in a sense it was worth doing. It still felt pretty stupid, and it was "mobbed up" even then — tremendously — by young men throwing fire-crackers and all that sort of thing. Getting obstreperous, throwing bread rolls. But Queen Charlotte's was all started by that remarkable, redoubtable lady, Lady Howard de Walden. She organized all that, and was the sort of doyenne of the Season.

The morning would have been spent rehearsing the elaborate ceremonies under the stern eye of Lady Howard de Walden herself. If 228 girls are to sweep in pairs down two staircases and curtsey in twos to the Guest of Honour and a cake, it has to be done with military precision, otherwise laughter — whether caused by nerves or by the comic spectacle they presented — could ruin the effect.

The cake was decorated with 195 candles, representing the number of years since Queen Charlotte's birth. (She was of course the first patron of the hospital.) The candles, unfortunately, were electric, not real. The royal personage who was Guest of Honour each year had to be descended from Queen Charlotte, but was never a reigning queen. (This might have implied that Queen Charlotte's Ball was usurping the role properly played by presentation at Court.) In 1939 the Guest of Honour was Princess Helena Victoria, the sixty-nine-year-old granddaughter of Queen Victoria. The quaint formalities surrounding the cake were accompanied by the music of Handel's "Judas Maccabeus", and were said to be derived from the original Queen Charlotte's favourite birthday ritual.

On the same night, also at Grosvenor House, the National Association for Local Government Officers gave a dance for 250 of their counterparts from Scandinavia. Imagination boggles at what some misdirected Norwegian local council official would have made of the scene, had he by chance found himself in the main ballroom and come upon nearly 250 eighteen-year-old girls dressed in pure white, discreetly jewelled, nervously awaiting their great moment. Initial relief, that the occasion was to be graced by a larger number of attractive young women than the invitation had led him to suspect, and gratitude to his hosts for having provided partners for himself and every single one of his Scandinavian colleagues would have been followed by incredulity as he observed them sink into deep curtseys in front of a gigantic, many-candled cake.

Absurd it may have been, but lots of the debutantes were thrilled by it all. So was the *Daily Mail,* whose breathless diarist informed the paper s readers that the 1939 debs were the prettiest and most aristocratic for years. It redeemed itself however with a touching description of the nannies who watched their former charges from the balcony overlooking the main ballroom :

> Hundreds of nannies settled like a flock of starlings on the balcony of the big banqueting hall at Grosvenor House just when the procession was about to begin. They looked earnest and protective, waiting anxiously, with their eyes glued to their girls, though one or two dashed over to give their last words of encouragement and a final pat before the ceremony began.[7]

Surprisingly, this was not the last Queen Charlotte's Ball for the next five years. It carried on during the war, though its date was later moved to December and the cake was made with dried eggs, the young men wore uniform and the debs' dresses were bought with coupons.

Marigold Charrington, whose dance came next on 18 May, remembers chiefly being worried about whether anyone would dance with her :

> I was frightfully anxious about whether anyone would want to dance with me. It mattered that you could *talk*. I remember an aunt of mine sending a note down the dinner-table to a young niece saying, "Talk, you loon," and of course she never spoke again. But you were not allowed to talk about money or the food or domestics.

This was the main point of the dinner-parties: to ensure that the girls (some of whom, certainly at this stage of the Season, might otherwise have known nobody at all) were supplied with at least two guaranteed partners. "The young men were in honour bound — and did honour it. Usually they did have to, however much they disliked, however much they thought she was simply hideous, dance with the girl beside them at dinner. Even if she was boss-eyed and the size of a hippopotamus. It was, so to speak, singing for your supper." Not that this would ever have been a problem for Vivien Mosley, who made that remark. Through family connections and her brother's Etonian friends, she had a wide circle of male acquaintances even before the Season began. But for girls up from the depths of the country whose social circle was local and limited, it was a godsend to know you would not have to "sit out" every single dance — the ultimate humiliation.

What were they really like, the young men who were such an essential component of every Season; and why did they always seem to be in short supply?

The truth is, they were not in short supply: only the desirable ones were. Men were desirable, in the words of one former deb, "if they were good dancers, good looking and amusing to talk to". In the eyes of debs' mothers, it was even more important that they should come from good fanulies. "Good", of course, meant aristocratic. Mollie Acland, whose mother used to bring her knitting to dances, says, "I could always tell what sort of chap I was dancing with by her expression — smiles for rich young lordlings, down to positive frowns for penniless subalterns!" Lady Cathleen Eliot (now Hudson) remembers another kind of popularity:

It came from aristocratic birth, being photogenic, and most of all from the glossy magazines of that time. The male "leading lights" of the year were Valerian Douro, now Duke of Wellington; Charles Manners, who was then Granby and is now Rutland — those two were both extremely good-looking — and Hugh Fraser, the younger brother of Lord Lovat.

Other names that were mentioned again and again were those of Dawyck Haig (who had been Earl Haig since he was ten years old, which caused him a good many problems at prep school); "Rowley" Errington, later the Earl of Cromer, who was popular not only because he was titled but because he was tremendously funny as well; Charlie Linlithgow's twin brother (now Lord Glendevon); Tony Loughborough (the late Earl of Rosslyn); Alan Cathcart, who had succeeded to the earldom aged eight; Martyn Beckett (who had succeeded to his father's baronetcy in 1937); Billy Hartington and his brother Andrew Cavendish. These last three were already deeply engrossed in the young women they were later to marry. Over a span of fifty years one must take it on trust that all these young men were charming and attractive; what cannot be disputed is that they all, without exception, came from aristocratic families, and most of them, if not already titled, would be eventually.

Several former debs also mentioned the names of some notable eccentrics: young men who were memorable for being different: Sir Iain Moncreiffe of that Ilk (whose very name gave him a head start); Ben Nicholson (not the painter — a namesake); Simon

Asquith; Ivan Moffatt; and Philip Toynbee. The last two would certainly be appalled at finding themselves listed among the young men of the 1939 Season, and one suspects that they were remembered chiefly because their political views differed so startlingly from those of their fellows.

There could never be enough "rich young lordlings" to go round, and next in the popularity stakes came younger sons — victims of primogeniture, in Waugh's phrase — who would not themselves inherit a title (though the war upset a lot of people's expectations) but would provide entry to a noble family. The girls themselves could always be charmed by a man who was witty (which implies intelligence as well) and a good dancer — whatever their mothers might have to say about his prospects. But all these categories together could not amount to more than about a hundred young men: and this when even the elite among the girls amounted to four times that number. The rest, brought in to provide dancing partners, were described over and over again — after fifty years the memory still rankles — as spoilt, conventional and dull. *They* were the "debs' delights": the chinless wonders of the time. In spite of this, the impression of a shortfall persists. Mollie Acland stresses:

The first thing to remember is that there were never enough: if for a dinner-party you had to fall back on a seventeen-year-old or a forty-year-old, that was a failure. The ideal age was twenty-three, but twenty-one to twenty-seven was good. They certainly enjoyed the food — dinner, supper and breakfast! — but also I think, like us, actually enjoyed just meeting other young. Don't forget that public schools were

145

still single sex, so for both boys and girls it was a first chance of limited freedom with the opposite sex.

Nobody expected the debs to work, and the very few who did found the summer a gruelling experience. Many of the men, on the other hand, did have jobs. The largest proportion were in the Army. "My clearest recollections are of the many, many young men with whom I danced who were killed in the war. We were all so *young*. Almost all, if not in the Regular Army by June, were in the Territorials or the RNVR or RAFVR" One of the debs escorts concurs: "Most of the young men who were on the List came-from the landed gentry, the aristocracy, the civil service and the armed forces." He was himself eighteen at the start of the 1939 Season: was he willing to be involved in all this?

Up to a point, yes. I was young and I enjoyed the company of pretty girls. I enjoyed my wine and food, and one was usually given a good dinner first, and then the whole party went on to the dance, wherever it was, and between midnight and two o'clock there was usually a very good supper served, with champagne. Later on there would be breakfast: eggs and bacon and kedgeree, and more champagne. But I was not prepared to do it every single night of the Season, otherwise one would have had no sleep. Then, the morning after the dance, one would send flowers — not to the girl, but to her mother, who had been the hostess. This was partly courtesy, and partly looked upon as an investment!

In addition to the men from the armed forces, there was a surprisingly large number of medical students. It was an infallible way of getting a free meal, and for young medical students or law students who did not have generous allowances from their parents, the endless supply of free salmon and strawberries was a godsend. Helen Vlasto, who was nursing as well as being a deb that year, recalls:

My husband, who had just come down from Cambridge and was a medical student at the London Hospital, tells me that on their "Mess" noticeboard, the names of hostesses and whereabouts of deb dances were displayed for anyone who cared to do so to make use of. Few could afford the travel, and by no means all had the right dress for such occasions. He did attend one or two, but I think found the whole world somewhat unreal, when he was treating the poor and the sick of London's East End!

Rhoda Walker-Heneage-Vivian remembers them too:

Apart from the Army and Navy men and a sprinkling of stockbrokers, there were also several medical students (particularly from St George's Hospital: perhaps because it was so central). They used to go straight into the wards from the dances having stocked up on the huge breakfasts provided in the early hours. My husband has reminded me of the practice of the dance hostesses of sending cards to Regimental Messes (usually the Guards) for officers to sign their names if they wished for invitations to the various dances. Even so, it was always a bit of a headache scraping up enough men to go round the dinner-parties and all sorts of ghastly cousins were pressed into service and ignored by Ann and me.

Brothers made up the shortfall, even if they were only seventeen and sometimes still at public school. But one deb's brother is another deb's partner, and the fact that the girl was doing a Season virtually guaranteed the suitability of her brother.

Even allowing for the men from the Army and Navy, the undergraduates, the medical students and a smattering from the professions, this still left a large number who did hardly any work at all. Lady Cathleen Eliot, the niece of the Duke of Beaufort, remembers many such:

> The young men of 1939 were often heirs to big estates learning in a most relaxed way to take over from their fathers. They spent their time hunting and shooting and fishing, and going to deb dances and getting free dinners on the way. Even the ones who were soldiers seemed to have a lot of leave, and hunted at least twice a week. It was considered common to work in the City or in trade.

Their lives cannot have been too demanding, and certainly left them plenty of time for the Season. For a man "in the forefront of the debs' delightery", to borrow one scathing expression, this idleness was an advantage:

> There was only a nucleus who either wanted or were able to literally dance the nights away five darn nights a week. So they went round and round and round and *round*, and I suppose they did get nobbled up in the end. But, you know, there were a lot who, other than in the most exceptional circumstances — like a great friend or a sister — would have *died* rather than attend a deb dance. And don't forget, it wasn't just the dances — there was Ascot and Henley and so on, and the whole shabang, the whole mobaroo moved round those as well: all just drifting round in the same galère.

One deb's brother, co-opted to dinner and dances, now says, "I found all the Seasons *fun* and not in any way a "social duty". During my time manners — good manners — were a *sine qua non,* although there were lapses by the occasional young man. It was also taken for granted that one dressed on all occasions in meticulous fashion, from head to toe." Anthony Loch adds a telling detail: "Since it was more economical to send white waistcoats to the laundry rather than the dry-cleaners, I found myself the possessor of something like a dozen."

Everyone is unanimous about the good manners of young men and women in Society in those last days before the War. One of the men who escorted many of the 1939 debs strikes a wistful note:

In my view, by the time of the 1939 Season, courtesy and etiquette had reached the highest level since 1913 and 1914. I think the survivors of the First World War were so shocked at what had happened, that first of all they let themselves go in the 1920s as a relief; but gradually it all began to come back in the 30s. I think there was a great nostalgia and yearning for Edwardian times, when we thought we were safe, we thought we were on top of the world; when living was gracious and people entertained, people still gave house parties and could afford to. And I think it was part of this yearning that created this climate for good manners, courtesy and consideration. Manners began to deteriorate as soon as the war broke out. Everyone was in a hurry. But I think manners today — which are absolutely appalling — are so bad because people are selfish. They just don't care about others.

He clearly has in mind two quite different aspects of good manners. There is conventional courtesy — the obligation to dance with your neighbours at dinner, or

149

to send flowers and a thank-you letter to your hostess the next day. But he also has in mind a more profound sort of manners, the manners of the heart: a rare and unselfish consideration for other people. Vivien Mosley made exactly the same point, but she sees it rather differently:

> All the men had beautifully superimposed manners. They knew how to behave impeccably and they were certainly well turned out. But on another level, I would not say that their manners were innately beautiful — by which I mean being sensitive to the person you're dealing with. I certainly don't think that applied. Whereas today people's manners are much worse — absolutely unpardonable, some of them. On both levels.

What, then — if they all had perfect manners — made a young man undesirable? Apart from the usual things like being boring or unattractive (which were much more serious handicaps in the case of the girls), men who were sexually predatory were disapproved of — particularly by the mothers. Lady Royds' List marked these off with the initials NSIT (not safe in taxis), to which the debs added a further category, MTF (must touch flesh). However, knowing that a man was NSIT added a certain frisson to his company ... and sometimes a certain disappointment. If one of these "taxi tigers" *didn't* pounce, the girl was left thinking, "Well, what's wrong with me?" So taxi tigers were quite an intriguing species, though the ubiquitous chaperones rarely gave them a chance to pursue their prey unobserved. They could sometimes entice one, of the braver girls to a nightclub and in the taxi on the way there or, more likely, on the way back hope for a kiss and a cuddle; but never, or only very seldom, did it amount to anything more.

One is left with the obvious conclusion that the least desirable young men were the dull ones — especially if they were conceited as well. The worst offenders seem to have been the very young Guards officers: "We thought they were frightfully stupid and unsophisticated and dreary." Remarkably few of the men seem to have been good dancers; indeed, one former deb said bitterly, "Good? Most of them were atrocious — *atrocious* —"

An awful lot of us that year loved waltzing more than anything else, Viennese waltzing, and one used to stand there with that silly programme and one used to absolutely *pray* and wait and look around saying, I do hope, I do hope . . . Well, there were about half a dozen real dab hands, and one simply didn't care, they could come up to one's knee and be covered in warts or anything — but if they could waltz well, I mean, one was so pleased.

The ritual of the dance cards still survived, although both sexes found it archaic. One man who was in attendance during the last two Seasons of the decade recalled how it worked:

The girl had the dance programme with a pencil attached on the end of a cord, and a young man would go round and say to a girl he liked the look of, "Are you free to dance the 12th?" (which might be a waltz, or it might be a two-step) and the pretty girls normally had all their programmes filled up. The ones who were not pretty, I'm afraid, indulged in a certain amount of subterfuge, and it was not unknown for a girl to fill

151

in her own programme, so that she would not lose face with her mother or her chaperone. She would say, I'm tired, I'm sitting this dance out."

Mary Pollock (now Mrs D'Oyly) tells the story of what she did when faced with an almost-empty dance card:

There was one dreadful evening at 6 Stanhope Gate when hardly anybody asked me to dance. I think I had two names on my card. I sat there feeling so awful — kept going off to the loo — coming back — still nobody — so in the end I rang up my parents. It was late, and they'd gone to bed but my father who was a frightfully kind man said, "Don't worry — I'll be at the door in half an hour." Just after, a young man came up to me and said, "Excuse me, I've noticed that you don't seem to have had many dances: will you come and dance with me?" I had to tell him that I was leaving in half an hour, but anyhow we danced for the rest of the evening, and I got to know him quite well. Next day he came to call on me. He became a good friend — no, I didn't marry him!

It is good to be reminded that the young could be spontaneously kind to one another.

Lord Cromer remembers the gamesmanship, as he calls it, attached to dance cards:

As far as the young men were concerned, a lot of them were very shy. The one thing you didn't want to do was to be left on your own. Of course it was always easier for the boys because at a party they could always go to the bar and have a drink. If a girl wasn't asked to dance then I think she had a very miserable time. At private parties, programmes were universal, and there was a great deal of gamesmanship in it. If a girl was pretty and much sought after, then you would say, have you a spare dance? And she would say, oh, I can manage number eleven and you knew perfectly well she'd made it up. It was all part of the sort of mating — well, not mating, that's too strong a word — dating ploy. It was a private piece of paper. A girl kept her programme, and only a very persistent young man would say, I want to see it. Now, having promised you number eleven she was honour bound to dance with you — *if* she was still there. But the party might have broken up. She couldn't though, say, "I've forgotten". That was bad.

A man might be conscious that he had been rejected; but for a girl a half-empty programme was a disaster. It was public humiliation to be seen sitting like a wallflower at the edge of the room while others danced. One deb remembers vividly:

> People used to gather in the entrance of the ballroom and you used to start off looking quite confident and then you'd start to look slightly worried and then you'd sort of look round and you'd look at your card as if someone had let you down, and hopefully someone would come and ask you to dance.
>
> And then there was the other thing: you used to go to the bar and pretend someone was getting you a drink. It was a tragedy if your programme wasn't filled. I never used to go and spend time in the cloakroom. You'd never get asked to dance *there*.

A young man who liked dancing was rated above one who was a good talker. Most of the debs positively expected to be bored in conversation. They were advised not to be too interesting themselves, in case it intimidated the men, and certainly not to display signs of intellectual prowess. "My mother said to me, 'Darling, boys don't like *bookish* girls.'" says Sarah

Norton — which must have been frustrating for her, since she was rather well read. Elizabeth Lowry-Corry had exactly the same experience:

> Setting the world to rights was not really one of my subjects, but I was in a way already becoming an intellectual. I had studied music in Dresden; I'd read a great many books by this time, and I think if I'd been able to talk about these kind of things, it would have been fine. But in fact none of the chaps I knew, or most of the girls either, believed in that line of country at all. And my father hated talking to intelligent girls. He didn't like it if you came out with anything, really. Perhaps one may have tried to say something, but it fell flat. So all this made conversation very difficult.

Even Priscilla Brett, who moved among an unusually bright and articulate young crowd, experienced the same problems as soon as she left the company of her close friends: "At the dinner-table, if you were put next to a stranger, the difficulty was to keep the thing going without saying anything very interesting, because that wasn't done." This remembered range of topics conjures up an image of a young man who expects to hold forth and a young girl who expects to have to listen: "Most of them liked telling you about their regiments, or their horses, or their hunting prowess, or their plans for the future; and occasionally their sad stories of disappointments with other girls." Lady Cathleen Eliot was even more unlucky:

> The main conversation that I remember was how many dances you were going to that week; which of last night's two or three were you at; and were you going to so-and-so's tomorrow A few of the men were of course intelligent, and that made them

good conversationalists, but on the whole they were dull. I was lucky enough to be a good talker, helped by the fact that my mother had a pilot's licence and used to fly me up and down to London from the country, which made me popular with the men. The war and politics were not talked about among my friends, so I thought that hunting, house parties and parties would go on ad infinitum until perhaps one day I would get married. I think debs at that time were very parochial and xenophobic, mostly because they'd had such a sheltered upbringing.

One senses that the young people for whose benefit the Season was so elaborately stage-managed were often scarcely more than children and, for all their beautiful manners, underneath that façade they were ill at ease, inexperienced and — especially the men — quite unprepared for emotional contact with the opposite sex. Prep and public schools ensured that, for ten years or more, boys had almost no knowledge of girls outside their immediate family. At the same time they were often indoctrinated with the belief that it was unmanly to show their feelings — not triumph or disappointment or pride, not tenderness or affection, and, above all, never a chink of vulnerability. Small boys despatched sobbing to prep school at the age of seven or eight, frightened and homesick in their scratchy new uniforms, came home after one or two terms with the concept of the stiff upper lip already firmly lodged in their minds. Tears and teddy bears were laughed to scorn and bullying was endemic. "From the age of eight I slept with a knife under my pillow," said one good-looking scion of the aristocracy. Adolescent sexuality took the form of torrid love-affairs with other boys or, more sinisterly, the organized brutality of caning. Boys were at a further disadvantage in that many of them were not allowed to betray signs of affection at home, either, and were much more subject to discipline than girls. Boys from aristocratic families usually referred to their fathers by their title at all times, except to their face, when they might say "Papa" or "Pater". Boys in their teens could be ordered around by any passing uncle or cousin — "Go and change your shoes before your father sees you" — and only the bravest or most devoted mother would demur.

By the time boys emerged from the public-school system at the age of eighteen, the worst of them had been rendered unimaginative and insensitive to the feelings of others, while even the best had learned all too effectively how to hide their feelings. Some never overcame this. Many Englishmen direct their strongest emotions towards their horse, their car, their club, their regiment or even their old school. Madeleine Turnbull looks back sympathetically at the gauche young men of her generation: "Public school certainly bashed an awful lot of emotion out of them, these terribly up-tight young men who had it all sort of bottled in and couldn't express it. It was terribly sad. While boarding schools for the girls were just the opposite ... hothouses of expectation and romantic ideas!" Girls might dream of love and aristocratic elopements as portrayed in the historical novels of Margaret Irwin or Georgette Heyer, but they never doubted that sex before marriage was taboo. "I think I was kissed twice before I met my future husband," said one, who is not untypical.

And so the young enacted, night after night, a formalized ritual of meeting, conversing and dancing in the most luxurious surroundings, while mutual misunderstanding and confusion were disguised by a set of social conventions from which few deviated. The miracle is that so many did have fun and most of them found marriage partners.

If failure at last night's dance, and growing apprehension at the prospect of the next, was the dominant thought, each night would have become an obstacle course between the Scylla of the chaperones and the Charybdis of the debs' delights.

Two days after Queen Charlotte's Ball, on 19 May, came a dance that risked breaking some at least of the bounds of convention. It was given by Lady Twysden at 6 Stanhope Gate, and was unusual in that it was not only a coming-out dance for her daughter Betty, but also a coming-of-age party for Betty's older brother, Sir Anthony Twysden, and younger brother Michael Blake. Betty was greatly in demand as a deb because of her two elder brothers, one of whom was a very good dancer. "The other", says Betty, now Mrs Morton, "danced like a large Labrador puppy!" It was mainly the boys who had insisted that this was not going to be the usual deb dance. In the receiving line at the top of the double staircase at 6 Stanhope Gate, Betty and her two brothers stood in a row with their mother to welcome guests, Anthony clutching a large bouquet of cauliflowers and carrots which someone had sent him from Moyses Stevens!

Our party was frowned on by some of the stuffier Mums who considered it shocking that we had a black band to play. Mother had been apprehensive but we assured her that Snakehips Johnson was marvellous, though I do remember her looking a bit taken aback when he arrived in his swallowtail coat and bowed over her hand. Some of the Mums took one look and carted their daughters off home. But I shall never forget the picture of Snakehips and his band leading all the little debs and their escorts in a whooping conga up one side of the double staircase and down the other side. The Mums were horrified but we thought it was tremendous fun.

The weekend was fun as well, with polo at Hurlingham and Ranelagh and next week's Derby to look forward to.

Fun in England, at any rate; in Poland a small but ominous incident occurred on the morning of Sunday, 21 May. Three Polish officials had driven to a village called Kalthof, on the Prussian-Danzig frontier, to investigate reported disturbances. Shots fired from their car, apparently by the chauffeur, killed a Danzig citizen of German birth. In the highly charged border atmosphere of the time, it was precisely the kind of incendiary gesture the Poles most feared, calculated to provide propaganda for the Germans. The area was a tinder-box; one man's death could have been the spark. But, for the time being, a sharp protest was the only apparent result.

The following week was dominated by the Epsom summer meeting, and was not an ideal week for dances. The last race at Epsom was run at 5 p.m., which meant a rush to travel back to London and change for the evening. Experienced mothers marked down Epsom week — like Ascot — as one to avoid, so that, although there were five dances, they were all relatively minor. The two highlights of the week were the Derby on Wednesday afternoon and the Oaks on Friday. The course was in excellent condition, the going should be perfect, and the weather was beautiful. The Hon. Anne Douglas-Scott-Montagu remembers when her cousins, Lord and Lady Wharncliffe,

took a double-decker red London bus. It was lined up somewhere on the Derby course and we had this wonderful party with a fantastic lunch, champagne, all spread out downstairs in the bus, and we all sat upstairs. I remember Diana and Barbara Stuart-Wortley, whose party it was — and that was one of the unusual, rather nice things I remember doing.

Blue Peter was favourite for the Derby, Galatea II for the Oaks. In the event, both duly won, Blue Peter by four lengths. He was a popular winner, being the Earl of Rosebery's first success in the Derby (the previous Earl had won it three times) and the huge crowd attracted by glorious sunshine cheered his victory ecstatically.

Many debs were racing enthusiasts, having been born and brought up with horses, and would have attended Epsom not just for the fashion parade which accompanied every one of its four days, but also because they were genuinely knowledgeable and interested in the racing. Surprisngly perhaps, they were allowed a discreet bet — two shillings slipped to an escort could be placed with a bookie, and it all added to the afternoon's excitement.

159

Marigold Charrington was one who was well informed about racing and horses: "Racing was part of our life — my parents' too — and we were knowledgeable about form and so on. In fact I went to see the horses far more than the people! Though of course one had to dress up — a different outfit for each day: new hat, new dress. Not bags and shoes — we made them do. It was a lovely week — wonderful weather." But, although the dresses and hats were once again faithfully reported in *The Times,* Epsom as a fashion event was definitely less important than Ascot. Although both the Derby and the Oaks dated back 160 years, and Epsom was firmly rooted in the Season, it was classless in its appeal. Less exclusive than Ascot — with its Royal Enclosure and rigid rules about who might or might not be admitted — it had long been a national rather than a Society occasion. The Derby is democracy writ large; and the upper classes have always had their doubts about democracy. Hoi-polloi make the oligarchy nervous.

Racing has always had a special fascination for the aristocracy. Selective breeding, the tracing of bloodlines down several generations, the inheritance of certain characteristics from sire to foal; the mitigating of the faults of one line by introducing a mare whose strengths will compensate — these mirror, in safely equine form, the obsession with blood that is crucial to the aristocracy's good opinion of itself. The English thoroughbred is lineage made visible. The use of racing slang to express approval of a woman is no accident. Besides enabling an Englishman to pay a compliment without feeling self-conscious, it conveys in terms that all around him perfectly comprehend the overriding importance of pure blood. So a girl can be called a "fine-looking filly", "a goer" or "a stayer" with a "mane" of hair; while the closer her legs approach to the narrow fragility of a race-horse's, the more they are likely to be admired. Lady Sarah Churchill recognized this quite explicitly: "I used to say to my mother, 'You know, we're just like fillies at a race track, we're being wandered around for sale to the highest bidder. Y'know, like horse sales.' She used to be furious: 'Don't talk such nonsense!'"

Two other events on Derby Day made news. The first was the King's Empire Day message broadcast from Winnipeg and relayed to listeners all over the world, including 1,200 guests at the Empire Day dinner in Grosvenor House. The speech was anodyne, as such speeches must be: what can a monarch say to several hundred million people that will offend no one? And so they heard "deeply moving experience . . . the march of progress striving to restore standards not in power or wealth alone Speaking directly to young listeners, the King concluded: "It is true, and I deplore it deeply, that the skies are overcast in more than one quarter at the present time. Do not on that account lose heart. Life is a great adventure, and every one of you can be a pioneer blazing by thought and service a trail to better things."

On the same day, a British military mission arrived in Poland; the Cabinet passed a plan for concerted action between Britain, France and Soviet Russia in case any one of the three was attacked; and a sale at Christie's in aid of Lord Baldwin's Fund for Refugees raised

£15,647. Many of the paintings and *objets d'art* were either given or purchased by Jews. The fund now totalled £481,646. It included £60 which was the proceeds of a dance given by the Whitechapel and Stepney Street Traders' Protection Association.

Friday, 26 May was the night of the Royal Caledonian Ball. This was the annual event which gave Scottish members of Society an opportunity to show off their reels. Men wore full evening tartan, women white evening dress, sashed with the family tartan, it being the only occasion in the year when it was considered correct to wear full tartan outside Scotland. Taking part in the reels was by invitation, and the dancers rehearsed assiduously beforehand. For Christian Grant it was one of the highlights of her Season:

The Caledonian Ball was basically for charity, but it was real fun. It was usually organized by a group of "senior" mothers from Scotland, of whom my mother qualified as one that year. It was held in Grosvenor House, being the biggest ballroom they could find in London. It started off with simple set reels. One had to be invited to take part, and if one wasn't, it would have been a pretty good disaster . . . it was rather an important thing, if one came from Scotland. So all the young girls from Scotland were paired up with all the most dashing or eligible young men from Scotland — because, of course, one qualification was that you had to be able to dress yourself up in tartan. All the men wore the regulation kilt and the girls white dresses with their family tartan draped round them as a sash and fastened on the shoulder with a silver brooch with your family crest. It must have been quite a spectacle, seen from the balcony at Grosvenor House. It was sort of Scotland's night out in London, and great fun for anyone who had connections with Scotland.

May had been a portentous month. Tension was increasing in Poland, and the British military mission sent to Warsaw, ostensibly to confer with officers of the Polish General Staff about military aspects of the Anglo-Polish agreement, in actuality, had been briefed to find out the truth about the number of border incidents, and to try and cool matters down. This was impossible, since Hitler deliberately exaggerated the incidents — many of them caused by German *agents provocateurs* in the first place — so as to stir up patriotic ardour in Germany. In Spain the Civil War had officially ended on 19 May, but general mobilization had been called for. After some weeks of tentative negotiations — was Britain to hug the Russian bear or gingerly accept its paw?, in Chips Channon's metaphor — the Anglo-Russian pact seemed on the point of being concluded.

In London, evacuation plans were being drawn up. Over two million copies of a pamphlet explaining who was entitled to be evacuated, and how it would be done, were delivered by post to households in central London and eleven boroughs. It was stressed that evacuation was entirely voluntary, although "a grave responsibility would rest on parents and guardians who nevertheless kept their children in London". A Civil Defence Bill, debated in Parliament throughout May, was organizing blackout facilities and air-raid shelters. Even the advertisements cashed in on the orninous mood of the moment. "You Must Be Prepared for Home Defence — Lay in a Store of Ovaltine Now!" ran one headline. The advertisement went on: "It is not only a wise precaution but conforms to the advice given by the authorities to housewives to lay in a reserve against possible emergencies. 1/1d, 1/10d, 3/3d per tin."

By this time some debs had already begun to prepare for the ordeal that had to come. Lady Brigid Guinness and the Hon. Aedgyth Acton were two who trained in first aid with the Red Cross during the summer of 1939. Others embarked on a practical nursing training, managing somehow to combine the rigours of hospital life with the contrasting — but still gruelling — rigours of the Season. One such was Helen Long, née Vlasto:

> The hospital to which I was assigned was Lambeth Infirmary — at that time full of terminal cases, and patients for whom there was little or no hope of recovery. Evacuation of other patients to alternative or country-based hospitals had already taken place, so close to war were we by then.
>
> A very diffident eighteen-year-old, I spent my days at Lambeth Infirmary and my nights at various West End hotels or private houses, attending deb dances. The contrasting scenes invalidated each other, and I felt I was living a double, and somewhat unworthy life. Only the hot and scented baths taken between my day and night life enabled me to replenish the energy required for both, and to face them with equanimity.[8]

Meanwhile, it was the Bank Holiday weekend. No rain had fallen since the washout of the Chelsea Flower Show, and although temperatures had been about average until now, Whit Monday was brilliantly hot and sunny. Parents and debs dispersed to their country homes, or one another's, for the long weekend, while the rest of the country lazed happily in thousands of deckchairs in hundreds of parks and on miles of beaches. London bus and train stations were packed solid with queues of people determined to see the — sea. The banks of the Thames were crowded with picnickers. Thousands went to watch cricket at Lords; thousands more to see the panda at London zoo or the lions at Chessington. Hampstead had its traditional Whit Monday fair, and ice-cream and whelk sellers, gypsies and fortune tellers, pickpockets and big dippers had a field day. Central London was practically empty, and museums showed unusually low attendance figures. It was a day for making the most of the present. The past threw long shadows, and the future did not bear thinking about.

CHAPTER SIX

The Last Three Months of Peace: one

The country basked in a smiling June. For the first ten days not a drop of rain fell. As usual in good weather, spirits soared. The Fourth of June was bound to be sunny; with luck the weather would hold until Ascot week; and meanwhile the Glyndebourne opera season opened on 1 June to long, balmy evenings.

An ominous and tragic accident sobered the holiday mood. On the morning of 1 June, a British submarine, the *Thetis*, underwent routine trials in Liverpool Bay. However, she failed to surface after a test dive, and rescue aircraft and ships circled the waters between Liverpool and Blackpool in search of her. The *Thetis* was soon spotted, indeed she surfaced; but it seemed that nothing could be done to reach the ninety-nine men trapped inside. Frantic efforts were made to attach the submarine to a cable — it snapped — and to cut through her hull, but the air supply ran out before the men could be rescued. All died. It was a grim portent.

There were other ships and other portents. A German liner, the *St Louis,* had been cruising for almost a month in search of a welcoming harbour for its 937

Jewish passengers. They steamed to Cuba, where entry permits had been promised, but after agonizing negotiations with immigration officials they were turned away and told they must return to Hamburg unless they could find a country willing to receive them.

There were others: the *Colorado*, with 226 Jewish refugees, refused admission everywhere; the *Liesel* whose 906 passengers were finally allowed into Palestine, but only on condition that the quota for other Jews would be reduced accordingly. Meanwhile, the sun shone and the debs danced on. Who wanted to talk politics on such golden evenings?

The first Saturday of the month was the occasion for that annual gathering of Etonians and all connected with them, the Fourth of June, at which they reaffirm to one another "their elegance, their ease, their pastoral urbanity".[1]

This event, which nominally commemorates the birthday of George III, is a reunion for Etonians past and present. They believe it is the best school in the country, if not the world; they believe that having been there marks a man for life. The least secure among them will continue to wear an Old Etonian tie or contrive — for the benefit of the uninitiated who do not recognize it — to indicate their privileged status, even if decades have elapsed since their schoolboy days.

The Fourth of June is a vast insiders' cocktail party; an opportunity for sociable or wary encounters and mutual appraisal; a day on which the school's special jargon bedecks the conversation like bunting to celebrate the triumph of the ruling caste. It is also a happy day, as one Old Etonian who was there in 1939 wistfully remembers:

It was a lovely social occasion, the Fourth of June with the fireworks. My brother and I were extremely fortunate in the housemaster who took over the house in the summer of '33. Hubert Hartley and Grizel Hartley have never been surpassed and probably never will be surpassed as a married couple giving their all to the boys in their house. They had a big house overlooking the field with a big garden full of lupins and irises and on the Fourth of June they'd have a huge lunch party for boys in the house and parents; and also for boys who'd recently left. In '39 I'd left four years before — I'd been captain of the house. It would have been a great meeting of old friends and the old Eton place, old Eton faces, absence, nostalgia, the fireworks — oh, I think it's a great family occasion, unique in its way. It's the best club in the world, and if the club is having a beano, you don't want to miss it.

Lady Anne Fitzroy, whose father had succeeded unexpectedly to the dukedom of Grafton in 1936, remembers attending the Fourth of June many times because her younger brother was at the school.

It was a family do really. You took a picnic lunch and had it wherever the car was parked — on some playing field — or, if it was wet, in the boy's study. If you were intellectual you could go and hear the boys declaiming in Latin and Greek. Then after lunch there was the cricket match, and you walked round meeting endless people who were all doing the same thing. That went on till about 5 o'clock. Then you had tea in the boy's room, and after tea there was the Procession of Boats, between about 6 and 7 o'clock. Then you had a picnic supper, preferably on the banks of the river — so there was lots of preparation needed, doing two picnics for about ten people. Then there were fireworks in the evening until about ten or eleven at night. They've stopped the fireworks now, I think, which seems a shame.

"Harrow may be more clever, Rugby may make more row, But we'll row for ever Steady from stroke to bow And nothing in life shall sever The chain that is round us now."

June was also the most crowded month for dances, two or three every weekday evening. One of the first that month was given by the Hon. Lady Bailey for her third daughter, Noreen (now Countess Raben).

I'd just spent two years in a French boarding school, I was meant to go to Austria and learn German as well but then Hitler walked in and that put a stop to that. Even Paris got filled up with Germans; I noticed them sleeping and sitting around in cafés and I didn't like that at all. Having been away so long meant that most of my girlfriends were long-ago childhood chums, and I had to rely on my older sister to produce the young men. I borrowed hers, really.

I think I wore a mauve and white dress from Jean Patou, and I remember that the Duchess of Gloucester was there, and oh my hat! old Lady Oxford and Asquith making a frightful nuisance of herself — my Mama said she didn't remember asking her. But it was all rather fun — very, very nice — especially having it in our own house at 38 Bryanston Square. The only bad thing I remember about the evening was Barbara McNeill being driven there by someone and being involved in a car crash, so she arrived with a cut forehead.

Apart from that it was a very happy occasion, and not so very frivolous. Just great fun.

She may have felt she knew few of her contemporaries but, all the same, Noreen Bailey was at the dance a couple of nights later which Lady Joseph gave for her two daughters, Rosamond and Cynthia. The familiar surroundings of 6 Stanhope Gate had been turned into an English country garden for the occasion, with banks of hydrangeas and delphiniums: a herbaceous border recreated just for one night. Cynthia, now Mrs Peter Dean, remembers that all their staff came up from the country for the occasion, including her nanny, whose job it was to iron the girls' multi-layered ballgowns.

On 8 June, memorial services were held at four different naval bases — Portsmouth, Devonport, Chatham and Birkenhead — for the ninety-nine men who had died in the *Thetis*. Their bodies were mostly buried at sea. St Martin's in the Fields was also crowded with mourners. Deaths like theirs still seemed outside the normal course of events, and people were shocked and indignant. Meanwhile, less remarked, the *St Louis*, the *Liesel* and half a dozen other refugee ships sailed on, desperate for some port that would let them anchor and disembark their unwanted, human, Jewish cargo. Other ships, in the light of their experience, were now unwilling to leave Germany, so that even those Jews who had managed to secure their release from concentration camps, and obtain the necessary papers and visas, could not escape.

To suggest that the debs should have known about these horrors, and should have done something to alleviate them, is asking a great deal of teenage girls; but in answer to the question, *could* the debs and their young partners have known what was going on, the answer must be unequivocal. Yes. Here is a memory from a very different milieu:

Surely anyone who knew what Hitler was doing, at home and abroad, must see that he was a unique epitome of all evils? I cannot help, even today, doubting the sincerity — or, if not the sincerity, the basic intelligence — of those with power and influence then who did not know what was happening inside Germany, and the fate in store for the rest of us should it be allowed to overflow. How did we, ordinary, uneducated working-class people, in a depressed town in a depressed area, half an hour's bus ride from Jarrow, know about concentration camps, about the final solution to the problem of inferior races, about the occupation of Europe, tomorrow the world? Well, you could read about it in the Left Book Club editions, in some papers, notably the *News Chronicle*, the *Daily Worker*, the *Herald*, the *New Statesman* — all of which I studied in the reading room of the library. You could always turn to *Mein Kampf* where Hitler's plans and policies are given in detail.[2]

The Season's next big dance was that given by Baroness Ravensdale, the eldest daughter of Lord Curzon, for her niece Vivien Mosley. Held on 8 June, this was one of the memorable parties of the Season. Its setting was romantic, melancholy, haunted, as Vivien (now the Hon. Mrs Forbes Adam) recalled:

It was held in a most peculiar house in Regent's Park that belonged to Maud Allen, the dancer. It was known as the West Wing, and it was . . . not ruined, exactly, but abandoned; not lived in. In her heyday Maud Allen had been a predecessor of Isadora Duncan, doing the same kind of dancing — all free spirit of the earth — and at the height of her popularity she had bought this house. But by 1939 she was well over sixty, and the house was very ramshackley, but rather beautiful. It had the most wonderful garden. Well, Maud Allen was a friend of my aunt, so she lent us this house. I don't think there was ever another dance like that. And the Duke and Duchess of Kent were at the dance — they had dinner with my aunt, Lady Alexandra Metcalfe, beforehand. They had been married four years earlier and the Duchess — my God, she was dazzling. Wonderful, wonderful.

Priscilla Brett, a great friend of Vivien, remembers dawn the next morning, as the party ended: "I remember walking in the Park in the daybreak, walking across Regent's Park at about five o'clock in the morning . . . that was wonderful. That was special."

Vivien's mother, Lady Cynthia, had died of peritonitis in 1933, and in 1936 her father, Sir Oswald Mosley, had married Diana Mitford. This strong cast of characters formed the background to her childhood and adolescence and made Vivien a forthright and unusual young woman. She was intelligent, well informed and took a lively interest in politics, without sharing her father's Fascist views. Already at the age of eighteen she was linked with families which — for good or ill — were among the most powerful in the country; she had travelled in France and Germany; and she had a circle of friends who were remarkable — at least among the debutantes — for their intelligence. Vivien would never have sat glumly on the sidelines at a dance waiting for her card to be filled up; indeed, she much preferred talking to dancing, and her chief memory of 6 Stanhope Gate is the peace and quiet of its sixth floor, to which she and her like-minded friends used to retreat, away from the band and the critical eyes of chaperones, to talk politics and speculate about the coming war. Why, in that case, did she agree to do the Season at all?

It was automatic. Everybody one knew a year older had done it and at the time one thought everybody was going to be doing it that year and so on. . . . In fact they weren't but that wasn't realized at the time. Meeting new friends certainly wasn't my intention; I had plenty already. In the end I did it just for the fun of it. But it was a most self-indulgent, invalid life, and I think, not everybody, but some of us were extremely aware of it and a bit ashamed of it. Not too ashamed, otherwise you couldn't have done it. You stayed in bed till twelve — got up — just managed to get to a girls' lunch party — perhaps a dress fitting in the afternoon — and so on and round you went, following the same pattern day after day. It was very jolly — I'm not denying it. Certainly I enjoyed it.

My friends were not typical debs at all. They were good liberal girls with, sort of, intellectual minds, and they used to get so fed up with all the nonsense, they'd disappear for ages, sorting the world out, and then they'd forget the passage of time and God Save the King would be played — it always was, in those days, at the end of a dance — and then they'd come tottering down from the upper floors and there would be all the old dowagers having an absolute fit, but all they'd actually been doing was talking — serious-minded people putting the world to rights. But these were people who came from political families and had been brought up with that and were much more interested in it than in the endless chitchat. In that sense it was almost like doing a few months at university. You'd argue your ideas with somebody else, only in between times you'd have to break it up to go down and do your stuff. I daresay we were interested in a very naive manner — we were only eighteen, which these days is very adult but in those days was not. And we weren't lascivious, either. There were a certain number of young men — not the ones who went to dances night after night; others, who occasionally went to parties — who would find it more rewarding to talk to someone away from the hubbub.

Who were the members of this unlikely intelligentsia amid the hubbub of the London Season? They formed a group so small and exclusive that many other debs remain to this day unaware that it even existed. Its members talk about it reluctantly; partly perhaps because, like most groups, its identity is more clearly defined in retrospect than it seemed at the time; partly because its preoccupations were so much at variance with the prevailing ethos of the Season.

Certainly during the late 1930s there was a group known as "the Liberal girls", most of whom would have denied that they "did" the Season in any real sense at all. They included Laura Bonham-Carter, who later married Jo Grimond, and her sister Cressida, who sat at dances and knitted to show her contempt for it all. They were clever, unconventional girls, whose male friends were clever and unconventional too. Many of them were left-wing, sometimes to the point of Communism. Coming from "good" families, or being friendly with girls who did, these young men occasionally appeared at deb dances, making the chaperones nervous. To most debs' mothers, a Communist might as well have had horns and a tail, so dangerous and exotic did he seem. They were men like Simon Asquith, Ben Nicholson or Ivan Moffat, and the trio of friends that comprised Philip Toynbee, Jasper Ridley and Esmond Romilly — the renegade ex-public schoolboy who had captivated Jessica Mitford before going off to fight in the Spanish Civil War. Such people, who questioned the assumptions of their parents and were sensitive to the social changes taking place, were aware of the anomalies — even the absurdity — of the rituals their coming out attempted to perpetuate. Shiela Grant Duff — another rebel — analysed it thus:

And so the struggle between my two worlds was engaged. The world I was moving towards won hands down through most of that summer, for life with Douglas [Jay] and his Oxford friends was, I hoped, the "real world" outside the confines, artificialities and conventions of "the Season" which, as much against the grain for my mother as for me, I was supposed to be having that year. The contrast was exposed, sharply and rather cynically, on the evening I was presented at Court. My grandmother had lent us her Rolls-Royce and her men-servants and my mother and I were sitting in that long cortége which assembles for such occasions in the Mall, dressed in our ostrich feathers and trains. Suddenly Douglas appeared in his macintosh and tennis shoes and jumped in to sit on the little seat between us and the glass panel which divided us from the chauffeur and footman. Perfectly trained, they never even turned their heads, and on that occasion Douglas had only cheered up the long and boring wait and not destroyed the glitter and glamour of Court. . . . When later, as a journalist, I attended royal ceremonies in Belgrade and Bucharest with considerable detachment, I was glad that I had joined "the real world".[3]

Although she agreed to be presented, Shiela Grant Duff refused to be "brought out" through the Season's interminable dances — one of just a tiny handful of aristocratic girls who turned their backs on the Season.

Its tyranny was such that only the most defiant girls dared defy it, as Jessica Mitford explained:

Now must follow, as inevitably as the sun rises, but never sets, on the British Empire, my first London season. There was no real alternative. College was out — impossible to qualify. What was going to happen next? The season might turn out to be fun. After all, one was bound to meet literally hundreds of people; among them there must be a few kindred souls, a few people of my own age also looking for a way out of their own particular fortress.[4]

Even Jessica could not escape what she calls "the specific, upper-class version of the puberty rite". In the end, she found it interminably boring:

Endless successions of flower-banked ballrooms filled with very young men and women, resembling uniformly processed market produce at its approximate peak, with here and there an overripe or underripe exception. . . . Smooth, fair, guileless faces, radiating the health bestowed by innumerable fresh-air-filled upbringings in innumerable country houses; straight or snub — features bearing ample evidence of years of rather more than adequate protein and fat consumption. . . . Opening gambits were generally restricted to two or three subjects: "D'you do much riding?" "Do you get up to Scotland much?" "Care for night-clubs?" Since, in my case, a truthful reply to any of the three happened to be in the negative, keeping the conversation going usually proved to be uphill work.[5]

Jessica Mitford proves that, in 1935 at least, it was possible, even for a debutante, to know what was really happening in Germany. That year, *The Brown Book of the Hitler Terror* was published.

The Brown Book detailed and documented as much as was then known of the revolting cruelties to which the Jews were being subjected in Germany.

It contained actual photographs of the bruised and bleeding victims of Nazi sadism, and related in horrifying detail how the new anti-Semitic laws were working out in practice. My parents maintained that the book was Communist-inspired, and that anyway the Jews had brought all this trouble on themselves, apparently by the mere fact of their existence.[6]

There seem to have been no debs as bold or as open-minded as Jessica in the Season of 1939, but some would have seemed politically unconventional. They included, besides Vivien Mosley, the Hon. Priscilla Brett, the daughter of Viscount Esher; Rosalind Cubitt — furious at being described in the popular press as "Deb of the Year", a title she despised and disclaimed — and the Hon. Sarah Norton. Priscilla Brett, known by her friends as "Pinkie", analyses what made them different:

Intelligence was not generally sought after in young men. Only, I think, by my little lot. We were all people who liked books and music. Intelligent people rather than not very intelligent people. I don't think we were typical — I or the rest of my friends. Our group weren't all debs, for a start, and not all the same age. Quite a lot were older, and certainly one or two were what they then called highbrows. There was a number of much older young men, who used to go to dances because it was rather fun, there was all that frightfully delicious food, and it was very glamorous. The Asquith girls were very much my old friends. They had this amazing governess called Miss Strachey, by whom they were very well educated. And then there were the men like Philip Toynbee, Ben Nicholson, Simon Asquith — he was extraordinary — who went to dances even though they were all older. But that didn't mean they were part of the Season. But we were very much in a sort of liberal establishment. My father was a Liberal, and all my friends were Communists — just to complicate matters. Philip was definitely Communist ... but then again, one wondered how serious he was. But on the whole we were very left. We discussed politics a great deal among ourselves. We all had a feeling that there was going to be a war. It was fairly obvious that it was getting nearer and nearer. I was actually rather a pacifist, unlike everybody else. Most of us were very anti-Munich, but I hated the idea of war altogether.

The last vignette from this unlikely group portrays the chameleon-like figure of Philip Toynbee as he flitted between several worlds:

Philip [writes Jessica Mitford] was our only link, if rather a disreputable one, with the now-estranged world of London society. Although a member of the Communist Party, he still found time to take in a good number of debutante dances during the London season, and he would regale us with accounts of these.

"Couldn't you take along a little paper bag and bring us back some of the delicious food?" we urged. But the most he brought back were bits of juicy gossip about my family and former friends, and stories of what was being said about us.[7]

Apart from the coming-out dances which now succeeded each other in nightly uniformity — "salmon and strawberries; strawberries and salmon", as one deb recalled with a weary sigh — there were other parties, too, as the Season approached its peak. What can the rest of London have thought, as taxis and private cars disgorged their passengers, to sparkle and giggle briefly outside a hotel or private house before disappearing into the brightly lit, musical mêlée within? Girls barely out of school, their long skirts held delicately above the dusty pavement, escorted by pink-faced young men in starched shirts and tails under the watchful eye of tiara-ed mothers — what did ordinary working people make of such conspicuous consumption? The Hon. Anne Douglas-Scott-Montagu (now Lady Chichester) retains a guilty image from that indulgent summer of:

> the very sad and embarrassing situation at 6 Stanhope Gate when the very elaborate and delicious supper was laid out in a room whose (uncurtained) bow window overlooked the street. One could see pathetic faces looking in, pressed against the glass at this scene of splendour and scrumptious food. I remember trying to sit far away so that I couldn't be seen — it quite put me off my supper!

The same thought occurred to Ruth Magnus, when she was a deb — a more thoughtful and imaginative one than most:

> In the streets of London it was a common sight to see a crowd of shabby passers-by watching richly dressed guests as they walked from their cars across a strip of red carpet into brilliantly lit houses where a dance was in progress. I used to wonder, with the fierce intensity of youth, what were the respective thoughts of the poor and the privileged, but the class system in those days was generally accepted as a law of nature, so probably the sight of the revellers aroused no more envy among the onlookers than some lush scene in a film.[8]

Charity events were fun and also a convenient way for people to silence the occasional qualm of conscience. A typical example is the "Naughty Ninety Night" held on 8 June — the same night as Vivien Mosley's dance — in aid of the Royal Cambridge Home for Soldiers' Widows. It was organized by Susan Hambro who had been a deb some seasons earlier. The tickets cost thirty shillings each (£1.50 — or about £30 at today's values) and covered supper, champagne, cabaret ("Miss Frances Day has very kindly consented to appear") and a band from Carroll Gibbons. The meticulously kept accounts for the night have survived, providing fascinating evidence of the cost of organizing what was — by comparison with the big deb dances — a fairly modest evening's entertainment for about 200 people.

The most expensive items, accounting for £235 of the total cost, were catering, by Jacksons of Piccadilly, at £141 7s 3d; wine, from Grants, at £57 10s; and the hire of Carroll Gibbons' band for the night, at £36 15s. For this sum, eight men played from 10.30 p.m. until 3.30 a.m. — five hours for what used to be called 35 guineas, or just under £1 an hour each. Other expenses were minimal: for the printing and postage of the invitations, just under £10; for tips to the butler and staff, £1 (not each — altogether). The list ends with two intriguing items: "Parrots, Hire of 2 . . . 10/-" and "Whiskers & glue . . . 10/-". The total cost of the evening was £250 14s 6d and the money raised by ticket sales was £249 10s. Fortunately, some guests made additional small donations and these amounted altogether to £12, enabling the Royal Cambridge Home for Soldiers' Widows to benefit by the sum of £10 17s 6d.

On 13 June, Governors Speech Day took place at Harrow — a more low-key event than the Fourth of

June, and in any case Harrow's great triumph of the summer was yet to come. On brilliant afternoons and during the long, light evenings, Harrow was preparing for its great confrontation, but that day of glory was a full month away.

The middle of June saw the apotheosis of the English Season, the four days of Ascot. Announcements in *The Times* the previous week had detailed the hosts and guests at forthcoming house parties arranged around the racing. Nobbscrook, Binfield Park, Queenshill and Little Paddocks all awaited their quota of racing enthusiasts and leaders of fashion.

"Entertaining for the meeting", it was reported, "promises to be on much the same scale as during the last few years."

With the exception of the floral decorations — always the last of the many preparations to be made at Ascot — everything is now ready for the opening. All the wood and ironwork at the stands has been repainted, and with the grass of the lawns and enclosures at its best everything looks fresh and inviting. The turf, too, is in splendid condition. Thanks to the system of watering installed a few years ago the dry spell of the past fortnight has not adversely affected it and the going should be perfect.

The Cavalry Club, the Highland Brigade, Buck's Club, and the Carlton, the Conservative, and the Naval and Military Clubs will, as usual, have their luncheon tents on the heath, and the Marlborough will again be in the paddock.[9]

The Irish racing fraternity was on its way over; only the King and Queen would be absent. Having visited the World's Fair in New York and been greeted by a crowd of 600,000 in Washington, they had returned to Canada, whence they would begin the voyage home. The visit had been a success. Americans adore celebrities, and the welcome they gave the royal couple had been warm and timely. It was a good moment to renew the Anglo-American alliance.

Royal Ascot provides the best four days of flat-racing in the year, as well as a chance to appraise the finest horses and the most elegant men and women. But it also offers something harder to define. It epitomizes what English society is all about — what it prides itself on, and what it does best. Against a glorious background of green and white, rails and stands and sky, racing silks and floating dresses, it shows society in its favourite setting, indulging in its favourite pastime. There is little to choose between the parade of the runners around the-paddock and that of their owners and followers in the Royal Enclosure. Both are faultlessly turned out; both under scrutiny by experts. As Lady Sarah Churchill has already put it tartly, "The debs, too, were under starter's orders: just like fillies at a race track, y'know, being wandered around for sale to the best bidder." What makes a winner on four legs or two is pedigree — looks, training, spirit and style. Horses prove, more reliably than the aristocracy, that breeding tells. Racehorses symbolize that alliance between money and breeding on which the success of the British upper classes has come to depend — which may be why the aristocracy are such keen racegoers. One deb's delight of 1939 was quite specific about the connection:

Racing and breeding thoroughbreds is a safe way of discussing and proving something that is a source of private satisfaction to them, though it — would be immensely bad form to talk about it in relation to their own families. Certainly of my Eton and regimental contemporaries a number are passionately involved in the racing world. It reminds me of an expression which occurred frequently in my grandmother's conversation. She was always referring to people's pedigree. That was the term she always used — *pedigree* — though if I were to use it, it would be in connection with the bloodstock industry, but she connected it with family. For "pedigree" read "good family".

The great owner-breeders of the twenties and thirties were Lord Astor, with the Cliveden Stud, and Lord Derby, with his Stanley House Stud. The latter produced the great Hyperion among many other classic winners. But racing was not merely an aristocratic preserve; there were many other, more raffish, figures, like the (recently ennobled) Lord Glanely, the first self-made man to be elected to the Jockey Club; the "Joel brothers; and, of course, the jockeys: small, starved, waspish men, the goblins of the pantomime. Racing appealed to its devotees for a number of quite different reasons. First, there was the skill of breeding. Next, the skill of the trainer in picking which races to enter his horses for, so as to give them the best chance of winning; and allied to this, the skills of the jockey in riding a race carefully judged according to the horse, the going and the course. Then, the excitement of betting. Finally, the sheer aesthetic pleasure of the spectacle.

A Totalizator — or Tote — said to be the largest in the world had been installed at Ascot in the late 1920s, and made gambling easier and faster. It had 360 windows in operation, and was manned by over 500 people. In the four days of Ascot, it took well over half a million pounds. Debs who attended Ascot in a family party might have been allowed to ask someone to place a bet — it would depend how strict their fathers were but most of them would have gone not to gamble, but for the exhibitionstic pleasure they gave, and derived, at the fashion parade. *The Times* printed its usual checklist of who wore what and with whom; but — although many of them pretended to despise photographers from Society magazines — it was much more fun to have one's picture taken in full fig for the *Tatler* or *Bystander,* or perhaps for the gossip column of a newspaper. These show a procession of intimidatingly smart and grown-up looking debs. It is hard to detect, behind their tailored suits or drifting dresses, chic hats and severe hairstyles, the nervous schoolgirls of just few weeks earlier. The Season was doing its work. The geese were turning into swans.

Mary Pollock was the type of girl who would derive most fun from Ascot, coming as she did from a family whose racing connections went back at least two generations.

I enjoyed Ascot enormously because racing was in my family: my great-uncle had owned racehorses and another great-uncle had been a gentleman jockey and twice came second in the

Derby; while yet another relation had a stud and trained horses.

You had to apply for the Royal Enclosure a long way in advance, and it was much more exclusive then than it is now . . . you couldn't have anyone divorced in the family.

I had rather a wretched dress that year — it was rather low-cut, which made me feel self-conscious; and to make matters worse I was catching the sun and I could feel myself getting red.

It all seems so long ago, and as though it were some other girl.

Susan Meyrick was another keen race-goer, and she loved Ascot.

We always stayed at Brown's Hotel in London as my family lived in Hampshire, and from the hotel we went to Ascot by train from Waterloo. That was ghastly. My parents thought it was much easier — it avoided all the queuing for the car park and made a much quicker getaway afterwards — but I found it very embarrassing being all dressed up and in large hats on the station and then in the train.

Once we got there we always went to Buck's Club tent, where we got a very good lunch. The racing was marvellous and it always irritated me that people round the paddock were more interested in looking at each others' clothes than at the horses.

Ascot then was much less crowded and you could always get a place in the stand in front of the Royal Enclosure, or you could go up on the roof.

We went on all four days in 1939, which meant you had that awful business of having to wear something different every day — especially on Gold Cup day, which was the big day.

Some debs went to Ascot because they were genuinely interested in the racing, but others went simply because it made a change, after all those ballrooms, to meet in the open air. Christian Grant came into this category: "I knew nothing about racehorses and so, frankly, I just betted on the jockey with the prettiest colours. One wouldn't dream of going to a bookie oneself: a young man put two bob on for one — and I didn't even do that much, because I was far too careful of my pennies. It was primarily a social event — one of the occasions to see and be seen." The weather held for the first three days of Ascot, only to break on the Friday into a spectacular rainstorm. Next day *The Times* reported sulkily:

> Yesterday it was a case of furs, some no doubt borrowed at the last moment from the hostess with whom visitors might be staying, of overcoats, of few silk hats and many grey ones, and still more soft hats or bowlers. It was indeed a sad Ascot from the point of view of fashion, whether of men's clothes or women's. It is many years since so few new clothes have been seen.[10]

Perhaps it had something to do with the absence of the royal couple, for (*The Times* again): "Ascot without the King and Queen is not Ascot at all: like being asked to dinner and being told on arrival that the host and hostess have gone elsewhere and would one make oneself at home and ask for what one wants?" There was no winner that year to match Brown Jack's stunning succession of wins in the early years of the decade; indeed, if anything, it was the French horses who came out best.

Lord Abergavenny had ceased to take much part in the Season by 1939, having the previous year married Mary, one of the eight Harrison sisters who came out over a period of eighteen years spanning 1928 to 1946. By 1939, too, Lord Abergavenny was a serving soldier with the Life Guards. But he was, from 1972 until 1981, the Queen's Representative at Ascot; and he believes racing is classless in its appeal.

All country people were used to breeding, owning, hunting and riding horses — they'd been around horses and dogs since they were in nappies — the only difference was that the upper classes were likely to have land on which they could breed horses, and this formed the original backbone of the bloodstock industry. Likewise, racing originated as matches — riding contests — between two aristocrats, who usually gambled on the outcome.

Until 1948 Ascot had just the one four-day meeting a year. It now has twenty- six days. It has always been more exclusive than Epsom, because Epsom was common land, which meant anyone could go; whereas entry for Ascot has always been charged.

What is special about racing in this country is the knowledgeable following it attracts. People have always taken a great interest in horses by name, and they know the breeding of each and why it is named that way.

Remember that in 1939 only certain classes had the leisure to follow racing regularly. Similarly, at that time many fewer people had cars, and in the days when there weren't always convenient train services — say, to Newmarket — people who hadn't the means of transport had less opportunity to go racing. Now, everybody has leisure and many more people have cars. That's why there's been such a huge increase in the number of days' racing in the year.

At the same time as Ascot, the Cambridge May Week and Boat Club balls were in full swing, while the Guards had combined the two into Boat Club Ascot ball at Maidenhead. (May Week, confusingly, was actually two weeks in June.) Sidney Sussex, Pembroke, Corpus Christi and King's all had May balls in the same two days, and no sooner were they over than Oxford's Commemoration Balls began on 19 June. These were balls held by each college in rotation over five years, and were not strictly part of the Season, since anyone who had connections with the college and could afford the two-guinea ticket could attend. Undergraduates would make up parties of a dozen to twenty, inviting their girlfriends, sisters, cousins for a long night's celebration of the end of term and, perhaps, of Finals, in a setting whose antiquity and beauty could only be rivalled by the greatest country houses. The evening often began with a dinner-party in one of the private college dining-rooms, it which college servants would serve five or six courses cooked in the college kitchens and presented on college plate to be eaten with college silver and accompanied by wine from the traditionally fine college cellars. The main rooms and most of the grounds were thrown open for the night. Young men and their partners could wander across manicured lawns — the product of centuries of mowing and rolling and weeding, weeding and rolling and mowing — and admire the gardens, at the peak of their June beauty, all through the fragrant summer night. Or, yet again, they could dance — not just to one band, but usually to two or three. Around midnight, a huge buffet would be laid out, consisting of such culinary extravaganzas as whole roast swans and haunches of venison. At dawn, breakfast would be served, and the balls traditionally ended with exhausted young women reclining in punts, being slowly propelled along the Cam or the Isis by the drooping figures of young men held upright only by the punt pole. *Gaudeamus igitur* . . .

On 14 June, the evening of Royal Hunt Cup day at Ascot, Harold Nicolson went to dine with Kenneth Clark. It was a gathering of men and minds with influence in a number of spheres and — inspired perhaps by the company — Winston Churchill, the guest of honour, made a defiant and uncannily prescient speech. Nicolson reported it apparently verbatim:

Winston is horrified by Lippmann saying that the American Ambassador, Joe Kennedy, had informed him that war was inevitable and that we should be licked. Winston is stirred by this defeatism into a magnificent oration. He sits hunched there, waving his whisky-and-soda to mark his periods, stubbing his cigar with the other hand. "It may be true, it may well be true," he says, "that this country will at the outset of this coming and to my mind almost inevitable war be exposed to dire peril and fierce ordeals. It may be true that steel and fire will rain down upon us day and night scattering death and destruction far and wide. It may be true that our sea-communications will be imperilled and our food-supplies placed in jeopardy. Yet these trials and disasters, I ask you to believe me, Mr Lippmann, will but serve to steel the resolution of the British people and to enhance our will for victory. No, the Ambassador should not have spoken so, Mr Lippmann; he should not have said that dreadful word. Yet supposing (as I do not for one moment suppose) that Mr Kennedy were correct in his tragic utterance, then I for one would willingly lay down my life in combat, rather than, in fear of defeat, surrender to the menaces of these most sinister men. . . . Nor should I die happy in the great struggle which I see before me, were I not convinced that if we in this dear dear island succumb to the ferocity and might of our enemies, over there in your distant and immune continent the torch of liberty will burn untarnished and (I trust and hope) undismayed.''[11]

Back to the Season — since, as one man who danced as gaily as the rest put it, ''If you knew the world was going to end tomorrow, and there was nothing you could do about it, wouldn't you have fun while you still could?'' On 16 June, the final — wet — day of Ascot, Mrs Humphrey Pollock gave a small dinner dance for her daughter Mary, at Grosvenor House. The word ''small'' could mean anything from 300 or 400 guests, and in some cases was used mainly to indicate that the dance would not be attended by royalty. On this occasion, however, it really did mean small. Mary Pollock, Mrs D'Oyly, admits frankly that her parents were not well off, and her Season had to be managed as economically as possible. In this instance, ''small'' meant a dinner dance for no more than forty people, mainly to pay back hospitality. Even so, they enjoyed a five-course dinner and quantities of champagne.

I wore my Court dress, which was of embossed silver brocade and had been made for me free by the Royal School of Needlework because my father, who was a doctor, attended them for nothing, and this was a nice way of saying thank you. My sister, who was three years younger, was at school still, but we thought it would be a great shame if she were to miss it, so she was allowed out for the evening. She wore the dress that

I'd worn for Queen Charlotte's, but of course it had to be taken in, as she was only fifteen.

I was always very shy and conscious that I didn't move in the grandest of circles. On top of that, I didn't have brothers, so getting partners was always rather an anxiety. In spite of that I enjoyed some of the dances enormously. It's an interesting thing to have done — I saw another side of life — and people were never snobbish, never; just friendly and giggly and rather fun. I got to know quite a few people, including some men, but nobody I really broke my heart over.

Mary was one of the girls — there must have been many — who resented the constant chaperonage.

One just *didn't* "go too far" — I wouldn't have dreamt of it — yet this business of being supervised everywhere was taken to ridiculous lengths. I remember at eighteen arranging to meet a friend from Heathfield, where I'd been to school. We met at Charing Cross and then went next door to Lyons' Corner House. To my horror, when I looked around, I saw one of our maids sitting at another table. My mother had sent her to chaperone me ... I was furious. But more than that: it actually made me rather frightened. One had heard of the white slave traffic, and that sort of supervision made you feel that it must be a real threat. In fact, nobody ever laid a finger on me, and I never heard of it happening.

If, at worst, the need for a chaperone to guard against nameless predators was frightening, even at its best it was often absurd. Mollie Acland recalls being invited to a small but very elegant dance at which — for once — chaperones were not present:

My mother was hesitant about letting me go, but she sent me in our car (a *very* ancient Rolls with a ladder up to the roof) with our head chauffeur Moore and strict instructions that he must bring me home.

Well, at about 4 a.m. Peter (now my husband) remembered that he had to go to work next day, so we went to find Moore and Peter told him he was going to walk me home. Moore was very firm. "Her Ladyship instructed me to bring you back, so *get in*, Miss Mollie." I said, "Oh Moore, it's only a few hundred yards . . . let me just walk home this time." Moore said, "You'll stick to the pavement then?" "Oh *yes*." So Peter and I walked home to Upper Grosvenor Street, not even arm-in-arm, with Moore following behind at a snail's pace with the headlights *full on* all the way!

Not for a moment was a girl allowed to be alone. Anne Douglas-Scott-Montagu recalls the horror that greeted her announcement that she had travelled to a party by bus:

That's something which my cousin Barbara and I laugh about now. Her mother had organized some party in a big house just off South Audley Street that they'd rented, I think just for the Season. So I found my way there by bus — I used to go everywhere by bus during the day, because I had quite a small allowance and my mother was very, very careful about money. And when I arrived at the door, Lady Wharncliffe said to me, "But who's brought you?" And I said, "Oh, nobody's brought me." So she said, "You came *alone*? In a taxi?" So I said, "No, no I didn't . . . I came on the bus." And she was even more horrified . . . to *think* that my mother could have let me come *alone* on a *bus* across *London*, to *their* house . . . she didn't think that was at all the form. And yet I didn't resent that a bit. I never thought it was odd.

Apart from being the peak of the house-party season, mid-June was also a time when most sporting events seemed to take place. The International Horse Show had opened on 15 June, and continued for the next ten days. The London Grass Court Championships began at Queen's on 19 June, to be followed shortly by Wimbledon. The RAF Rifle Meeting began on the same day, at Bisley. The two-day race meeting at Sandown Park was imminent, as was the first Test Match against the West Indies at Lords.

Ascot provided a great excuse for house-parties — at Cliveden especially — but they happened every weekend throughout the summer. They were the *fêtes champêtres* of the Season. There must have been something preternaturally beautiful about the great houses and gardens of England then as, full-blown, like a carefully tended rose at the very height of summer, they trembled on the edge of the moment when they would fade and decay. Roses were lovelier then . . . old varieties grafted on to old stock; not yet rendered garish or unperfumed by crossing with too many hybrids. Gardeners were still plentiful, with six or eight at least to look after the gardens of private houses; and in the midst of the grand gardens lay the great country houses, also poised on the brink of change. Today, many no longer exist; while many more have been converted into schools, old people's homes or time-share properties.

House-parties were given for a number of reasons apart from straightforward hospitality. They were a way of asserting the intimacy of a group of friends, or of deciding whether to admit a new member. They could be used to throw two people together for longer than just an evening, affording them a better opportunity to get to know each other. They could even be used to test the social skills of a new girl. She might be very presentable across a dinner-table or in the familiar setting of a dance, but would she — or, for that matter, he — stand up to scrutiny over a whole weekend? Were clothes, manners, even sporting prowess up to scratch? But most often a house-party was simply an opportunity to get away to the country after the rigours of a week in London.

In spite of this, the conventions that governed it were still narrow. Rhoda Walker-Heneage-Vivian has vivid memories of those weekends:

Oh yes, they were enormous fun. People arrived by car with lots of luggage as we had to change for dinner every night (three different dresses) and needed tennis things, etc. The proverbial huge breakfast under silver dish-covers was served, and then something planned for the morning — usually walks to somewhere or a trip into the nearest town. After lunch (again huge, with a starter, hot meat, cold meats, pudding and cheese . . . heaven knows where we put it all!) we played tennis or croquet or swam in someone's pool or rode someone's horses. Dinner was formal, with seating arrangements, taking turns for a seat by one's host (the girl's father) and after dinner billiards, gossip over the coffee cups (*no dirt!*) or indoor games. Sometimes we'd dance to records. One game we played was called Truths and consisted of awkward questions being asked, which you were sworn to answer truthfully! Bed at about 11 p.m. There *was* corridor-creeping — in my case only once, when I recall lying in a sort of Madame Récamier pose on the divan and *talking* until 3 a.m. to a charming man in the Hussars who groped occasionally round the bosom area and I thought I was being very daring!

During the Season we had three big house-parties in Wales for Easter and Whitsun, spent lying on the beach, mostly. We also organized Scavenger Hunts and roped in local friends. These were motorized treasure hunts with an almost impossible list of objects to find in pairs and get home first. I remember borrowing a policeman's helmet and catching a live wasp in a match box and wildly searching for a tabby cat. There were more house parties in July and August when the Season ended, until war stopped it all.

One unchanging feature of country-house parties was an institution simply called The Game. It had certainly been around in the last decade of Victoria's reign, made popular by the fiendish mental agility of the Souls, that unusual set of late-Victorian aristocrats. The Game (pronounced as though it were all one word, like M'tutor — Th' Game) had no other name and no rigid rules. Lady Anne Fitzroy (now Lady Anne Mackenzie) describes the version she used to play:

You have two teams in separate rooms and each team must select a subject for every member of the other team: let's say about eight. Then you all sit round in one room, and one by one your opponents are taken aside and their subject is whispered to them, and they have to act it. If their team guesses it correctly, they get a point, and at the end the one with the most points wins. There are variations, like whether you are allowed to use standard gestures to indicate whether you are acting out the title of a book (both hands exposed, palms upwards) or a film (hand turns imaginary projector beside head). It could vary from the easy to the almost impossible — from *Gone with the Wind* to Full Fathom Five, depending how skilled the players were.

Certain families had games which were peculiar to themselves, which they always played and which they made their guests play.

These indoor games, a hangover from the Victorian and Edwardian craze for esoteric acting games or elaborate word games, were a favourite pastime at country-house parties; though Lord Haig recalls that he eventually got bored with them:

We usually played those sort of games when we were staying with the Buccleuchs. I was always very bad at it because you had to be a bit inventive. You'd all be sitting round and you had to think of the name of a painter beginning with A and all that sort of thing; or else there were acting games — a sort of glorified charades. When I was younger I played Sardines and Murder, but one had slightly matured into less boisterous games — after all, in 1939 I was twenty-one — past the Sardine age!

I remember a lot of large, marvellous weekend parties in those days, with people like the Moynes and the Buccleuchs. Not so much as part of the deb scene — it was a way of being in touch with a lot of the political figures. I saw quite a lot of Philip Sassoon at that time, and had interesting weekends at Trent and Lympne with people like Churchill and Eden and Morrison sitting round the table discussing the difficult problems which faced the country at that time. Probably there wouldn't have been many young girls there. But those happened with great regularity, and of course it was all backed up with marvellous breakfasts and footmen and every comfort; lovely games of tennis — idyllic places to live in. But it absolutely depended on having a large retinue of servants ... It's gone out now, I think.

It certainly has. Who could now afford the splendour that Lord Boothby describes at Lympne?

all set against a background of mingled luxury, simplicity and informality, brilliantly contrived. The beautifully proportioned red brick house, the blue bathing pool surrounded by such a profusion of lilies that the scent at night became almost overpowering, the flamingoes and ducks, the banks of exquisite flowers in the drawing room, the red carnation and the cocktail on one's dressing-table before dinner, were each and all perfect of their kind.[12]

Debs had to observe certain rigid conventions before they might accept an invitation to a weekend away. Sarah Norton, who was very beautiful and popular, was invited to many that summer:

Country-house weekends were very important and one did them regularly. The hostess always had to write to your mother first, asking if she could invite you. Lots of us would go — there would be fourteen, eighteen or sometimes even more in the party. I remember Michael Astor inviting me to Cliveden, and I had to say no, I can't, not unless your mother writes to my mother. At Cliveden in the summer we used to take out the boats or play tennis; swimming pools didn't really exist much. In the evenings we used to play games — especially The Game. We also played Murder and Sardines. There were slips of paper and you all drew one and if you were the murderer you didn't tell anyone. Then you all went off and disappeared and hid in cupboards or under beds or behind curtains and then the murderer struck and somebody was the detective and had to discover who the murderer was; and he — the murderer — was the only person who was allowed to lie. Sardines was a great excuse for flirting — though we were incredibly circumspect. Sex was something we didn't understand at all.

A number of these weekends were organized around a dance, since a few debs chose not to give their coming-out parties in London, but at their own homes in the country. Sonia Denison has hazy memories of one of the best dances that summer:

I was staying in a house-party, I can't now remember where, but it was all arranged for one of the most wonderful balls in an enormous house — that I can remember well — miles and miles of passages. What normally happened is that your mother would send you with a maid, and she would unpack for you and look after you. Then you would go up and change for dinner, and your dress — perhaps tulle, or a satin dress with a great skirt — would be laid out for you. Then there'd be an enormous dinner-party at about half-past eight. The actual dance would start about eleven, with people arriving from other house-parties all around. The dance would go on until all hours — four or five in the morning, with everyone marvellously dressed. We did wear lovely clothes. There'd be two bands, and more wonderful food, and no chaperones — not in the country — the people we were staying with looked after us.

Those were the summer parties; in the winter things were less formal, in Susan Meyrick's experience: "I went to the country-house parties for the Hunt Balls, usually in Northamptonshire or Gloucestershire. After the ball we usually went to the meet next morning. It was all much more relaxed — the men would wear dinner jackets; dinner was at 8 p.m. and we did *not* get up very early in the morning!" One weekend right at the end of the summer, when the official Season was over, remains Mollie Acland's outstanding memory of that year:

> Our summer home was at Seaview, Isle of Wight. We needed young men for the house-party and also to sail and crew in the regattas. So I asked my favourite from the Season, Peter Tabor, to join us there with his younger brother for the last week in August. One evening we went to a party at Bembridge — I was wearing my black and white taffeta dress — and there on the beach we decided we were definitely meant for each other. But that's another story . . . starting 9 December, 1939, and still going strong!

As Lord Haig pointed out, the servants were the *sine qua non* of this lavish hospitality. They were the worker bees who made things hum. Many of the young people of the time insist that their servants were well treated and had good lives — "better than working in a factory or a shop, certainly". It is clear from their accounts that they were often devoted to their family servants; but, however friendly the relationship between servants and children, they were not, and never could be, friends. An unbridgeable social chasm lay between them. Friendship demands equality, and servants and masters, though they were mutually dependent, were never equal.

The helplessness of people used to being waited on hand and foot is extraordinary. One young man, on first living by himself in London, said to his mother: "But who will turn down my bed for me, or answer the telephone when it rings?" He literally could not imagine doing these things for himself.

Some of the debs were beginning to feel uneasy about the difference between their lives and that of the servants who looked after them. Ann Schuster, although only seventeen at the time, was one:

I do remember feeling guilty about our huge staff at home. My mother had her personal maid; I had a personal maid to look after my clothes who was my age, and I used to feel terribly guilty when she said, "What are you going to wear?" and then, "Ooh, isn't it lovely?" and I knew she'd never been to a dance. I think a social conscience was just beginning to arise. I did have one sweet boyfriend who was very badly off and really did come along for the evenings just to get a meal. He was about the only one who didn't have a car, and used to whistle along on buses, and I think he gave me very much the other point of view. I saw this world and it was tough. But otherwise, one had led such a sheltered life — none of my grandchildren or even children could ever believe that I could be so sheltered.

The size of the establishments kept by upper-class families varied according to their wealth and the size and number of their houses. There cannot be anyone in Britain today, with the exception perhaps of two or three royal households, who lives in the style of dozens of the great families in 1939, while those same great families now maintain hardly a quarter — often a tenth — as many servants as they did fifty years ago. Between the wars only some 5 per cent of private households had a resident domestic at all; but the families whose daughters were presented at Court would certainly have fallen within that 5 per cent. For them, even those with a relatively modest middle-class background, half a dozen servants would have been considered the minimum necessary to run a house. The basic six would have been a cook-housekeeper, a nanny or, later, a governess, a couple of housemaids, probably a ladies' maid, and a chauffeur/handyman. No lady expected to do her own housework, and few knew how to, let alone how to cook. The families from which the debs were drawn would have had between eight and a dozen servants as a rule — even if this subjected them to personal hardship. In Evelyn Waugh's A *Handful of Dust* (1934), Lady Brenda Last says,

> Do you know how much it costs just to live here? We should be quite rich if it wasn't for that. As it is we support fifteen servants indoors, besides gardeners and carpenters and a night-watchman and all the people at the farm and odd little men constantly popping in to wind the clock and cook the accounts and clean the moat. . . .

The great aristocratic households were run by many more people. Lady Astor's personal maid, Rose Harrison, gives a table showing the hierarchy of staff kept at the Astors' five houses and it totals 127. Even allowing for the fact that servants' wages were low in those days (hence the increasing difficulty of hiring them), the cost of feeding, housing, paying and buying uniforms for all these people was immense. Yet in some respects Lady Astor could be mean. She took on Rose as her maid in 1928 at a salary of £75 a year. Six years later Rose — who had discovered by that time that the job was for eighteen hours a day, seven days a week — asked for a rise, and was given an extra £5 a year. Stung by this — for it amounted to 3d a day — she never asked again; and was never offered an increase in her remaining twenty-six years of service.

Similarly, Chatsworth — one of several houses belonging to the Duke of Devonshire — was still run in 1939 by a staff of over fifty, of whom forty lived on the premises. Here too wages were not generous. A house-keeper earned between £100 and £140 a year, depending on the size of the house she had to run (this would be £2,000–£2,800 in today's money); a house-maid between £35 and £45 (£700-£900 would be the modern equivalent). While it is true that all their living expenses were paid for them, living in the house had a number of disadvantages. It was almost impossible for servants to have a truly private life. Love-affairs and marriages among servants were discouraged, so although they sometimes happened nevertheless, it was in the face of opposition, and they were forced to keep their relationships secret. The Duchess of Devonshire writes about the 1930s in the household she married into in 1941:

Chatsworth had a reputation for poor wages. There were no rises and the under-servants did not stay long. . . . The housemaids were supposed to have one afternoon a week and every other evening off, but there was usually too much work for this and they had very little free time. They had to be in by nine-thirty in the winter and ten o'clock in the summer.

When tea was substituted for beer, cash was paid in lieu, hence the "beer money" [a bonus equivalent to about 25 per cent of the wages] in addition to the wages. In 1931 income tax rose to 5s in the pound under Ramsay MacDonald and Granny decided on stringent economies and stopped the beer money. As it was a considerable part of the wages and was in the contract of employment it rankled terribly, and no wonder.

The housemaids had to buy their own uniforms: print dresses for morning, black with little white aprons for the afternoon and black for the evening, and white organdie caps which were fastened with elastic at the back. They made these themselves.[13]

By 1939, lesser households were finding it more and more difficult to attract, and keep, good servants. The tradition of domestic service died hard among employers, but among working women a generation almost swept it away. By the 1930s there were many alternative forms of work available to young women, and while they may not have paid significantly more (taking into account the free board and lodging supplied to domestic servants), they all without exception offered more freedom. A survey carried out by Miss F.A.F. Livingstone in 1934 revealed that among the 200 working-class mothers and daughters whom she questioned, the mothers were still divided as to whether domestic service was a good way to earn a living, but the daughters were almost unanimously against it. The job had very low status. Hours were long. Living and working conditions could be appalling. Servants often slept two, three or four to a room, with no privacy, little furniture and no comforts. Employers' attitudes could be arrogant and unreasonable. Rose Harrison records a telling exchange with Lady Astor:

"The difference between us, Rose, is that I was born to command and have learnt through experience how to deal with people."

"The difference between us, my lady," I said, "is that you have money. Money is power, and people respect money and power so they respect you for having it."[14]

One cannot be certain that this exchange ever really took place, for Sarah Norton, who married Lady Astor's son Bill, reports that Rose's memory was selective, and she often told stories as she wished they had happened, rather than with strict regard to the truth. Either way, the anecdote is revealing. Equally revealing is this description, by a man who had better be anonymous, of his family's attitudes towards their servants:

My parents' generation knew how to treat their servants and it got a very good response from them. Nowadays you're supposed to behave, so to speak, as if they were equal human beings. But then, when your personal servant addressed you, they might have found you pompous, but familiarity breeds contempt. Nowadays, people treat their servants very, very well — and they lose them. Our servants were never overpaid: but they never went. There were certain people who had been with us for a very long time, and they could really speak their minds: the very, very old servants. I think we were frightened of them, in a funny sort of way. Looking back, you could say we were inconsiderate in what we expected of our servants. But we got it.

Lady Troubridge's *Book of Etiquette,* first published in 1926, is a guide to what she described as "the technique of the art of social life". Among the minutiae of correct observances that it details, there is a section on servants. Under the heading "Manners in General" Lady Troubridge advises:

A servant should never be noisy when on duty. He is not supposed to whistle or sing, talk loudly, or call to his fellow-servants. He should not bang doors, and run about or move noisily. He should speak gently and clearly and, if he meets one of the family or a guest upon the stairs or in a passage, he should draw aside and allow them to pass.

It seems extra hard on the servant that, having been instructed to maintain this prim and self-effacing demeanour, he is then also told that it is his duty to be *cheerful*.

Young working-class men and women possessing an education, the vote and above all a range of alternatives to domestic service saw few advantages in the servant's life. Phrases about the honour or the dignity of service began to ring hollow. As they turned elsewhere in search of satisfying work, the whole edifice of gracious living and hospitality which had depended upon their labour began to crumble. Certainly the Second World War hastened the process, just as the First had done, but it would have happened in any case. Employers were seldom imaginative or generous towards their servants, and saw no reason to improve their working hours and wages, or to make their lives easier by introducing cleaner forms of cooking and heating such as electricity. (As late as 1936, only 6 per cent of households cooked with electricity. The vast majority still used old, cumbersome coal-fired ranges, unreliable to cook with and a nightmare to clean: not at all like the gleaming enamelled Aga of today.)

The attitudes towards servants and the conditions in which they were expected to live and work un-complainingly were hard to change because they became fossilized by the memory of the older generations. An upper-class mother brought up in a grand Victorian household in the days when girls were reasonably happy to enter domestic service would often fail to realize how much things had changed since then, and would criticize her daughter for what she saw as a lowering of standards. Attitudes were passed on from elderly mother to middle-aged daughter, and from her to teenage debutante. The world changed, but employers preferred not to — since it meant losing the comfort they had grown up to expect. Evidence of these changes can be read between the lines of comments from the more intelligent or sensitive girls — like Sonia Denison, now Mrs Heathcoat-Amory:

One sometimes wondered if it could all be justified — the luxury and the waste. Because we were aware of the unemployment and the poverty. I suppose one thought all this — our world, the dances, the clothes — made employment. But ... the lavishness of the suppers: and a lot of it just thrown away in the end. We were very conscious and ashamed of it really — well, I think a lot of people were.

I remember my father saying, if you were to do a job — as I wanted to — you are taking a job from somebody who needs it. None of us worked — none of us earned our living. That was the great difference then. We didn't need to, but on top of that we weren't *allowed* to. I'm sure a lot of brains were wasted. It was a really idiotic life. It was. But we did it and enjoyed it and it's finished. We were very spoilt — looked after hand and foot. I'd never cooked or so much as packed a suitcase before the war. And then of course all that changed very quickly when war broke out. We were all VADS [Voluntary Aid Detachment] and things, and then we really got to work. That was a big change. But it was a very luxurious life before then. Extraordinary.

Yet the depression did not see any increase in the number of domestic servants. Instead, electrical devices to make housework easier were gradually being introduced. Vacuum cleaners — invented as long ago as 1903 — were becoming more common and so were electric irons.

Meanwhile — watchman, what of the night? War was now less than three months away. There were still many people who believed that Hitler would back down. In a speech he made at Chatham House at the end of June, the Foreign Secretary said quite plainly: "We know that, if international law and order is to be preserved, we must be prepared to fight in its defence." He went on,

> We are creating here a powerful weapon for the defence of our own liberty and that of other peoples. With every week that passes, that effort gains momentum, and on every side of life, political, administrative, industrial, we have abundant evidence of how firmly this national effort is driven and supported by the people's will. Behind all our military effort stand the British people, more united than ever before. . . .[15]"

Brave words, when Lord Halifax must have known that the results of an opinion poll carried out that same week showed that 57 per cent of those polled believed that the risk of war had decreased since the previous autumn, and 13 per cent were "don't knows". This did not, of course, mean that 70 per cent of the British people were not prepared to fight; but it certainly meant that they did not expect to have to do so, let alone so soon.

The German people felt exactly the same. There is no poll to give a precise figure for their opinions, but the *New York Times* correspondent in Berlin reported that 90 per cent of the population would have liked to rest content with the land Hitler had annexed so far, and they did not wish — or believe — that Germany would go to war.[16] They knew Britain and France did not want war either, and from this naive and optimistic belief in the essential peaceableness of the ordinary man, they drew comfort from the belief that there would therefore be no war. The Germans too had vivid and recent memories of the slaughter of the First World War.

The truth was simple. People have an indestructible tendency to look on the bright side until faced with dark evidence that there is no bright side; and in a green and sunny June the prospect of war was hard to face. Harold Nicolson wrote to Vita, his wife:

> June 19, 1939
>
> Why can we not be left alone? We are doing no harm. We care for fine and gentle things. We wish only to do good on earth. We are not vulgar in our tastes or cruel in our thoughts. Why is it that we are impotent to prevent something which we know to be evil and terrible? I would willingly give my own life if I could stop this war. I am so unhappy about the outside, and happy in my own little orbit.[17]

Plaintive, peaceable, passive ... it was how most people felt.

The last fortnight in June was the very peak of the Season. *The Times* listed at least two dances every night, sometimes three; and there were many people who — perhaps for fear of gatecrashers — preferred not to have their dance announced in the Social Column. Susan Ridley (now Mrs Chaplin), whose dance was on 26 June, recalls the problems uninvited guests could cause:

My dance was given at 54 Mount Street, in a house that belonged to the Dowager Viscountess Cowdray. (Her daughter had married my cousin, so we were sort of related.) There were always quite a lot of gatecrashers around at deb dances — it was a risk you ran, because everyone knew whose the next party was, and if word got round that it was going to be good, you'd have lots of uninvited guests. Lady Cowdray insisted that we had someone at the door to keep them out, who checked everyone's invitations — it was, after all, a private house. So we did very well, and only had two gatecrashers, who were caught red-handed trying to get in with two young men, and they were removed from the dance. They were — I won't reveal their names — but they were ex-debs who'd got a bit past it, but knew the routine and hoped for some free food and a drink. That sort of thing used to happen a lot.

In the end the party was a huge success — it ended at about five o'clock in the morning, so we all got to bed very late. I adored it.

On 22 June, the King and Queen returned from their tour of Canada and the United States to a triumphal welcome. The weather, which had hampered their arrival in Canada seven weeks earlier now hampered their return. Mist and rain made it necessary to cancel the spectacular naval and air ceremonies which had been planned. In London, however, the sun shone, happy crowds lined the streets, the little princesses looked sweet in pink coats and white socks and the King looked tanned and the Queen smiled her radiant smile. The bunting and decorations to welcome them back fluttered along the streets and at Waterloo station, where their train drew in from Southampton.

The same decorations had given quite unintended pleasure to a group of 287 Jewish refugees from the *St Louis*, the ship that had sailed to Havana and back in a vain attempt to find safe harbour for its passengers. Britain was one of four countries that had finally, reluctantly, agreed to accept the 900 stateless Jews between them. Britain's quota arrived at Waterloo Station on 21 June, the day before the royal return, where the children were thrilled to find such a lovely show to herald their arrival, at last, in their new country.

The royal visit had in fact achieved little beyond flattering publicity for the royal couple. The King might have hoped for an unequivocal declaration of American support in the event of war, to be given in practical form: arms, troops, commitments. The Americans hoped to be able to steer clear. A poll among the intellectual readers of the American political weekly the *New Republic* had asked them what America's foreign policy should be if war broke out in Europe. Of the 144 replies it received, 47 readers voted to help Great Britain with positive aid — armaments, supplies and, if unavoidable, fighting men; 42 favoured a rigorous policy of keeping well out of it. That left 55, well over a third, ambivalent or undecided. It was not an encouraging response. A question had been asked in the House of Representatives, "whether the unprecedented visit of the King does in fact signify an entente between the administration for the preservation of the British Empire at the expense of American blood and American treasure?'' — a loaded question, it might seem. America was finding it difficult simultaneously to preserve neutrality and express its proper democratic hatred of the Fascist dictatorships. America temporized. The King returned empty-handed.

One of the four dances taking place on the evening of 22 June was given for Eunice Kennedy, the third daughter of Ambassador and Mrs Kennedy, at their official residence at 14 Prince's Gate. Her elder sister Kathleen (always known as "Kick") must have been a hard act to follow. Kick's wild success as a debutante the previous year had made her one of the most sought-after girls in the young set. All doors were open to her. Everyone solicited her company. Voted "the most exciting debutante of 1938", she had a large circle of friends. Elizabeth Leveson-Gower knew Eunice quite well; indeed she was a friend of all the young Kennedys:

They all had this quality of liveliness — Eunice too: she wasn't classically good-looking, and certainly not as attractive as Kick, but she was so lovely and energetic, and that was attractive. She had a rather wide face, but her figure was good and she was tremendously good company. Jack was very intelligent — too intelligent and political for me. He liked to dominate the conversation at a dinner-table; he wasn't interested in making small talk. He wanted to discuss serious issues.

I remember sitting next to Mr Kennedy at the dinner-party they gave before Eunice's dance. I liked him. A lot of people since have said he was anti-British, but I found him easy to talk to and a good host.

211

That was her account of the evening; but her diary for the whole day is worth quoting in full, for it conveys the sheer crowdedness of a deb's day:

Thursday, 22 June: Lunch Ursula Wyndham-Quin. Watched King & Queen in the Procession on their return from Canada from Lord Caledon's house. Dined Kennedys for their dance — I sat next to Mr Kennedy. Complete riot at end. Everyone formed a chain and ran round the house landing on the floors.
Home by 4 a.m.

Joseph Kennedy had come to London in 1938. In the great tradition of American ambassadors, he was a self-made man — and it was not advisable to enquire too closely into just how he had made himself. He had also made a marriage, to a wife of iron will and rigid Catholicism — and they had nine children. Their births spanned seventeen years; from Joe Jr, born in 1915, to little Teddy, born in 1932. At the older end of the family were three who took an active part in the Season: John (later Jack) Kennedy, born in 1917 and thus an ideal age for escorting debs; Kathleen, who grasped the rules of the Season instantly, and played its games with skill and vivacity; and Eunice, who was born in 1921 and was presented at Court in 1939, under the auspices of the diplomatic list. There was another daughter of the right age — Rosemary — but she was backward, more so than her mother would admit, and so, although dutifully shepherded from dance to dance with the other girls, she was something of a liability.

Ambassador Kennedy claimed — in one of those anecdotes that pepper American history, as though events turned on a chance or a joke — that he outbluffed the President, Franklin Delano Roosevelt, to get the job. The story is told in a biography of the Kennedy family:

When Kennedy was ushered into the Oval Office, the President asked him to step back by the fireplace so he could get a good look at-him. Puzzled, Kennedy did as he was told. "Joe," the President continued, "would you mind taking your pants* down?" Kennedy stared back in disbelief, then slowly unhooked his suspenders,† let his pants fall to the floor, and stood in his shorts†† looking silly and embarrassed. FDR broke the silence. "Joe, just look at your legs. You are just about the most bow-legged man I have ever seen. Don't you know that the Ambassador to the Court of St James's has to go through an induction ceremony at which he wears knee breeches and silk stockings? Can you imagine how you'll look? When photos of our new Ambassador appear all over the world, we'll be a laughing stock. You're just not right for the job, Joe."

Kennedy looked straight at Roosevelt: "Mr President, if I can get the permission of His Majesty's Government to wear a cutaway coat and striped pants to the ceremony, would you agree to appoint me?"

"Well, Joe, you know how the British are about tradition. There's no way you are going to get permission, and I will name a new Ambassador soon."

"Will you give me two weeks?"

FDR nodded and Kennedy pulled up his pants and went out of the door, leaving the President chuckling. Not long afterwards he returned with the permission he had promised to obtain.[18]

It is said that President Roosevelt appointed Joe Kennedy because he did not want an Anglophile ambassador, but one who would be disinterested in his

* Trousers.　† Braces　†† Underpants

reports on the European situation. Anglophilia was certainly not Kennedy's problem. In spite of that, he was determined to secure for himself and his children the kind of social acceptance that had eluded them in Boston, where "the Lowells speak only to Cabots, and the Cabots speak only to God". Be that as it may, they did not speak to the upstart Roman Catholic Kennedys, nor did they let Joe join their clubs, and the snub rankled bitterly.

Reinforced by the palatial setting of the American Embassy and its neighbouring residence in Prince's Gate; buttressed by his personal wealth; and helped most of all by three socially talented children, Kennedy achieved much of the success he had hoped for in London Society. Kathleen, his eldest daughter, acted as co-hostess for him with her mother. She was sent — as were so many debs — to Madame Vacani to learn how to do a proper Court curtsey for her presentation in 1938. (Madame Vacani's immortal words to the fledgling debs were: "Throw out your little chests and *burst* your little dresses!") Curtseying was the only skill Kathleen needed to learn. Her American confidence, her vigour and energy and her propensity to tease made her instantly popular.

Her father's popularity posed much more of a problem. He was coarse, brash, vulgar with money; he was an unashamed womanizer; and, above all, he seemed far too impressed by Hitler and the Germans and was, as a result, outspokenly in favour of appeasement — even at a time when the British government had abandoned the policy. If he could not stop the war, he would do everything in his power to

214

stop American involvement in it. He was anti-Semitic. His political judgement was poor — as well it might be, since he had virtually no previous experience of politics. His judgement of people was little better, and he dismissed Winston Churchill as a drunkard. Perhaps most damning of all, he allowed his privately held, extreme right-wing views to dictate his conduct while he was the official representative of his country. A scathing paragraph in Claud Cockburn's political magazine *The Week* informed its readers:

There are those in "high places" in London [meaning those who supported Sir Oswald Mosley] who regard it as axiomatic that the war must not be conducted in such a manner as to lead to a total breakdown of the German regime and the emergence of some kind of "radical" government in Germany. These circles are certainly in indirect touch with certain German military circles — and the intermediary is the American Embassy in London (after all, nobody can suspect Mr Kennedy of being unduly prejudiced against fascist regimes, and it is through Mr Kennedy that the German Government hopes to maintain "contacts").[19]

By 1939 Ambassador Kennedy's clandestine and self-serving behaviour was practically public knowledge. He was accused by the exiled Czech, Jan Masaryk, of having sold Czech securities so as to secure for himself a profit of £20,000. He was accused of having packed his family off to the safety of Ireland at the time of the Munich crisis, thereby setting a poor example and lowering morale. He was accused of being too sympathetic to Nazism. He made no secret of his belief that, when the time came, Hitler would march right over Poland and then it would be Britain's turn next. Yet none of this seemed to have harmed his daughters.

One deb, impeccably bred but far from rich, commented, "It was hell to go to dinner with the Kennedys, as they were fearfully squashing to anyone who was not in their close-knit circle." Since July 1938, that circle had included Billy Hartington, heir to the Duke of Devonshire. The family owned 180,000 acres and several residences, among them Chatsworth in Derbyshire, Lismore Castle in Ireland, Bolton Abbey in Yorkshire, Hardwick Hall and several London houses. Kathleen's popularity compensated for the bad impression created by her eldest brother, Joe, whose abrasive manner and cruel humour were the obverse of Kathleen's energy and teasing wit. Joe was known to have a violent temper, and — used to the greater licence permitted to young women in America — he could be sexually aggressive. His next brother, Jack, who was also still at college in America but made frequent visits to London, was better looking and more personable, and better able to keep his sexual aggression in check for the benefit of the gently reared English debs.

With such formidable siblings, Eunice's debut cannot have been easy. Her father determined to launch her with a spectacular dance. Although announced in *The Times* as a "small dance", this was merely a signal once again that the King and Queen would not be present — hardly surprising, since they had only the same day returned from their tour. The guests at the dinner-party beforehand included some of the leading lights of the Season, while the young men who partnered them offered a dazzling selection of suitable escorts and potential husbands to the Kennedy daughters. If not already titled — like Earl Haig and the Marquess of Hartington — they were likely to inherit a title in due course. The hostesses giving dinner-parties for other guests were brilliant figures in their generation, though the list is unusual in that two young, unmarried women also gave dinner-parties: the Hon. Deborah Mitford and Miss Jane Kenyon-Slaney (now Mrs Robin Compton). Eunice — or perhaps the choice was dictated by her parents — selected her intimates from the highest rung of society, and given that it was notoriously difficult to penetrate the upper ranks of the upper classes in one generation, let alone after a single Season, the Kennedys had done very well. It was not all due to Kathleen's skill and charm. Sarah Norton, another friend of the whole family, speaks warmly of young Jack Kennedy:

> He was much the nicest of them all . . . very personable and attractive, with beautiful manners and a nice sense of humour. Joe the eldest was anti-British — even then, and as for his father . . . after the very first air-raid during the Battle of Britain, he took the whole family to a house in the country and then himself skedaddled back to the States as fast as he could!

Vivien Mosley was a member of the group of rather clever, rather independent, very upper-class girls who were Kathleen's chosen set, and she became friendly with Eunice in the summer of 1939:

> She was a terribly nice girl, actually, though shyer, much more reticent than Kick. Now Kick had established herself as a tremendous character, almost as soon as she arrived, but

Eunice was a different kettle of fish. She was awfully sweet, though and pretty — very pretty. Rosemary was around quite a lot as well — she was the one who was sort of . . . slightly . . . I don't know that one could say she was exactly . . . well, she was shy. Eunice was always very tactful about her. And Joe didn't play very much part, because he was already heavily involved with his flying.

Eunice's pictures from that year show a classic Kennedy face, brimming with health and energy. Wide sparkling eyes and white sparkling teeth, in conjunction with a slightly more gentle and serious manner than her glamorous elder sister, must have guaranteed her success with young men. She was intelligent, too, and her American talent for swift repartee made her conversation livelier and more unexpected than that of the sheltered English girls. But it was her naturalness that charmed most: even if it sometimes stemmed from ignorance. The *Tatler* for 12 July tells an anecdote from the Blenheim Ball, at which, the magazine said, "No seventeen-year-old looked half as alert as Lady Cunard, with the possible exception of the second Kennedy daughter, Eunice, a complete unselfconscious darling of a girl who rushed her partner up to the Duke of Marlborough with, "Let's ask this man the time!""

Eunice's dance was on a Thursday. The two dances the following night — for Lorna Campbell and her cousin Helen Campbell; and another for Priscilla Hale and her brother Michael — were both held in the country. Friday night was, for obvious reasons, a favourite for country dances. It provided the perfect excuse for a country weekend, with everyone congregating at house-parties given by local hostesses, who would each give a dinner for their house-guests and "then arrive in a group for the evening's dance. (By one of those curious coincidences which demonstrate the essential continuity of the English upper classes, the Hales' dance was given in the house in Plumpton, East Sussex in which Rosalind Cubitt lives today.)

It was Midsummer Day next morning, Saturday, 24 June, but the brilliantly sunny days had ended. The weather broke on 17 June and was cool, pale, unsettled right through until the end of the month. This has not prevented the debs of 1939 from describing it over and over again as "a brilliant summer", "wonderful weather for just weeks on end". The same was said of the whole Edwardian period, although scrutiny of the records of the Meteorological Office shows that in both cases the weather was no better than average. In 1914, the last summer of peace was indeed brilliant: a heat-wave hung unnaturally over the country for weeks on end, and August was still and scorching. This memory seems to have been suspended, so that in retrospect it bathed the whole decade in its stifling, airless heat. Nineteen-thirty-nine was a typically cool English summer. Yet it seems as though, once again, the fact that the country was enjoying a heatwave when war broke out has preserved that weather in amber, exotically golden and heavy with the buzzing haze of heat and idleness, and *that* is what people remember.

The first Test Match began at Lords that Saturday, against the West Indies, and on the Monday, 26 June Wimbledon fortnight opened. It was a mediocre year for tennis lovers. R.L.Riggs took the men's title, although his "robot rallies" bored the crowd; and Alice Marble from the USA took the ladies' title. A few debs went along to watch — those who were keen on tennis, or good at it, for Wimbledon was not a fashionable occasion — and had their photographs taken for the *Bystander*. Although journalists were much less intrusive fifty years ago, there was a lively interest in the goings-on of Society, and photographers attended all the main social events. Leading debs would find their picture in the *Daily Express* gossip column next morning; the difference being that its writer — Tom Driberg — was not likely to reveal any scandal until it had become common knowledge to everyone except the readers of the *Daily* Express. The *Tatler* would not then dream of doing what is common practice now — catching an unflattering or compromising photograph of a girl looking undignified or in the wrong company. The upper classes were avid for gossip, but believed that its circulation should be restricted to those of their own kind. The habit of discretion persists to this day. Research for this book revealed a few girls who had deviated from the code that demanded virginity until marriage; but this information — always concerning the same half-dozen names — was divulged in the strictest secrecy, and only in return for a promise that it would not find its way into print.

The tone of Society magazines of the thirties is one of brittle and snobbish frivolity rather than the veiled spite which often characterizes them today. The following three captions are all drawn at random from a single page in the *Bystander* for August:

"Beetle" — Edith Lambert is the real name of this attractive young creature, the only child of Lord Cavan's brother and heir-presumptive.

The Hon. Deborah Mitford, 19-year-old ex-deb, sat on a paddock seat with Lord Andrew Cavendish, who is the same age.

Two 1939 debs, Osla Benning and the Hon. Guinevere Brodrick, daughter of Lady Dunsford, had Ian Farquhar to talk to them between races.

The oddly stilted tone of these remarks is due to the fact that they are, in magazine jargon, justified left and right: which means that they had to form a perfect rectangle with no short lines. This involved the laborious counting of letters and re-arranging of words so as to ensure that the caption fitted exactly into its space. The captions provided an insider's guide to who was with whom, and a snobs' guide to family networks. The two main Society magazines of the time were the Tatler and the *Bystander*. The former was rather more cosmopolitan and contained gossip about Society members in New York, Paris and the French holiday resorts, as well as several pages in each issue covering theatre and cinema and the private lives of the stars. The *Bystander* was more old-fashioned, confining itself largely to the events of the Season. It, like *The Times*, was the notice-board of the upper classes, but with pictures. Every week it published pictures of debutantes, engaged couples, weddings, young mothers with babies, so that the provincial gentry could keep up with what was going on.

The debs, while pretending to find all this frightfully embarrassing, were not in truth averse to being photographed, as is proved by the many who carefully cut out and kept these pictures. They paid lip-service to the belief that it was *infra dig* to have one's name in the papers, other than *The Times'* Social Column, or listed under "hatches, matches and despatches". The title "Deb of the Year", insofar as it existed at all, was bestowed by popular newspapers in return — it was rumoured — for payment; thus none will admit to having been Deb of the Year in 1939. Some of the more pushy mothers *were* prepared to pay for publicity, and then the girl in question would find a posse of photographers waiting for her outside every dance and clustering around her at Ascot. This was thought ineffably vulgar by the others, but it sometimes worked. Margaret Whigham had been Deb of the Year in 1930; she and her mother discreetly orchestrated her flattering press coverage and it certainly did not handicap her marriage prospects. American mothers were particularly good at stage-managing this kind of attention for their daughters. South African mothers did it too, despite knowing that this was frowned upon by the English. "IDB," people would murmur, looking askance at a woman bowed down under the weight of her tiara. It meant "illicit diamond buying" and was much disapproved. One former deb has never forgotten the behaviour of one of these wealthy South Africans:

There was a terribly vulgar woman in London before the war and she had three children. My mother was at a lunch-party one day, just a small one, and she was sitting next to this woman. Well, in her guileless sort of way she said, "I can't think what to do, I've got so-and-so's presentation in about a fortnight and I've got a tiara of course but it's at Asprey's and won't be ready. I wonder how I can get one?" All perfectly innocently meant. So this woman, Mrs, well I won't mention her name, nudged my mother and she said, "Don't you worry about that, Lady x, I'll lend you one of mine." You know . . . one of her tiaras. Whereupon my mother got a sharp kick in the shins from the other side and this was Mrs x, an old friend, and she whispered, "Don't you borrow one from that woman. I'll lend you mine."

Anyway this South African woman did very well, she succeeded in marrying all three children — she had two daughters and a son — into titled families.

The week beginning Monday, 26 June started with two dances and a charity ball. The Hon. Mrs Milles-Lade gave a dance for her daughters Diana and Isabel (now the Countess of Derby), which they shared with Sybil Jennings. Lady Diana — older by one year than her sister — remembers it with delight:

We were terribly lucky because we had Carroll Gibbons to play for us. That was considered a great privilege; but he was a friend of Sybil's father, so he kindly came and played half the night for us, which was wonderful. First we had our dinner-party at Claridge's, and then we all went and stood at the top of the staircase at the dance: the two mothers and we two sisters and Sybil, to greet our guests. Stanhope Gate was lovely — it was like your own house; smaller than a hotel and much more friendly. Goodyear — they were florists — did the flowers for us, pink and white carnations all round the rooms.

Everybody was so well behaved in those days and everybody looked so nice — they're all so frightful nowadays, but still. . . . The men were beautifully groomed in their white ties and tails and with a red carnation. There was nothing sort of evil, one just enjoyed it. Everybody went swinging around in a very, very friendly sort of way. I had to dance with everybody and see that they were all right and there weren't any girls standing miserably against the wall — and I had to look after Carroll Gibbons. That meant seeing that he had a drink. There was a picture in the *Tatler* of us receiving the guests, which I take out and look at now and again. It was all such fun.

The following night was Elizabeth Hambro's dance, shared with Hersey Williamson and given at Lady Forres' house at 41 Chelsea Square. Elizabeth, now Lady Bonsor, says, "One young man climbed up the marquee in the garden, which I remember annoyed my father very much — but yes, of course, I enjoyed it all very much. It was fun while it lasted. We knew it wouldn't last. Everybody was talking about the war: by now you couldn't be unaware of it."

Matters were coming to a head. Hitler's harassment of Danzig was becoming ever more blatant, and he was beginning to intimate that he would not be satisfied with just Danzig any longer; he wanted the whole of the Polish Corridor. Danzig was now effectively German — as were 90 per cent of its citizens. Its administration was controlled by the Danzig Nazi party and in all but name it was already part of the Reich. But President Moscicki of Poland — to whom name mattered, and who saw that Danzig would not satisfy Hitler — said in a speech on 29 June: "Any attempt to change the status quo in Danzig, either by a move within or from without, would be a cause of war." Winston Churchill, not at this stage a member of the Cabinet, had made a speech at the

Carlton Club the day before in which he addressed himself, dramatically, directly to Hitler. Churchill must have known that war was, at best, a matter of months away. Chamberlain was burned out by the responsibilities and stress of the last year; a man haggard with physical and mental exhaustion. He had been showing signs of strain for months, as even his supporters had to admit. The pressure for Churchill to be included in the Cabinet was coming to a head, but Chamberlain was inclined to compromise on the Danzig issue, while Churchill would not. So Churchill, unable to urge his views upon policy-makers in Britain, addressed them instead to Hitler:

Pause. . . . consider well before you take a plunge into the terrible unknown. Consider whether your life's work — which may even now be famous in the eyes of history — in raising Germany from defeat and frustration to a point where all the world is waiting for her actions, consider whether all this may not be irretrievably cast away.[20]

After this shrewd appeal to Hitler's vanity and his hunger for the acclaim of generations to come, Churchill went on, speaking now to his audience:

Considering the German preparations, the tone of the government-controlled press and Party leaders, there can be no conclusion but that the worst could happen and happen quite soon. I must consider — I think we must all consider — July, August and September as months in which the tension in Europe will become most severe.[21]

Churchill had thrown down the gauntlet, even if

Chamberlain would not. Those who prevaricated, claiming that Danzig and its 400,000 citizens were not sufficient justification for a war risking the lives of millions, were missing the point. The point was that Hitler would not take Danzig and then stop; he would demand and threaten and take, and then find fresh demands, just as he had always done in the past. There had to be a geographical and political frontier at which he either stopped, or fought. Danzig — Poland — was that frontier.

That day, Chips Channon wrote in his diary: "The whole outlook is appalling, Hitler is a bandit; we are all mad; and Russia is winking slyly — and waiting."[22]

It was now the end of June — and still the dances went on. The next, yet again at 6 Stanhope Gate, was for Rhona Wood and Eve Bannerman, whose mothers were great friends. Rhona — now Mrs Peyton-Jones — recalls the blissful, light-hearted extravagance of it all:

Our decor had as its centrepiece a fountain which shot water up high into the air. They'd decorated the place beautifully — it was all done by Searcy's. My mother had said, "When you've had your dance, darling, then you can go out with a young man". Otherwise you were never allowed to be with a chap alone.

Mummy bought me a very, very expensive pink net dress. It was skin-tight down to the hips and then it flared out in layers of net. It had thin shoulder-straps with full-blown pink roses on them. I kept it till after the war and went on wearing it — because of clothing coupons, you know, you couldn't buy anything. The dance was the most enormous fun. You knew everybody there by then, you'd seen the girls at all the same dos night after night, and the young men — though some of them were ghastly and you tried to avoid them.

And then afterwards — I think this is right; I'm sure it's right and it was that same evening — because I was now "out" I went off to a nightclub for the very first time. It was the 400 of course — *naturally* it was the 400! — the Embassy was much more down-market. The 400 was *the* nightclub; everybody went there. René, who was the head waiter, got to know me, and he'd keep my same table for me every night. And Tim Clayton had the band and played the piano, and when he saw you he'd play your special tune. Yes, I remember what mine was, but I'm not going to say!

The Friday of that week was the last day of June, and the month culminated with one of the greatest and grandest dances of the Season. It was given by the Duchess of Sutherland for her niece, Elizabeth Leveson-Gower. Both her parents were dead; her father had died in the year she was born and her mother in 1931, when Elizabeth was ten. As the only child of Lord Alastair St Clair Sutherland-Leveson-Gower, Elizabeth would one day succeed to the earldom of Sutherland and the barony of Strathnaver in her own right. Thus, although paradoxically she was only a "Miss" among a gaggle of Hons, she was in one sense the most titled of them all. Dunrobin Castle was the ancestral home of the dukes of Sutherland; Sutton Place, near Guildford, was their country house in England, and it was here that the coming-out ball was held on 30 June.

Elizabeth's memories of the day of her dance are surprising:

The garden directly in front of the house looked a bit sparse, so we rushed out to Woolworth's and bought a mass of artificial delphiniums and things and stuck them in among the real ones to make them look a bit better. If anyone noticed they were too polite to comment! Topazia [her great friend, an Italian girl] and I spent two hours the day before, picking lime leaves off the branches of the trees, to leave buds for decoration. The house was relatively small and not ideal for a dance. We used one of the long galleries for dancing, up on the first floor, which had to be shored up with pillars to support the weight of all that activity. We disguised them by entwining them with leaves and flowers. Looking back, I think it was a mistake not to have hired professional florists. We tried to do it all ourselves, which took hours, and in the end didn't look as good. Some of them were paper, too, and I overheard one guest saying to my aunt, "What wonderful flowers you always have, darlings, and how good they smell!"

I had a yellow dress with satin bows all over it and a high square neck.

All my clothes were chosen for me, and it never occurred to me that I might have any say in the matter, though I didn't like most of them. They were always pink or white or yellow, which were colours I hated and that I thought didn't suit me.

We had fifty for dinner beforehand, and I sat between Jack Kennedy and George Townshend. The dance itself was quite hard work, in a way, because being my own dance, I had to dance with everyone who asked me. You couldn't say no.

The gardens looked wonderful after all — everywhere was floodlit and the swimming pool was surrounded by fairy lights. In the end it got quite cold, and people started coming indoors. Breakfast was served from about four o'clock onwards, but the dance didn't end till 5.30.

That evening is one of the half dozen of the Season that has stayed in everyone's memory. The garden — whatever Elizabeth Leveson-Gower says — did look marvellous, and people remember strolling through its floodlit borders in the balmy, light evening of late June, conscious that it was an extraordinary moment.

When dances were given privately, in people's own houses, the guests usually included a wide and cosmopolitan selection of the hostess's friends, and not only debs of that Season. Lady Sarah Churchill remembers the dance at Sutton Place for two reasons. One is that the Duchess of Sutherland — Elizabeth's aunt — looked "simply wonderful". The other is more unexpected:

> I also remember getting ticked off thoroughly because I danced with the Aga Khan's son, Aly. Coming back in the car with Mummy I was told that I didn't dance with those sort of people. But Daddy was saying, "Well, tell her why." You know the sort of thing — and laughing. I knew I wasn't to dance with married men, but I didn't. know why I wasn't to dance with Aly. And it turned out it wasn't because he was a foreigner or his religion was different or anything like that. It was because he was an older man! There was a bit of a frown on for that.

On the same evening — that of the last day in June — Margaret Proby and Elizabeth Lowry-Corry had their dance, too. It was in London, at 96 Cheyne Walk, in a house that belonged to Rick Stewart-Jones. He was a wealthy young man who had used a legacy to preserve beautiful houses, and 96 Cheyne Walk was one of the loveliest of these. He had bought it from Bryan Guinness, and its large ballroom was a perfect and unusual private setting for a deb dance. It easily accommodated the 200 people invited that evening.

Elizabeth Lowry-Corry had spent some time in Dresden — a city where, she believes, many people disapproved of the Nazi regime and its treatment of Jews. She returned just before the Munich crisis, and was one of those who undoubtedly knew what was happening in Germany. Perhaps in part because of this, she could not throw herself whole-heartedly into the Season, though she admits to having enjoyed it. She and Margaret Proby were "country cousins". They both came from country families, not especially grand and not especially rich. Neither of them was part of a debby "set". They were practical young women: Elizabeth was combining the Season with a typing course at Queen's, and spent every morning there, "dotty with sleep".

She still has the dress she wore for this party, a fragile bell of white silk taffeta, embroidered all over with tiny forget-me-nots. It is a dress such as Marie-Antoinette might have worn in her fantasy as a shepherdess, with its wide neckline and ruched bodice over which a little corset of turqoise blue lattice-work was tied with narrow satin ribbons.

I had been looking forward to my dance, and as it was towards the end of the Season one had become more confident. I knew that people would have to dance with me, which they did, thank God, though at other dances that was not always the case.

I remember we had a house-party in the country the following month and one of the guests — Edward Imbert-Terry, who was my father's godson — wrote in his thank-you letter that he had joined his regiment. He was in the Coldstream Guards.

You knew by then, you couldn't help knowing, that there was soon to be a war. You simply couldn't imagine what it would be like. Not the slightest conception.

Margaret Proby, now Mrs Harrison-Cripps, was a most unusual deb. For one thing, she spent that summer living in Bethnal Green, in a house belonging to her aunt, who ran a settlement there. This, she says, was considered a joke by the other debs, few of whom ever moved beyond the charmed circle of Mayfair, Belgravia, Knightsbridge, Kensington and Chelsea. The East End was just a name to them, a symbol of poverty and working-class deprivation; they could hardly imagine how one of their number could actually *live* there.

Margaret Proby never took her Season too seriously. She did it because her mother thought she should; but at the same time her parents took it for granted that in due course she would get a job. Her sister had been to university; Margaret herself attended the Royal School of Music. All this gave her a sense of proportion that was quite lacking in most of her contemporaries. She was very different in one other respect; not just different, but unique. Her family not only knew what was happening in Germany, they actively did something about it.

I went to Germany with my mother in 1938 and I can still remember seeing a large mural, and people around us whispering, "That's where the concentration camps are." We didn't understand what they meant. One couldn't imagine that anyone could be so perfectly awful. But we saw little boys

231

from the Hitler Youth being drilled in the streets of Munich, and although people said Hitler had given them jobs, given them prosperity, given them hope — which he had — one always felt there were overtones. . . .

My aunt was involved in getting children, Jewish children, out of Germany and we used to have young Jewish girls working for us as kitchen maids. They didn't like it very much, but at least they were out. We also had a Jewish doctor living with us for some time, who — despite many years of hospital practice — was forced to redo her medical training here before she was considered qualified to work.

This aunt was tremendously courageous; she went into Germany several times to get Jewish people out. She used to smuggle their jewellery out as well — which was forbidden by the Germans, of course; they'd let the people leave but they weren't allowed to take anything of value with them — and on one occasion she was found by the border police with a whole lot of rings that she'd hidden. She claimed they were hers, so the police said, "Try them on and we'll see if they fit"; so my aunt had to put them on her own fingers, having no idea if they would be the right size — but thank God, they were.

Margaret's aunt, Miss Barbara Murray, is still alive and still, at ninety, perfectly clear-headed in her recollection.

It was Bishop Bell of Chichester — a most remarkable man — who started the whole thing in about 1937. He formed a committee of people who were concerned about what was happening to the Jews of Europe. He had been to Germany and seen for himself their ill-treatment so he made contact with sympathetic priests from the German Lutheran Church. I was a member of this committee, which used to meet in London to plan how Jewish people — could be got out and found homes and sponsors here in England. We managed to get free places in schools, too, for some of the children.

Yes, I suppose it was quite an unusual thing to do: but most people in England didn't know what was going on, or if they did, didn't care. They didn't care what happened to Jews. If it wasn't ignorance it was indifference.

We mostly placed them in middle-class homes: with the clergy, or with teachers, and from there quite a number went over to America or Canada after the war. No, I can't remember any upper-class families taking one of our children. I may be wrong; but I don't remember a case.

In *The Times* for 1 July there are nine insertions commemorating young men killed on active service: rather fewer than might be expected, since it was the twenty-third anniversary of the first day of the Somme: a — day which was marked by the deaths of 19,249 young Englishmen. It is not that parents forget the death of a son; but perhaps after twenty-three years the ritual of the In Memoriam column had come to seem pointless or even — with another war looming — tactless. It is interesting to note that, of those nine names, two are Jewish.

CHAPTER
SEVEN

The Last Two Months
of Peace: July

July started badly. It rained. For 3, 4 and 5 July, Evelyn Waugh's diary recorded "Continuous rain" and, on 6 July, "More rain."[1] This meant that the hundredth Henley Royal Regatta, which opened on 3 July, was a pretty miserable affair for all but the most dedicated rowing enthusiasts. One such was Tom Vickers, a young bachelor living in digs in Ebury Street and working at the Colonial Office. He attended many deb parties that summer — he was especially popular because he was a good dancer and delighted in waltzing. A great friend of Rosamund Neave and her family, he soon found other invitations coming in. His name began to crop up on other mothers' lists, he enjoyed the dances, and found that the main disadvantage of the Season was the very large laundry bills incurred in washing and starching all those white shirts.

Rowing had been his passion, both at school and university, so Henley was a welcome break from a demanding London life:

I went to Henley in 1939 for two reasons. One is that the King's College Boat Club were able to send a full eight to row at Henley that year, whereas the previous year [his final year at Cambridge] we could only send a four. The other reason was that my twin brother was still at Trinity, Oxford, and he was going to be rowing in the Trinity second eight. As far as I remember I went on my own, because I still regarded myself as more part of the rowing fraternity than the London Season. I wanted to be able to watch the rowing, to retire to the Angel — the pub just by Henley Bridge — with my King's friends. I was more interested in doing that than in having girls and their mums tagging on. I think they would have been in the way.

Henley was then, and still is, dominated by the Stewards and Leander. It's essentially a *male* event. The old boys like to come out if they've got an Oxford or a Cambridge Blue. Of course . . . you want to put on your Blue cap or you want to wear your Leander tie and your Leander socks — it's not really a Society event. I mean, there are no top hats at Henley: the emphasis is quite different. So for Henley I would have worn my King's first-boat blazer and a King's tie and a King's cap probably; I mean, I would have worn what was expected. You were only entitled to wear the blazer or the cap or the tie if you had actually got it. It showed you were a rowing man.

The tie of all ties during Henley week comes from membership of the Leander Club. To aspire to that, a man has to have rowed in a winning event at Henley, or rowed in a boat that went head of the river at Oxford or Cambridge. It is an honour granted to few, and those few celebrate it, wearing a particularly bright salmon pink, in Leander's pretty Edwardian club house beside Henley Bridge. To this day, fifty years later, no women are allowed to row at Henley. It is, as Tom Vickers said, a very male event.

There were of course some debutantes there: what would Henley have been without its quota of girls in pretty frocks (rather damp and drooping frocks that year) even if they were sweetly ignorant about who was racing and who had won? Lady Elizabeth Scott was there with Lord Haig and Katharine Ormsby-Gore, photographed by the *Tatler* in an elegant group. Christian Grant was there, "mainly because my future husband, who was then a sort of boyfriend, had been in the eight at Eton and so was passionate about rowing". The weather prevented any really good times — in both senses of the word — for the wind was too strong for the boats and the rain too heavy for the debs. Most people sheltered in one of the many club tents as soon as they decently could, and the "wet-bobs' Ascot" was a bit of a wash-out. A pity: for it was not only the centenary year, but very possibly the last Henley for some years.

Increasingly, as month succeeded tense month in the summer of 1939, leaving less hope that war could be averted, people took part in the Season with the unspoken fear that each event could be the last; or, at any rate, their last. The young men who rowed at Henley, or watched others row, were mostly training for war by July. Many of the girls had embarked on some sort of preparation, nursing with the Red Cross perhaps. For almost a year people had convinced themselves that Munich had worked; but as the Polish crisis deepened it became clear to anyone who was at all politically informed, and especially to those with access to Establishment sources, that this time there was to be no way out. The stratagems put forward to placate Hitler were increasingly dishonourable. In early July there was a flurry of correspondence in *The Times* from people claiming that it was not worth starting another world war over Danzig. Better to annex its 400,000 citizens for Germany (most of them were German anyway). But Lloyd George had predicted twenty years earlier that Danzig and the Polish Corridor would trigger the next war, and he was right. Whatever the justice of the territorial boundaries redrawn by the Versailles agreement, Poland was always the weakest link. The only thing Munich had achieved — perhaps the only thing it could ever have hoped to achieve — was a year's breathing space, during which Britain could partly remedy the dangerous arms imbalance between herself and Germany.

Lord Hood describes the attitudes that resulted from this sense of fatalism:

One was hoping against hope that it could be avoided, as it was at the time of Munich, and I don't think the young realized what mobilization and all that would mean. But there was nothing they could do about it — there was nothing I could have done about it — and so I went on with my work and my ordinary play. It was a matter for governments to try and negotiate, and for the armed forces to get as well prepared as possible. I don't see anything unreasonable or wrong about the Season going on. In fact I think it would have been looked upon as panicking if it hadn't. And so we went on living the way we normally did. It didn't harm anybody.

I think by then everyone must have realized that war was imminent; but if you were out on an agreeable party you didn't think too much about it. There you were, you were having a good time, and that was enough for the evening.

Lord Haig reflects on the realities as they seemed at the time:

I couldn't say now whether most of the girls knew much about the likelihood of war but certainly I think most of the young men were only too aware of it. We'd been let off at the time of Munich when we were already expecting to be called up and sent off so it was a year's grace really. But the realities of it were only too clear and one knew what one was going to have to do. The difference was that one wasn't expecting this highly mechanized sort of war. One was being brought up in the aftermath of the trench war, the static war, and really wasn't expecting the Blitzkrieg. As for what was happening to the Jews in Germany, at the time, the short answer is that we just didn't know. I believe there was an occasional touch of anti-Semitism among the upper classes — among certain people you saw signs of it — but I certainly don't think that even they would have countenanced what was happening, if they'd known about it.

And so the last month of the last Season of peace carried on much as usual. Lady Kemsley gave a splendid dance for Ghislaine Dresselhuys, her daughter by a first marriage to an American. It was held at Chandos House, which was at that time the Kemsleys' London house. It was a beautiful Adam house in Queen Anne Street, one of the few such houses in London then remaining in private hands. (Its history since then has been chequered. It changed hands several times after the war, was for some time the premises of the Royal Society of Medicine, and in 1988 was sold yet again.)

The dance was given royal status by the presence of the Duke and Duchess of Kent. It was attended by two other duchesses as well, besides a glittering array of all the most sought-after debs of the Season and all the most distinguished young men. The music was by Nat Gonella and his Georgians, a new dance band whose music was closer to jazz than the usual popular songs to which the debs danced night after night. Ghislaine was a poised, beautiful and therefore much envied deb, and at this late stage of the Season it was necessary to produce some fairly startling element to a dance if it were to stand out from the nightly procession of all the other dances. Even salmon and champagne and Tubby Clayton pall eventually; but Nat Gonella livened things up considerably, and the sophisticated young guests who thronged Chandos House that evening welcomed music they could swing to.

The hesitant girls, awkward in their new ball dresses, who had ventured into their first dances at the beginning of May were now poised, almost blasé. Going to nightclubs now became a daring and frequent pastime. The smartest and most fashionable of all the clubs was the 400. Situated in Leicester Square, it was the mecca for London's chic night life and thus the mecca for debs. One of the men who escorted many of the 1939 debs recaptures the clandestine excitement all this entailed:

The great trick was when the chaperone was upstairs playing bridge — there was usually a separate room provided for them, where they had their own champagne and could play bridge or talk — the trick was to say to the pretty girl, let's nip off to a night club, this dance is rather boring, don't you think? And she would say, yes, actually. I've never been to a night club. So one would say, well, where would you like to go? Would you like to go to the Astor, the 400, the Orchid Room, the

Milroy, and so on? And she would select the club. One would take her to the night club and have a few dances in close proximity in semi-darkness, and then return to the ball in time to deliver the girl to the waiting chaperone who felt she'd been doing her duty all along. This was considered very dashing and was quite innocent. There were, I suppose, a few cases where it was not innocent; but generally it was a question of having a dance, tightly entwined, and a few kisses in the taxi coming back.

But it was quite expensive. You had to be a member, and the annual subscription was between ten shillings and a pound a year. For a young man who may have had three or four pounds a week, that could be too much.

Several young men of that year confirm this. One who was already earning his own living as a junior civil servant, says ruefully, "I never had the money to go on to the 400 after a dance, although that was where a lot of my friends would congregate. They would go from one dance to another and end up at the 400 — but that was going to be a pretty expensive evening by the time you were finished. Drinks and taxis and everything."

Ronnie Kershaw was a favourite escort in 1939 and one of his great attractions must have been his passion for the 400 Club.

The 400 was something on its own. It was the best place — I think it was the greatest place *ever*. There will never be another one. Mr Rossi was the head waiter. He always got you a table if he knew you. Then there was the fat man who played the piano: Tim Clayton. The atmosphere there was absolutely incredible. I went there an awful lot, with various people. It didn't cost a great deal. If you were in the Army you seemed to be allowed to do things at a very cheap rate . . . it can't have been more than a fiver at the most: maybe not as much.

You didn't go there to meet other people, in fact a great many went there not to be seen! It was so dark, it was quite difficult to see where anyone was. The atmosphere of that place was something indescribable.

The girls were — or it suited them to be — sweetly unaware of the expense involved. Anne Douglas-Scott-Montagu, now Lady Chichester, adored the 400, although her trips there did not become frequent until during the war, when it was a favourite haunt for people on a brief leave in London. "We always went dancing at the 400, which was great. We'd sometimes have dinner there, and then dance through to the early hours of the morning. But I've no idea what they cost — I never paid, so I wouldn't know. Poor young men: I suppose they had to pay, but I've no idea what they cost. I don't remember even thinking about it."

The Earl of Cromer, then Rowley Errington, also relished the night life that London's clubs and restaurants offered, at prices which, in retrospect, seem startlingly low.

The form very much was that if you were going to a dance later on you might take a girl to the theatre first, or dinner or something — it was all very cheap. None of us had much money. Well . . . a few did, but the majority didn't. You could take a girl out to dinner and the theatre then a nightclub for well under a fiver, even in the money of those days. But even so, you didn't do it too often because, obviously, you didn't have the cash. And of course it was *absolutely* out of the question that the girls should ever pay. But the restaurateurs, they all knew the structure and they encouraged the young

241

people to go in the hope that later on, if they'd got the money, they'd come there to spend it. It was purely commercial, but they were nice about it, too.

His favourite place was the Café de Paris:

It was downstairs in the basement of a building in New Coventry Street. The floor wasn't very big — only about 30 feet square: almost a club within a club, except that you didn't have to belong to it. It was run by a man called Pilsner, who welcomed the young. Then the favourite place after that was the 400, which had a sort of reputation all of its own — I mean a nice, happy reputation. Then there was Ciro's, which had a dance floor made of glass, with lights shining through: that was in Orange Street. Then there was another one called the Florida, just off Berkeley Square, which had a revolving floor — quite a novelty in those days. I don't remember any really sordid ones — I mean with telephones between the tables, where you could pick up a girl. You read about that sort of thing happening in Paris or New York but not in London, no. You went there with your girl. No pick-ups.

Yet here is quite a different point of view from Lord Hood, also a popular young man that year, though far too preoccupied with work to qualify as a "debs' delight". He had started doing the round of deb dances in 1932, so by 1939 the Season had to offer either a very splendid ball or a dance given by very close friends for him to find it amusing.

It was certainly considered "fast" for a debutante to go to a nightclub, because the chaperone would not have been around. In any case, I couldn't have afforded it. I was fairly impecunious and saw no reason to go. I went out and had a very good dinner and then I went on to the dance and after that I wanted to go home to bed, as I had to work the next day. So I don't recall ever having gone to a nightclub. There were of course the rather grand, rich young men who could, and did it, and thought it amusing and, you know, rather audacious and smart and so forth — I didn't; and there were a great many like me.

That was the men's point of view. For most of the girls a visit to a nightclub was nothing short of rapture. It was daring, delicious, a chance to be alone with a favourite young man, and thus forbidden and flattering. There were still, of course, many debs who obeyed their mothers' strict injunction not, ever, in any circumstances, no matter how attractive or safe, to venture into a nightclub. Mollie Acland says, ruefully, "Nightclubs were not merely fast: they were absolutely *forbidden* your first Season." So she did not go. Lady Cathleen Eliot (now Lady Cathleen Hudson) was also forbidden to go to nightclubs by her mother, but she went all the same — not least because her mother took an unconventional view of her duties as a chaperone, tending to consider them at an end when she had dropped her daughter off at the beginning of each week:

> She was a pilot with her own aeroplane and deposited me in London (Northolt) on Monday and collected me on Saturday, leaving strict instructions that I was not to go to nightclubs. But most of the debs did in fact go to them — it was only considered *slightly* fast — and I went to the 400 a few times, since that was the smart place to go.

This was the practical view taken by another very aristocratic deb: "Yes, it was thought fast for a deb to go to a nightclub, but we went all the same. The most fashionable was the 400, though the Paradise, the Suivi and the Nuthouse were also popular, and the Florida." The mothers were obviously fighting a losing battle, though Mary Tyser (now Lady Aldenham) remembers her mother's disapproval: "I remember her commenting on one or two girls who were known to have done so [i.e. gone to nightclubs] and unfortunately I never thought of evading my chaperone: I was far too gauche and childish, I suppose. Anyhow I never went to a nightclub in 1939." Lady Elizabeth Montagu Douglas Scott, now the Duchess of Northumberland, said:

> Not many girls could go to nightclubs as they were too strictly chaperoned, but I have to admit that from about halfway through the summer I did slip away quite often, but would return before the end of the dance and was only caught twice! This was probably because my mother would leave a ball quite early and go off to a nightclub, so I would have to enquire at the entrance whether she was there or not! My favourite place was the 400, so we would go there first and find out from charming Mr Rossi — who knew everyone — and he would welcome one *in* or *warn* one if there was danger! Then we could go elsewhere — such as the Café de Paris or the Florida. The 400 was, definitely a part of life then and all through the war and into the fifties. It had a wonderful band with a lovely huge fat brilliant pianist and leader.

The five or six nightclubs mentioned were only those most frequented by the debs, but London had dozens, many of which thrived all through the war — the Nest (known as "London's Harlem" because of its black band and its jazz), the Blue Lagoon, the Midnight Room, Hatchett's, the Hungaria, the Berkeley,

Quaglino's — all of them, say the habituées of those years, *much* more fun than anything London can offer today.

Why were the chaperones so adamant in forbidding nightclubs? A smooch in a dimly lit (but overcrowded) room, a cocktail or two, surely . . . ? The answer is that nightclubs were, they believed, hot-houses for people who were having — or about to have — an affair. Deb dances were all romance and prettiness, luxury and display and invigilated courting. But nightclubs were dark and secret places, their gloom pierced only by arabesques of cigarette smoke and the stimulating or melancholy music of jazz and the blues. They were, in a word, for sex: that untried and uncontrollable quality that all debs yearned to know more about.

Although the Season — like Jane Austen's novels — was based on sex, it was never mentioned. In the eyes of the mothers marriage came first. They all believed implicitly in the unwritten upper-class code, that only when marriage had produced a son and heir to safeguard the family property could a woman begin to think of making her own sexual choices. Married women were allowed a good deal of freedom in conducting affairs; and, indeed, the chaperones should not be thought of as stout, ageing ladies for whom sex was a thing of the past. Most of them were still comparatively young — certainly in their forties, or, in a few cases, their thirties — and several were themselves engaged in more or less public affairs with someone else's husband. But that was different. They had married; established a household (or, just as likely, inherited one); and given birth to children who would ensure that the line continued.

After that, if their marriages were less than happy, they were free to look elsewhere. But the debs were different, and their virginity had to be cherished. It was thought — by the mothers — to be the most valuable commodity they possessed. Few of the girls questioned this assumption and, if any did, there was also the fear of pregnancy to restrain them. "Every time you went to bed with a man you took your life in your hands," said one former deb, speaking more of her wartime escapades than her year as a deb.

Sex and nightclubs were both dangerous, forbidden territory, best left to the grown-ups, and in consequence oh, so desirable! There were of course some girls mature enough to ignore or flout these conventions. In any group of several hundred marriageable young women — or even the hundred who represented the inner circle of debs — there are bound to be some who do not conform. They may have been highly sexed; they may have been natural rebels; they may have been seduced at some stage of childhood or adolescence; they may, best of all, have been in love. But the majority, the very great majority, observed the conventions. It is significant, perhaps, that one debutante's first reaction to enquiries about the behaviour of her generation was to say that, certainly, the debutantes were all — as she was herself — entirely innocent and virginal. However, the enquiry made her wonder, after all these years, and she discussed it with her cousin:

She was a 1938 deb, and a very "go-ahead" and well-informed person, in the adventurous set and very social. She told me I must have been very naive to have thought that, on the whole, the debs were an innocent lot. Apparently that was not at all the case, either in '38 or '39! It would seem I must have been a real country cousin to have thought it quite dashing to see the dawn in at the 400 Club and not in the boyfriend's flat!

Ursula Wyndham, who was a few years older than the debs of 1939 but moved in the same family circles, said matter-of-factly, "There were always some who did and some who didn't. But most didn't." This is confirmed by the debs themselves. Lady Cathleen Eliot says: "Very few girls went 'the whole hog', as the expression was in 1939, but I knew of one or two who had to disappear for a few months. Having chaperones helped to keep one on the straight and narrow, but occasionally one could give them the slip. I was very seldom chaperoned but much too frightened to do anything too naughty."

"Naughty" — how revealing that childish word is of the docile attitude of a good daughter. Vivien Mosley calls it "getting up to mischief", a slightly racier term.

Some of the girls did — though I can't imagine how, with all those poor wretched chaperones sitting around — but they did manage to get up to mischief. One knew exactly who they were, and exactly what they were up to, and exactly where they were up to it. Nobody thought any the worse of them for it — not among their own contemporaries; there was no censoriousness about it all. In any age, whether it's called permissive or puritanical, there are some who will and some who won't.

Rhoda Walker-Heneage-Vivian puts it much more emphatically:

I really think we were pure as the driven snow — unless it is just that I was an innocent. I can recall no scandal or spicy gossip, but perhaps it just never came my way. I think our parents were still Victorian in manner — mine certainly were — and, although the maids got into trouble, it just never happened "above stairs". There was a great deal of chaperoning at all the dinners and dances, and really no place to get away from watchful eyes; and the disgrace and shame which any hanky-panky would arouse was just not worth it. I imagine the debs'' delights were brought up to think of us as untouchables anyway.

I remember at the age of fifteen years getting a card out of a slot machine on Mumbles Pier at Swansea telling me "I was fond of the opposite sex" and feeling hot with shame. The word "sex" was what threw me — it was never even *said* in our household!

All that changed during the war, however, when protected young girls suddenly became self-reliant young women with important jobs to do. Then, she goes on, "Wartime was a different kettle of fish and I had a splendid one — falling in and out of love with regular precision, to the horror of my father, who eventually when my husband asked if he might marry me said, "She'll never stick to you — I give it two years." I wish he could see us after forty-seven years of joy."

Even the most beautiful and worldly girls, though they may have been the most ardently pursued, were not necessarily caught. They found themselves in a double bind, which for young women who were more physically mature, or more independent-minded, would have been intolerable. The predicament was that their parents required them to be untouched; but they were worldly enough to know that the men preferred them to be sexy. Elizabeth Lowry-Corry summed it up:

248

It was definitely our mothers' intention that we should remain virgins until we married — and not just because they were old-fashioned and prim, but because many of them were also very Christian. And from our point of view, quite apart from the general pressure on virtue, you might very well have a baby: and *that* was quite a consideration: that *would* have been damaging.

But the trouble is, that men like sexy women. And so the women who were sexier were likely to "go a little way", and in due course that might lead to "going all the way". So your mother had the idea that a man wanted you to be a virgin, but the men didn't always seem to think so. It was all very confusing.

Sarah Norton (mentioned by many escorts of 1939 as one of the loveliest debs in Society) says today,

Sex was something we didn't understand at all. I was never told about it by my mother and, even though I was brought up on a farm, I never associated it with humans. I thought if you held hands for too long you'd get pregnant! Later on I knew that it was all right to be given a discreet kiss by a man labelled on the mums' list as "NSIT": not safe in taxis. We knew what the more daring girls were doing. They were the ones who usually went out into the shrubbery at dances and these girls had a "reputation" because the boys always talked. We were amused by it and always giggling, but as far as I was concerned it was all much too frightening for me to do it. I remember saying about one girl, "The trouble with her is, she's *crossed the Rubicon*." However, these incidents never — as far as I know — resulted in pregnancy.

You were supposed to go to the marriage bed as a virgin. There was no such thing as birth-control so if a girl got pregnant, she married almost immediately. I don't remember ever hearing the word "abortion" mentioned. If a girl did have a "reputation", then when she got engaged his parents wouldn't be very happy about it. Not that we were in any way frustrated — quite the opposite: we were having a very good time.

Anthony Loch has reflected on this innocence among young women who were, in many other respects, thoroughly poised and sophisticated, and concludes:

As regards morals, girls were not so knowing as nowadays, having been spared television and films with a high sex content. Even a good-night kiss tended to be a hasty rather than a torrid business, and not even a matter of course. I do not suggest that debutantes were not aware of the facts of life, and no doubt in some cases had been able to read *Lady Chatterley's Lover* on the sly, but the plain fact is that the pill had not been invented and drugs in one form or another were not common currency. It was even rare to see a girl clearly the worse for drink. As for the young men, whatever they did about sex, the debs were not an accepted target for serious business.

The girls may have been having a very good time: but what about the men? Only one man who was around during that Season has mentioned the obvious expedient — keeping a mistress — and he evidently took it for granted that you would keep her in Paris, which must have added to the already considerable expense. So this was a solution open to few. It is true that, if the girls were younger than their years in 1939 — at least by today's standards — so too were the men. They were only recently schoolboys, and may often have been closer to homosexual adventures than to marriage. But many more seem to have found the friendship and *camaraderie* of university or regiment a fulfilling, if platonic, substitute for sexual relationships. Lord Haig confirms this:

The awful thing is that I think a lot of the young men in those days were not terribly interested in the opposite sex. One had the feelings and had relationships and so on but not in any practising way — not outgoing at all. One was simply so taken up with serious problems — you know, of life, and responsibility — and my great relaxation and fun were always horses; so that the physical thing . . . well . . . Obviously one was enchanted by the whole aesthetics of it — the marvellous dinner-parties and lovely bands and lights and so on, all going on in lovely houses; aesthetically, the dances were a wonderful experience that you couldn't but absorb with the greatest enjoyment. But as for the debs: they were just a sort of great mass of sweet young ladies. The beauty of the dance convention was that you were always handing them on to someone else! I'm no authority on what their sex life was like and what they did, but I would think there was very little cohabitation between the sexes. Certainly for my generation that was so. It made the whole thing very unreal. And then, apart from anything else, on top of all these deb dances I was doing my Finals and also playing polo in the Oxford University team round all the tournaments. So all that burned one's energies out a bit!

Lord Hood also found that relationships tended to happen within the context of a group, and for two people to pair up as a couple was fairly unusual:

The idea of attaching yourself to one person has developed recently but it didn't apply so much then, I wouldn't have thought. You probably knew a group of people particularly well, and you went in a group to a dinner-party and then you went on to the dance. But it was considered rather unusual — and indeed the mother would probably disapprove of her daughter always dancing with the same young man.

Dinah Brand also retained the impression that it would be unusual for a girl to confine herself to just one partner:

Quite a lot of girls had several people around, and they would be flirting with five or six, probably. I think it was more fun in that way. You were seen with a lot of different young men, without that terrific emotional commitment which is quite hard work for a young girl: besides which there was always the risk that she was going to be the loser. They might go off with someone else. For us, it didn't usually get so involved — although at times, of course, there were terrific upsets and tears. But mostly you may have *thought* you were madly in love, but it hadn't got the same deep emotional thing, and not the physical pull at all. But on the whole you just met loads of people and emerged with far more friends than when you went in. That included men, too — you certainly made male friends, in the platonic sense, and you kept them for years.

There were, inevitably, a number of young men who were predatory. Did they pester the virginal debs? Or did they concentrate on those desirable commodities, the very few girls with a reputation for being fast? Basil Kenworthy thought they did. "In general, yes. The news would get around that so-and-so is easy. But to be fair, the girls, the majority of whom were virtuous, were respected by the young men, *because* they were so innocent. But their innocence sometimes made them rather boring. The fast ones were more amusing." Nevertheless, the girls were not allowed by their mothers to forget that, in the end, making a good marriage was the underlying aim of the Season, and the imminence of war as well as the fairy-tale atmosphere of the dances resulted in some very early engagements. Basil Kenworthy is quite unequivocal about this:

These very rapid engagements which took place between couples who had only been acquainted for a few weeks largely took place because of the romantic surroundings. Here you had a girl who had been produced from the hot-house for the debutante season; she had expensive clothes, sometimes good jewellery, she had always been to the hairdresser on the day of the ball, usually the young men had had too much to drink and there was romantic music, everyone felt good, they were unaware of any depression outside in the world or disaster — for the time being it was a ball. And I think that had a big effect. Sometimes they fell in love and sometimes they thought they fell in love.

The other big category was that of people marrying girls who lived in the property next door. I think that happened in many cases; but of course they had known the girls from babyhood, the parents approved, obviously it would be an advantageous marriage as well as a marriage for love. And finally, there were gold-diggers of both sexes.

Elizabeth Lowry-Corry talked eloquently of the paradox created for girls who had been brought up to believe implicitly that they must marry well — someone of their own kind — yet whose adolescent longings made them dream of marrying for passionate love:

I think we were both very worldly and yet unworldly, in that we wanted to marry within our own class, it seemed important to us and we were conscious of class; but at the same time we wanted to have a great passion. — I can't think where those tremendously romantic ideas came from, but we certainly had them. Being beautiful was terribly important. My mother was extraordinarily beautiful, and my brothers were very good-looking, so I didn't see myself standing beside some undistinguished-looking chap. Your eye has got to be caught, to trigger this passion we were all looking for.

Some couples did fall in love. Everyone from 1939 remembers Lord Andrew Cavendish (now the Duke of Devonshire) and Deborah Mitford. She had come out the year before; she was attractive in the unmistakable Mitford fashion, with piquant, witty expressions offset by classic English country looks, while he was the *beau idéal:* tall, dark and handsome with that air of detachment that would be called indifference in all but the aristocracy. But the main thing that was memorable about them was that they were so obviously, romantically, *appropriately* in love. They suited each other so well, they looked so right together. They were, says one deb wistfully, "the most romantic couple I've ever seen — very young and obviously hopelessly in love. They were so ethereally and beautifully dressed and they were so much in love and I wasn't a bit jealous, I just thought it was beautiful." Another recalls seeing Debo draped wearily at the foot of a long flight of stairs in the hall of some great house. "What are you doing, Debo?" she asked. "Oh, same as usual," sighed Debo; "waiting for Andrew." It is such a trivial exchange — why should she have remembered it? Perhaps — because Debo

Mitford epitomized what every girl would have liked to be. She was lovely to look at, popular, well connected, wonderful company — and she had found a man whom she loved *and* who was highly eligible.

Those two did not marry until 1941, but several debs married almost as soon as war broke out. One was Margaret Clifton-Brown, one of the great beauties of the Season, whose father was MP for Newbury. She had known her husband-to-be all her life but, as he was nine years older than she was, their relationship was neighbourly until the Season began. Then, inspired perhaps by the attention which other men were always paying her as much as by the sight of the gawky country cygnet suddenly transformed upon the picturesque lake of the Season into a swan, he fell in love with her. Their feelings for each other progressed so rapidly that by August they had become engaged.

> We decided to get married when he was posted back from Liverpool to Windsor. He rang me up and said, "Come over," and I went and he proposed and I accepted. Then I had to get home on a train with no lights, hoping no one would attack me, and I was so excited and happy that I went to the wrong station and had to go to a policeman, who took me home in a police car. I got married in a flurry ten days before war broke out — I didn't get anything new except a veil. There wasn't time. I was ridiculously young. We had six months together — longer than we'd expected; he thought he would be sent abroad immediately — and then he went away and I didn't see him again for four and a half years.

Rosamund Neave was another deb who married in a rush as war broke out. Her future husband also lived locally; she too had known him for years; but it was not until the night of her own dance, very early in the Season, that they began to fall in love. For her the Season was heaven after that: the most wonderful background to their relationship, ensuring that they would see each other often while their commitment to each other gradually developed and became a certainty. They married six days after the outbreak of war.

The women who were debs in 1939 consider themselves fortunate to have been spared the sexual pressures that their daughters and, even more, their granddaughters have had to learn to cope with. Young men were rarely importunate. If a girl had a reputation for being "naughty" or even "wicked" (to use their own terminology) she might find herself being propositioned — and she might accept. Her contemporaries would be curious, might even in an odd way envy her, but they were not censorious. The innocent girls were protected by their innocence, and very rarely had to ward off the demands of an over-heated young man. This was not only true within their own class. Lady Cathleen Eliot remembers with incredulity that all during the war she used to hitch lifts back from London in the small hours of the morning with lorry drivers, and nobody ever made sexual approaches to her. "There I would be, done up to the nines in evening dress, dripping with diamonds — well, not exactly dripping, but did have a lovely pair of chandelier diamond earrings that I had inherited — and none of them ever laid a finger on me. Quite the reverse: they used to share their sandwiches with me. You couldn't risk that today."

Rosamund Neave recalls her outrage on the one occasion when a young man overstepped the mark:

This was at a very well-known country house where I had gone to stay for the weekend. A young man came into my room and — said, "You know this is it. You know this is it. You know I want to sleep with you." I got very frightened because my hair was in curlers and so I said, "No, I'm not going to sleep with you and I do not like you, will you please go away." And he said, "Well, I'll go away if you meet me tomorrow morning, outside this house" . . . And so the next morning, early, when the housemaid came in I said, "Would you please tell your mistress that I wish to go home; I'm not feeling very well." And so that's how I got out of it.

But this incident is exceptional. By and large, debs were allowed to refuse any sexual advances.

The summer was now reaching its climax: sporting, social and political. Wimbledon was well into its second week, and a dull, wet week it was. Even the men's singles final sounds boring, in the account in *The Times*: "Somehow we had a touch of Edgar Allan Poe in the Centre Court: the unfathomable Riggs deliberately finished off his man by slow torture, and if it was of absorbing interest to students of stroke and strategy, those who like a dash of blood and sawdust with their tennis went out to tea."

The deb dances continued, with the prospect of four outstanding ones in the country to round off the three last months of nightly froth and sparkle. On 5 July — the night after the American Independence Day Ball at the Dorchester, at which the Kennedy family headed the cast — there were three dances. Rhoda Walker-Heneage-Vivian, the bright girl from a castle in Wales who had done the Season on what was, relatively, a shoe-string, describes hers:

It set my father back £600, which was a vast sum in those days. [Today's equivalent would be £12,000.] I wore the best of my seven evening dresses: an ice-blue satin one, with a brocade evening coat. Seven dresses sounds an awful lot, but it was nothing, compared with some debs. The dance was heaven . . . the first time I had been the most important person . . . and I carried a huge bouquet of stephanotis and wore long white gloves.

On the same evening, Margaret Clifton-Brown's mother gave a small dance for her ("only about 300 people") which she says she did not enjoy at all. It was marred by the fact that the man who was very soon to be her husband was not given leave by his regiment to be there:

By the end of June, early July, people were making the most of what they deemed to be their last hours on earth. Because of the awful slaughter in the First World War, a lot of the men thought the same thing was about to happen to them.

My parents were elderly, and one had to try to keep any worries away from them. So the dance went ahead, even though by then an awful lot of people were training hard and — like my friend — couldn't get away for the dances. So my wonderful slinky silver lame dress by Norman Hartnell was a bit wasted.

I'd done the Season mainly because it was my parents' wish, although I would have liked to take up nursing, and still wish I'd done so. I didn't get a chance to nurse during the war because by then I was already married and my son was born at the end of 1940. So I spent the war trying to run this rather wet and boggy farm in Norfolk. It was very quiet and dull and lonely, although I had great support from all the kindness of the village people.

Our son was four and a half years old before his father saw him, and although as time went on they came to love each other their first year together was very difficult as they were both so jealous of each other.

But that's leaping ahead a long way. The Season: to me, after my experiences in Austria, it all seemed unreal. One had to suppress that feeling and just keep going as long as possible. One didn't want to seem to panic. But I suppose, — if I'm honest, I didn't really enjoy the Season. I hadn't got my heart in it. It was all so artificial — a frivolous waste of time.

The second of the three great dances which took place in July, in the closing weeks of the Season, was held the following evening, Thursday the 6th, for Rosalind Cubitt. It was a very good dance and — with over a thousand guests — a very crowded dance. But the thing that made it remarkable, that everyone remembers with elegiac clarity, was its setting: Holland House. This great house, the first part of which was built at the beginning of the seventeenth century, but much added to during the passing years, was like a country house in the middle of Kensington, with grounds so vast that Lord Ilchester, its owner, held pheasant shoots there. The house features over and over again in the political and social history of the last three centuries. It was a centre of intrigue during the war between the Cavaliers and Roundheads — the first Earl of Holland lost his head for his ultimate loyalty to the royal cause — and was for a time a meeting place for Dr Johnson's circle, since Joseph Addison lived there for some years. The lovely and fascinating Lady Holland made it a great Whig centre at the beginning of the nineteenth century. It was a house redolent with history; and its own history ended violently in 1942, when it was bombed to destruction by the Luftwaffe. Ros Cubitt's coming out ball, attended by English and Spanish royalty, was thus its last great social occasion; and the beauty of the house has been preserved, like a still from some great historical film like the Russian *War and Peace,* in the minds of the guests who were there on 6 July 1939.

Other dances blur in the memory. Most debs — though not all — remember their own dance; the rest have merged into a composite patchwork of flowers, dance cards, chaperones on hired gilt chairs surrounding — the dance floor, and lavish quantities of food and champagne. The three dances, however, that stand out clearly as the epitome of that extravagant summer — the last and wildest waltz of an elite that took its pre-eminence for granted — were those at Sutton Place, Holland House and Blenheim Palace. Coincidence decreed that they should all take place within the span of a week; nothing quite like them would ever be seen again. Some girls sensed it, even then. One was Elizabeth Leveson-Gower, now the Countess of Sutherland:

I think I felt life like that couldn't and perhaps *shouldn't* go on — this tremendously rich life; these extreme privileges. One knew that the ability of people to give these beautiful dances in great houses with wonderful gardens and lovely flood-lighting — one knew that *must* change. Perhaps one didn't enjoy them quite so much at the time — in any case, the grand dances weren't in fact as much fun as the smaller ones — but I knew that one would look back on it all with great nostalgia. It was obvious that something was going to happen, and I just felt it couldn't . . . it must finish.

For Rosalind Cubitt herself, the dance should have been the climax of a brilliant Season. In fact, as she says, "I remember very little about it, as I had *very* bad 'flu and was doped to the hilt!" This may be why Rosalind did not accompany her parents to the dinner-party given before-hand by the Earl and Countess of Ilchester (who had lent Holland House for the dance), which was attended by the King and Queen. The presence of royalty, the brilliance of the dinner, she herself the focus of the evening — all this would have presented an ordeal even to a girl as poised as Rosalind. But when the girl was half-dead with 'flu and only kept on her feet with large doses of medicine to control the fever, it was clearly an impossibility. So Rosalind dined instead with her best friend Sonia Denison, at an intimate and undemanding dinner-party given by Sonia's mother and Brigadier-General Beale-Browne, and arrived at Holland House just before ten o'clock, as the dance was beginning. Sonia stayed next to her throughout the evening, as Lady Chichester remembers: "I can still see the big staircase, and Ros standing with Sonia at the bottom of the stairs. It was a lovely party, but I have a sort of memory of it being very, very crowded. I don't know how many they invited, but it was more I think than the house should have had." Lord Cromer, who was also there, says the same: "It was most beautifully done — it was magnificent — but my chief recollection is that it was enormously crowded. It was a goliath sort of dance — there must have been over a thousand people present — enormous. And that didn't necessarily make dances more fun; on the contrary. . . ."

Of all the dances given that summer, Holland House was the — only one that Lord Cathcart attended, and the sight of the house as he arrived made a lasting impression upon him: "I remember coming away from a dinner-party and turning in at those magnificent gates off Kensington High Street and going down the drive to Holland House which stood there, splendidly floodlit."

Any dance at which the King and Queen were present was always glittering. Women had to wear tiaras, for example, men wore decorations, everyone was on their best behaviour. There was an extra *frisson* given by their presence at this particular ball, for Rosalind was the daughter of Sonia Cubitt, who was herself the younger daughter of Mrs Keppel, the celebrated last mistress of Edward VII. Mrs Keppel had understood perfectly the conventions of behaviour in her role, and had been careful never to embarrass Queen Alexandra. All the same, it was regarded as a striking act of tolerance on the part of George VI to attend a dance given by the daughter of his grandfather's mistress. Christian Grant certainly remembers people talking about it:

It was rather special, because there was that slight aura of naughtiness about it — Mrs Keppel having been Edward VII's mistress and the Royal Family being there. We all thought it was rather broad-minded and nice of them to accept the situation, but it did make it a bit conspiratorial and glamorous.

Lord Hood was another who went to Holland House that night. 1939 was the seventh Season that he had taken part in; and by this time, although he received dozens of invitations, he went to very few dances:

I was working quite hard by then, so I never stayed very late, and probably went more to the kind of dance where not just the very young were present, but also the middle-aged, which I found more amusing. I remember particularly going to Holland House, because I'd never been there before: and of course, never went there again, because it was blitzed. It stretched right down to Kensington High Street and I don't know how far north. It had a big park in those days, and a red brick Jacobean house full of a lot of very lovely things. The best way I can describe it is by saying that it was just like a country house in London. Before the war, when the monarch dined out, the men might well have been asked to wear knee breeches; though I'm sure we didn't wear breeches for the Holland House dance. The card would have said, "To have the honour of meeting their Majesties the King and Queen" — or something like that — and then, "Dancing, 10 p.m. Decorations."

The Ilchesters had invited the King and Queen to dine, so they were already there before the rest came, and then the hostess — in this case Mrs Cubitt — would ask friends to give dinner parties. I dined, I remember quite well, with a strange lady called Mrs Corrigan. She had taken Lady Ward's house, Dudley House. Why Lady Ward let it I can't think; she didn't need to; but anyway Mrs Corrigan paid some huge sum for the house for the Season, and I remember dining there. I remember driving in her car to the party, and there was the most terrible queue of traffic, as you can imagine, trying to get there.

The same traffic delayed the Queen of Spain, who had not been invited to dine, and so she arrived very late. Lady Ilchester had given up waiting by the entrance to receive her, and when word came that the Queen of Spain was at the door, she had to struggle through the crowd of guests to try and get there in time to meet her. In the end they met in a passage, and there was a flurry of mutual apologies, with Lady Ilchester going, "I'm so sorry Ma'am that I wasn't at the door to meet you" and the Queen of Spain saying, "I shouldn't worry about that ... it's all the fault of the traffic ..." I remember the scene very well.

That was not the only *faux pas* of the evening. Another occurred when Lindsey Furneaux, in the crush of people on the dance floor, somehow collided with the Queen: "I was being whirled around by some chap and I knocked her over! I think it was me that was responsible — in fact I'm sure it was." Lord Haig describes the relaxed atmosphere of these parties: "The King and Queen were both very unstiff about everything. King George VI enjoyed his social life and he wasn't at all rigid about things. Formality had broken down a lot since King George V and they — the King and Queen — had encouraged everyone to let go in order to adjust to the realities of the time. They knew that all this stiffness and stuffiness wasn't really what mattered. They started out in a very democratic sort of way to change it." The royal couple made a great impression on Lord Savile:

I remember the Queen coming down the staircase at Holland House looking like a Winterhalter — perfectly wonderful. That was at one o'clock when they were leaving to go home.

I also remember for some reason that it was the last ball that Mrs Ronnie Greville ever attended. She'd been very ill, but the Queen said to her, "You *can* come — you *can!*" and so she did. John Fox-Strangways wheeled her into dinner, but then she went home afterwards.

They had Ambrose and his band of fourteen musicians playing that night, all the best dance tunes of that year — Cole Porter and so on. And there was a Sir Roger de Coverley, led by Lady Ilchester. The ladies wore tiaras, and I, because I didn't have any orders or decorations, wore a carnation. But then, I was only twenty. We don't belong to the same world today. . . .

Finally, here is a contrasting description from someone who, despite her fragile beauty and aristocratic background, found that crowded, competitive evening an ordeal — Lady Elizabeth Scott, now the Duchess of Northumberland: "My recollection is of a nightmare — finding myself swept along in a milling mass of strangers — separated even from my parents. As soon as I found them (by which time I was nearly in tears) I begged to be taken home!"

Everyone agrees that dance tunes were much better than they are today: easier to dance to, more romantic and with "much nicer words". Naturally, different tunes have special significance for different people, but the ones that were named over and over again include "Deep Purple", "Jeepers Creepers", "My Heart Belongs to Daddy", "Smoke Gets in Your Eyes", "You're the Tops", "Dancing Cheek to Cheek", "Tiger Rag", "I Like New York in June", "The Lady is a Tramp", "Change Partners", "The Umbrella Man", "Night and Day", "A Nightingale Sang in Berkeley Square", "I've Got You Under My Skin", "Hold Tight", "Three Little Fishes", "Miss Otis

Regrets", "A Foggy Day", "Oh Play to Me", "Gipsy", "Nice Work If You Can Get It", "One Night of Love", "Remember Me", "Popcorn Man", "Begin the Beguine" ... and so on and on and swirling, twirling, spinning, swooping on. "The Big Apple" was a jazz number of the day, and many dances ended with that or with a mad gallop before the National Anthem, so that the younger guests could let their hair down for the last dance before being rounded up by the chaperones and taken home to bed.

The same bands played night after night. Ambrose was the smartest name to secure for a coming-out dance, but Carroll Gibbons and the Savoy Orpheans were also popular, and after these two came Jack Jackson, Tommy Kinsman, Tubby Clayton, Henry Hall, Geoffrey Howard, Geraldo, Harry Roy, and others forgotten now but much loved then. In addition, nightclub bands could sometimes be coaxed out for the evening to play at a deb dance: men like Tiny Tim Clayton and his Whispering 400 Band, Roy Fox and his band from the Monsignor, and Ken (Snakehips) Johnson, the black bandleader who played at the Café de Paris (and was killed there when a bomb fell on it in 1941). They were kindly, even fatherly figures, who knew many of the debs and their escorts by name and would sometimes be deputed by the mothers to ensure that a daughter did not stay out too long. Ann Schuster (now Mrs Archie Mackenzie) recalls visiting one favourite night spot when she was only just seventeen and still very new to the Season:

My mother had allowed me to go to the Berkeley on my own as a very great treat with a young man who was only just eighteen: in fact I think the occasion might have been his birthday. He was a neighbour and I'd known him ever since I was a child. However, behind my back she'd gone to see the *maitre d'hôtel* — an Italian called Ferraro who knew all the mothers, and took a fatherly interest in everybody — and she had asked him to keep an eye on me and make sure I didn't stay too late. So, to my dismay and shame, at midnight he came over and tapped my boyfriend on the shoulder and said, "I'm sorry, Sir, but it's time now" — and he actually saw us into the taxi and made sure everything was all right.

Nice men — great dance bands — memorable tunes, as is proved by the fact that their titles, fifty years later, still set off a hum in the mind.

There was one final, crowning dance to come: an event which, like the last spectacular setpiece at a firework display, illuminates the dark sky and creates magic and wonder for even the most jaded spectators. It was the great ball given on 7 July by the Duchess of Marlborough at Blenheim Palace for her daughter, Lady Sarah Spencer-Churchill. The Blenheim Ball still has the power to make people's eyes light up, fifty years later. It was huge, it was floodlit, it was Society's last great extravagance before the coming of war. Invitations to this ball were avidly — desperately — sought after. Girls would fake illness rather than admit they had not been asked. "Everyone who was anyone" — in that phrase riddled with elitism, the more so because it is unconscious — came to the Blenheim Ball. Exaggeration is impossible; hyperbole pales beside the ancestral splendour of this, the greatest social event of the summer of 1939.

Lady Sarah was a magnificent-looking young woman, as her photograph from that time shows: magnificent, rather than pretty. She was very tall and slim, with long slender legs; not a bit embarrassed by her height, she was high-spirited, energetic and bold. She had a typically Churchillian face, with large blue eyes and a pursed mouth: and she too was, she says, a complete innocent:

> We had not been brought up like children are today. We literally never saw other children. We lived in a house called Lodesby House in Leicestershire and in those days it was sort of frowned on for us to see other children — it wasn't for snobbish reasons, but in case we caught measles or any other disease. So we never saw anyone except maybe our own relations, a few cousins: nobody else.

She had been "finished" in Paris, at a small and very exclusive establishment run by a Madame d'Aunay, which she attended with her friend Lady Elizabeth Scott. Because of this they had missed the "little Season" — the chatty lunches at which girls got to know one another, made friends and found a niche among the bewildering variety of strange faces. Lady Sarah arrived in London from Paris in mid-May and was catapulted straight into the Astorian splendour of Dinah Brand's dance at 6 St James's Square. The veneer of sophistication which Paris had given her, helped by a wardrobe of magnificent ball dresses chosen for her at Worth by her grandmother, Mme Jacques Balsan (Consuelo, the American heiress whose first husband had been the ninth Duke of Marlborough), made her seem outwardly formidable.

Her social pre-eminence ensured that she was in demand for every dance, and at dinner-parties would always be given the best seat at the best table, according to strict rules of *placement.*

> The dinners before dances were rather boring because one always sat next to practically the same people. Being a duke's daughter, it was done in order of precedence, so usually whoever was on either side of me had a girlfriend below the salt and I had a boyfriend below the salt, so one was never sitting with anybody one wanted to be with. I used to vary between Prince Frederick of Prussia (who's now dead); the present Lord Salisbury, who was the Hon. Robert Cecil; Billy Hartington (who's dead); and Rowley Errington — Lord Cromer. I used to guess my seat, and most times I wasn't very far out. I got switched around sometimes, it changed a little — but very little.

It was hard for her dinner and dancing partners to realize that this tall, aristocratic, wealthy girl was, underneath, much like any other seventeen-year-old. Her childhood had been even more sheltered than most of her contemporaries' for she had never been to school and emotionally she was still completely immature. "We weren't like seventeen- or eighteen-year-olds at all — more like today's twelve-year-olds. Our relationships were very innocent, absolutely. Totally innocent relationships: like you might find between a boy and a girl aged twelve and thirteen today — or even probably younger, because they're so sophisticated. My granddaughter aged seven knows much more than I did at seventeen." In the course of the Season she developed a warm affection for Mark Howard. Four years older and very good-looking, he had already left Trinity College, Cambridge, and was serving in the Coldstream Guards. The eldest of three sons, he would, had he lived, have inherited Castle Howard. He was killed in action in 1944. He was at her dance on 7 July, but Lady Sarah cannot have been able to spare him much attention for she was the focus and the *raison d'être* of the great Blenheim Ball.

Preparations for it had lasted throughout the preceding week:

> I remember the preamble to it . . . the work by the electricians because the house was going to be floodlit; all the work with the tent going up in the garden — there were all sorts of things going on, and all that took about a week.
>
> On the night of the dance we had a band playing outside on the lawn, y'see. And I remember the arcade rooms all being emptied of their furniture — because we had a supper-party down there. And I remember also the gardeners were told to grow malmaisons — great masses of pink malmaisons were all over the house. I don't think they grow malmaisons any more, I don't think there's a market for them, they're too expensive. Great big pink carnations: they were huge. So apart from the electricians and the workmen there were all the gardeners as well running about getting the flowers arranged. . . .

Blenheim Palace was filled with relatives and some of the more privileged guests who were staying the night. Vast as it is, the house was so crowded that Elizabeth Leveson-Gower remembers having to share a room with Lady Mairi Stewart. House-parties were held at all the neighbouring houses as well, and few if any of the hundreds of guests who thronged the great house and its park would have returned to London that night. The ball was not only — not even mainly — for the younger generation. Politicians, diplomats, members of the far-flung Marlborough family down to the remotest cousins were all there. Lady Sarah's grandmother travelled from France to attend.

In 1939 I went to Blenheim with anxious forebodings, for the international horizon was dark. At dinner, sitting next to Monsieur Corbin, the popular French Ambassador, I found it difficult to share the diplomatic detachment his conversation maintained. Yet at that same dinner, at my grand-daughter's table, was one of the sons of the German Crown Prince, whom, I was told, Winston had suggested using as a perfect counterfoil to Nazism under Hitler. Monsieur Corbin, the perfect diplomat, avoided such issues, preferring a personal topic. . . . I suffered the same unease that had afflicted me once in Russia when, surrounded by the glittering splendour of the Czar's Court, I sensed impending disaster. For again, in this brilliant scene at Blenheim, I sensed the end of an era. . . . But on that evening, the scene was still gay, and my pleasure great in meeting so many old friends. I supped with Winston and Anthony Eden and wandered out to the lovely terraces Marlborough had built before his death. With their formal lines and classic ornaments, they were the right setting for so imposing a monument as Blenheim Palace.[2]

Churchill, of course, was also at the ball that night, and Mollie Acland remembers him:

I "sat out" — i.e. walked about — one dance with a rather blasé young would-be politician and on the terrace were Winston Churchill and Anthony Eden, chatting and smoking. "Oh," said my partner, "look at that poor old has-been. My

271

father says he's still a potential trouble-maker, but he won't get any more public life now!'' And this was in July '39!

Back to the younger members of the family. And perhaps the youngest to attend that night was Lady Sarah's middle sister, Lady Caroline: ''My recollections are rather hazy as you can imagine — the sixteen-year-old sister being allowed to attend the ball and being mortified that my dress was the same colour and the same material as my sister's but a totally different style. I can remember that they were yellow organza; hers rather décolletée and my one high at the neck with a ruffle.'' Memory *is* hazy. Lady Sarah is convinced that her dress was in cream satin, a quite different material from her sister's; though she does agree that it was décolletée: so much so that her mother insisted on raising the neckline so as to cover more of her bosom. It was the most splendid of her four ballgowns from Worth, and to see her, fifty years later, rise to sketch its outline with her hands — a wide fanning movement around the shoulders to indicate the ruffle, a long smoothing gesture down the hips to demonstrate its narrowness — convinces one that it was very splendid indeed.

Lady Sarah's closest friend was Lady Elizabeth Scott, who was of course at Blenheim that night, and who retains an almost dream-like impression of its beauty:

The dances in the country stand out in one's mind as being the most fun of all. Blenheim and Hever in particular were wonderful: floodlighting and music and the lights in the garden and amongst trees and shrubs, making them magical, romantic and memorable. I was particularly lucky as most of my parents' friends lived in lovely houses — which would now be known as stately homes — and we went willingly to these dances, which were exceptional parties given by people one knew. There was so much going on that summer that my parents didn't even consider giving a ball for me! I was only seventeen and they probably decided to wait a bit. The whole summer seemed to be given up to having a good time. I was very lucky to have come out then, as I was younger than most of my friends and might easily have been kept educating for another year.

Lindsey Furneaux had had an exceptionally tiring summer, for as well as going to a good many dances she was also busy training to be a nurse at Colchester Hospital during the day:

I remember driving to Oxford to stay at Charlton with my aunt Lady Birkenhead and going to Blenheim for the dance. I was dead — really dead. I sat there collapsed over an armchair and Sacheverell Sitwell came up to me and said, "What would you like to do?" and I said, "I'd like you to show me the pictures here." And he was so divine — I can't tell you how sweet he was — and he showed me all round the house and told me all about the pictures and I didn't dance at all, and that was *heaven*!

That evening — night, really, since the dance went on until dawn broke over the lake — was remarkable for many things. One was the fact that it was the last occasion in England when footmen, wearing eighteenth-century Marlborough livery, powdered their wigs. This archaic procedure was loathed by the men themselves, for powdering took hours to do and even longer to undo. The fine white powder (usually flour from the kitchen) drifted everywhere, getting under their collars and making their necks itch, and since water had been added to make it adhere, it dried solid and felt unnatural. But it was undeniably grand. It was a refinement of grandeur indeed, abandoned even for Court Balls; and it never happened in England again at a private dance.

Yes [says Anne Douglas-Scott-Montagu] I remember them all in their footmen's uniform: knee breeches, and the Marlborough livery — I think it was blue and yellow. It was a wonderful dance, it really was. I remember dancing, dancing masses of waltzes, in that huge room. I also remember that on all the marble statues all down the long passage to the front door, people had draped coats: fox fur stoles and capes and scarves, all draped on the statues all the way down the passage.

I also remember this enormous organ, in the room we danced in towards the library — I'm not sure what the room was called — but there was this huge room with an organ painted white and it looked exactly like an iced sugar cake, with all the candles, which were the organ pipes. And Sarah enjoyed herself enormously. She was very energetic, full of energy and enthusiasm and fun. She wasn't at all beautiful but she was a terrific character: most amusing. Very tall and thin.

The only sad thing about that party was that halfway through it poured with rain. They'd had an outdoor floor put down, all floodlit, and some of the band were going to play outside, in the garden. But we never could dance out there, it was too wet, and everything had to be brought in.

Others who were there have forgotten the rain entirely; they only remember the magic. Rosamund Neave says, "Fantastic. It was fantastic. At a certain moment — at eleven o'clock or something, Sarah pressed a button and suddenly the whole of Blenheim was floodlit. Oh, fantastic!"

Few people except the victims, realized that Blenheim was the scene of a burglary that night. Lady Sarah Churchill, however, can remember it all too well:

> Then of course we had the big problem at that party ... that big burglary. The ball sort of rather backlashed. Quite a lot of fur coats disappeared. The cloakroom was in the present dining-room at Blenheim and all I know was that one lady went to go home and she couldn't find her coat so she thought someone else had taken it by mistake. But then it got to be bad, with more people missing their coats and in the end — I don't remember exactly, but the figure seventeen seems to ring a bell. The police came in — I can't recall how it was cleared up but it was all over the headlines the next day. Somebody was definitely in there, because they'd picked out all the best coats. So it rather backlashed as a party and we were all very upset.
>
> I remember the sun rising, the big doors open — it was five or six in the morning and we were all going to bed and everything had gone so beautifully except that, boom, all these coats were gone.

Here, finally, is Chips Channon's bedazzled account of the ball: —

> In the afternoon I drove to Weston to stay with the Sitwells for the Blenheim Ball, which was stupendous. I have seen much, travelled far, and am accustomed to splendour, but there has never been anything like tonight. The palace was floodlit, and its grand baroque beauty could be seen for miles. The lakes were floodlit too and, better still, the famous terraces, they were blue and green and Tyroleans walked about singing; and although there were seven hundred people or even more, it was not in the least crowded. It was gay, young, brilliant, in

short, perfection. I was loathe to leave, but did so at about 4.30 and took one last look at the baroque terraces with the lake below, and the golden statues and the great palace. Shall we ever see the like again? Is such a function not out of date? Yet it was all of the England that is supposed to be dead and is not. There were literally rivers of champagne.[3]

Behind such lavish displays of ancestral pride and social magnificence, the debutantes remained very young girls, anxious to please and be pleased and well able to enjoy simpler pleasures. This extract from Elizabeth Leveson-Gower's diary of the weekend at Blenheim describes what happened after the huge, waterlogged marquee had been taken down and the house began to return to its normal weekend state (if Blenheim Palace could ever be described as normal — or, indeed, as a house):

Saturday, 8 July: Got up at 1 o'clock. Raining. Played backgammon. Went to film in Oxford by bus. Had to miss the end. Played sardines.
Sunday, 9 July: Church. Played tennis. Elizabeth swam and we were all thrown into the pool in our clothes.

It sounds much like the aftermath of any other dance. Midnight strikes and the coach turns into a pumpkin. The fairy lights are taken down, the fairy-tale is over, and life goes on.

There was, however, one authentic Cinderella figure whose elusive shadow flits in and out of the Season, occasionally glimpsed, never there for long. No one remembers her, and she cannot be found in any of the reference books through whose columns the upper class trace one another's passage through life. Her name was Doreen Davison, and she was the protégée, that Season, of Lady St John of Bletso.

There is a studio portrait of Doreen reproduced in the *Tatler* for 19 July. It was taken by Paul Tanqueray, a brilliant photographer of the inter-war decades who was a precursor of Cecil Beaton and many other Society photographers. The lighting is masterly; the modelling of the face is undoubtedly flattering. Even allowing for all that, it is a handsome, brooding, intelligent face. Doreen has intense dark eyes with thick lashes; good features; and heavy but expert make-up. More than most girls of that Season, she looks mature and intriguing, a girl whom one would like to know better. Yet she has apparently vanished. No one from the debs of 1939 knows her today and not even the people who were pictured in the *Bystander* sitting out at her dance can remember her. One has to assume that she was the archetypal *nouveau riche,* whose mother (named once, and once only, as Mrs Malcolm Arbuthnot) hoped that her striking looks could lead, perhaps, to a titled husband. There could be no other reason for her parents paying — reputedly — £2,000 (£40,000 today) and then retiring from the scene for the whole summer, leaving their daughter in the plump hands of Lady St John of Bletso. For Lady St John did not do things by halves. She took a girl into her own home at Ennismore Gardens in South Kensington; lodged her, groomed her, chose her dresses, took her to mums' lunches and girls' teas, and with exemplary thoroughness launched her into Society ... for three months. After that, the girl was on her own. Back she went to her parents, with an address book full of names and telephone numbers and half a dozen less than pristine ball dresses.

Lady St John had slipped up badly when she chose the date of Doreen's coming-out dance. The debutantes who had been at Blenheim would have been scattered around several different house-parties afterwards, and must have exchanged their various memories of the evening as soon as they met up again at Doreen's dance on the evening of Monday, 10 July. Doreen herself, who was not at Blenheim, had to sit and listen to them comparing notes, knowing that her own dance paled into insignificance beside the splendour of the Marlborough ball. However, Lady St John delivered the goods as far as press coverage was concerned. Both the *Tatler* and the *Bystander* carried a number of pictures of Doreen's dance (unfortunately, in more than one case, they are the same pictures) and these show a handful of younger guests sitting out rather glumly on deckchairs, as well as rather too large a proportion of much older people. There is one of Doreen, flanked by two young guests. None of them looks vivacious. That evening is the first and last time that Doreen's part in the Season is acknowledged by anyone. One hopes that she — like most of her contemporaries — derives some satisfaction from telling her grandchildren that she was there.

In the middle of that same week two final Courts were held on the 12th and 13th for the last of the year's 1,657 presentations to the King and Queen. The Court on 12 July was the smarter of the two and Lady Sarah Churchill remembers her mother's chagrin that a last-minute bout of illness forced her to make her curtsey at the second and final of the year's five Courts, where she knew nobody. Certainly the Fourth Court included many of the *crème de la crème* of that year's debutantes: Lady Elizabeth Scott, in a silver lamb dress with a train of white net edged with silver, was presented by her mother, the Duchess of Buccleuch. Elizabeth Leveson-Gower in an Empire dress of pale satin trimmed with pearls, and a matching train, was presented by her aunt, the Duchess of Sutherland. Lady Alexandra Metcalfe presented Vivien Mosley, wearing white tulle embroidered with pale gold leaf, with a gold lamb train; and Eunice Kennedy was presented by Mrs J.P. Kennedy under the auspices of the diplomatic corps in an ivory tulle crinoline. We know exactly what they all wore, because *The Times* printed six and a half full columns the following day, inserted by the dressmakers, giving details. Reading them is like counting sheep. White taffeta (over) . . . cream silk (over) . . . white net (oops) . . . pale blue chiffon (over) . . . enlivened all too rarely by a spectacular and endearing piece of vulgarity like the mother who wore "a train lined with turquoise chiffon to match her jewellery". The Throne Room must have been a shimmering tribute to the products of the British Empire, as mothers and daughters glided and dipped, their heads bobbing with ostrich feathers, their bosoms (well, the mothers' bosoms, at any rate: the girls wore pearls) palpitating with diamonds.

At the Fifth Court Lady Sarah Churchill and her mother, both dressed by Worth, were the lonely stars of an otherwise low-key collection of debutantes. And, with them, the last of the presentations of 1939 was over: not for a year, as most people must have assumed, but for seven years. They were suspended during the war, resumed in 1947, and discontinued for ever in 1958. The pre-war evening Courts, held at 9.30 p.m. and followed by a light buffet, were also abandoned, which meant that debs no longer wore evening dress, but day dresses with hats. The change from the elaborate, archaic uniform of Prince of Wales feathers, long train, long dress and white gloves symbolized the change in the Season itself. The days of ornate excess were over; austerity was imposed by the exigencies of the forties and fifties, and with it a recognition that the display of wealth and privilege was inappropriate in post-war Britain. There was food and petrol-rationing for the first few years, and even fashion took some time to shake off the simplicity of uniform and return, with Dior's New Look of 1948, to full-blown, full-skirted, tight-waisted glamour.

On Friday, 14 July, there appeared in *The Times* a half-page advertisement with the almost incredible headline: "GERMANY Land of Hospitality". Germany, it said, "offers everything you could wish for your holiday this year", with 2,000 miles of unique Autobahn, numerous exhibitions and festivals — including an opera festival at Munich from 29 July to 10 September — and (towards the bottom, in rather small print) Vienna, which most English people probably still thought of as being in Austria. All these pleasures could be had at a bargain price: 60 per cent reduction on rail tickets purchased outside Germany, and 40-50 per cent currency savings for people who made use of "travel Marks". Southern Bavaria, the area which Hitler made his holiday base, promised "rest and enjoyment for everyone".

One is aghast at the naivety, both of the German Railways Board, which placed the advertisement, and of those people who — presumably — took advantage of the proffered reductions. One is mildly aghast at *The Times* for accepting the advertisement. War was now seven weeks away: did people really think a holiday in Germany was desirable? Maybe they did. Chips Channon, who as an MP had no excuse for ignorance of the situation, wrote in his diary on 11 July: "The war seems a little more remote; perhaps it will never come; it seems less of a reality, perhaps because there is no news. . . ."[4] Many people still believed that, if Danzig were conceded, war could be averted. They wrote letters to *The Times* to that effect. Britain's pledge to Poland was not taken seriously, and few believed that the present Cabinet would honour it. As long as Churchill and Eden remained outside the Cabinet, Hitler had no reason to believe it either. The London *Evening Star* wrote: "Those who know the Nazi psychology best say that the return of Mr Churchill and Mr Eden to the Cabinet would do more than a hundred speeches to convert the Nazis to a belief in the sincerity of our intentions."

Meanwhile men and arms continued to pour into Danzig from Germany, and the British pact with Russia in defence of neutral and independent states inched no nearer to agreement. There were no sound reasons for optimism, but people have an inveterate tendency to hope for the best. As the *Tatler* put it on 12 July, "Despite the none-too-good news from Europe the social racket still goes gaily on and quite right too, for what is the use of squealing before you are hurt?''

From mid-July onwards the London Season was winding down. The rest of the month was marked by a series of sporting events, beginning with the Eton and Harrow two-day match at Lords on 14 and 15 July. This annual event had been a feature of the debs' summer for nearly a century. It reached its culmination in the years immediately before the First World War, when playing for one's school and fighting for one's country were seen as two manifestations of the same set of values. Both embodied unthinking loyalty/patriotism, team/regimental spirit; athletic/military prowess dedicated to a common cause. The Eton and Harrow match was played by clean-cut young sportsmen in symbolically pristine white (the literal opposite of the Blackshirts), embodying the traditional rivalry between England's two top public schools.

Few debs — whatever their brothers' past triumphs — were greatly interested in the game of cricket. The two days at Lords were largely taken up with strolling around the ground, meeting friends and relatives, or sitting in coaches on the Mound. Their clothes were, as usual, described at length in *The Times*. Christian Grant sums up what it was like:

It was great fun because one was still very young and of course a lot of the boys one was going out with were eighteen or so and had probably only just left either Eton or Harrow. Eton figured pretty large among the people who were around at deb dances, and one saw lots of people. At Lords you can walk all the way round the big circle, so you walked round clockwise for a bit and then you turned round and walked back anticlockwise, so you were quite sure of seeing everybody who was there, one way or another. Unless they turned round at the same time! I don't think, frankly, we took much notice of the cricket. I think one pretended to if one was with somebody who had been a dry-bob at Eton or had been in the Eleven or something But I was mortified when Harrow won, because all my family was at Eton Probably if that was happening I wasn't *allowed* to watch.

Elizabeth Leveson-Gower and Eunice Kennedy nearly did not get there at all. They had arranged to go to the match together, so Elizabeth picked Eunice up after lunch and drove her to Eton College by mistake. The school must have been as empty as the *Marie Celeste,* but they found someone to explain to two embarrassed girls that the Eton and Harrow match took place at Lords. Gamely they drove there, and arrived in the late afternoon. They took refuge in Billy Hartington's box to watch the last hour of the first day's play.

Marigold Charrington, who also went, recalls the mad frenzy that Harrow's victory the following day provoked: "It was a very exciting day and at the end everybody just went mad. They all rushed on to the pitch, throwing their hats into the air, and it was an extraordinary and really a wonderful sight." Not everyone viewed it quite so indulgently. Baroness Ravensdale, who was there with her niece, Vivien Mosley, called it:

A most disgusting riot and shambles. It was not mere top-hat bashing: middle-aged men rushed in and were bestial and

283

savage in their onslaughts on boy and older youths alike; one small boy was badly hurt and was carried off; the savagery shown was sickening, even trying to debag people! Eyes, teeth and noses risked being smashed.[5]

The reason for this near-riot was that, in 1939, Harrow won for the first time in thirty years. The player chiefly responsible for this great victory was one E. Crutchley, who scored the only century (he made 115 in Harrow's first innings) and whose father had been equally instrumental in securing the school's last victory in 1909. It is precisely the sort of demonstration of continuity and skill handed down from father to son that the English love, especially when it happens in a context that unites two of their ruling passions; and Crutchley was wildly fêted at the ball in honour of the match at the Hurlingham Club that night.

The account by *The Times'* cricket correspondent is so rapturous and so unlike any sports report that might be written today that it is worth quoting at some length:

The drought is over, the Arctic night is past, the chains are burst, the clouds have lifted from the Hill — no metaphor can do justice to the feeling of long-deferred satisfaction with which lovers of cricket in general and of this match in particular saw Harrow beat Eton on Saturday by eight wickets.

. . . Thirty years is a long time, and the last Harrow victories are brilliantly associated with the names of Crutchley and Anson and Cowley. History repeats itself, and it is pleasant to imagine, at least in two of these cases, Hamilcars impressing

on their infant Hannibals the necessity for undying hostility
and ultimate vengeance upon the ancient foe.

... It was to be and was, as the old lady said when she
married the footman: that, and the fact that the match is now
alive again must be Eton's present consolation.

... Nothing short of an air-raid could stop Harrow's serene
advance to the land of their 30-year-old dreams.

... Harrow cheers were now the shout of them that
triumph, the song of them that intend shortly to feast without
stint or misgiving. Lithgow (the Harrow captain) was chaired
to the pavilion in the traditional manner, in which there may
be little comfort to the limbs but surely an abundance of glory
to the soul. The customary scenes of enthusiasm and hat-
smashing, honoured by time but not perhaps by much else,
followed, and the heroes of the drama had to take their
calls. . . . Then the lowing herd wound slowly o'er the lea, and
soon nothing remained on the scene of Harrow's splendid and
deserved success save a raffle of old school ties and what, 48
hours earlier, had been new school hats.

It is a wonderful piece of writing, and — with its
references to everything from Hannibal to air-raids —
entirely characteristic of its time.

The Season was now on its last legs as far as dancing
was concerned, though some of the major sporting
events were yet to come. Fewer than half a dozen dances
were listed for the next three weeks, and of these the
main one was Gavin Astor's coming-of-age at Hever
Castle on 18 July. The previous evening, however, saw
one final pastoral entertainment which rounded off the
summer typically and gloriously. It was given for
Barbara McNeill, a charming and popular blue-eyed
English blonde and everything a deb ought to be, who
showed when the war came that she was made for much

more than just the adornment of Society. Her mother, Mrs John Dewar, lived near East Grinstead in Sussex, in a beautiful house with spacious grounds called Dutton Homestall. Barbara's step-father was very rich, and the party was a suitably extravagant climax to three months of gaiety. Mollie Acland was flattered to be invited, as the guests were — for once — mainly those who were genuinely friends of Barbara or her mother, and not just names plucked from a list. "There weren't many debs or young men and it was very sophisticated. I remember sofas and lying-down chairs with white satin cushions and masses of caviar." Elizabeth Leveson-Gower was there, too; and dined with the Dewars beforehand. "Great fun," she recorded in her diary; "garden floodlit and woods too. Everything looked beautiful and there was iced fruit on the tables." She, like most of the guests, finally got home at five-thirty next morning. A week later she was already aboard the *Empress of Britain* en route for Canada, where her uncle's ocean-going yacht with its crew of twenty-seven was waiting.

Although she was one of the earliest debs to leave, the holiday migration was beginning. People were anxious to get to the sun and seaside as quickly as possible, just in case . . . *The Times* prefaced its list of those who had taken grouse moors for the (shooting) season with the glum words:

The state of world affairs and their uncertainty has had a serious effect on the letting of grouse moors and deer forests in Scotland during the early part of the year. It is expected that quite a number of moors which have failed to find tenants will be shot over by the proprietors. It is certain that there will be fewer Americans than usual out on the Twelfth. The counter-attraction of their own World's Fair and the uncertainty of the European situation are responsible.

The country still did not know what it wanted. As late as July the *Daily Express* carried a daily banner on its masthead that proclaimed "THERE WILL BE NO WAR IN EUROPE THIS YEAR OR NEXT". Those who were politically aware (whose number seldom included the debs) ranged from one extreme across to the other: epitomized by members of the Mitford family, whose opinions shaded from deep red to brightest blue, right through the spectrum to Fascist black. Their memoirs make interesting reading. The Hon. Lady Mosley (then wife, now widow of Sir Oswald Mosley, the charismatic leader of the British Union of Fascists) writes in hers:

In July 1939 M. had an immense meeting and demonstration for peace in the Exhibition Hall at Earls Court. It was the culmination of several months' campaign all over the country. Tom [her brother], hoping for peace but seeing that war was probable, had joined a territorial regiment, the Queen's West minsters. He gave the fascist salute as M. marched up the hall, and this was reported in one of the newspapers with a comment implying that an officer in the army could not at the same time be a follower of Sir Oswald Mosley. Tom's Colonel strongly upheld him and said he was not going to be deprived of one of his best officers; no more was heard of this nonsense.[6]

In complete contrast, here is Jessica Mitford — by then the wife of Esmond Romilly. Although both held extreme socialist views, they were not members of the Communist Party. "The Bermondsey Labour Party was much more to our liking. At the monthly meetings . . . vigorous discussions would take place on the important political events of the day . . . Fund-raising campaigns for milk for Spanish orphans or for aid to Hitler's Jewish victims were planned and carried out."[7] On one occasion, at a Labour Party parade, several members of the family found themselves at the same meeting, though on opposite sides:

> We had been warned that the Blackshirts might try to disrupt the parade, and sure enough there were groups of them lying in wait at several points along the way. Armed with rubber truncheons and knuckle-dusters, they leaped out from behind buildings; there were several brief battles in which the Blackshirts were overwhelmed by the sheer numbers of the Bermondsey men. Once I caught sight of two familiar, tall, blonde figures: Boud [Unity] and Diana, waving Swastika flags. I shook my fist at them in the Red Front salute. . . .[8]

But such issues, passionately felt, were only a microcosm of the great concerns preoccupying the statesmen of Europe. A statement by the Prime Minister in the House of Commons earlier in July had promised unconditionally that Britain would support Poland against German aggression: "We have guaranteed to give our assistance to Poland in the case of a clear threat to her independence, which she considers it vital to resist with her national forces, and we are firmly resolved to carry out this undertaking."[9] In spite of this crystal-clear expression of support, the British Ambassador in Berlin, Sir Nevile Henderson, reported back a few days later that Hitler was convinced that England would never fight over Danzig. Henderson reiterated to the Under-Secretary at the German Foreign Office, Baron von Weizsäcker, that "if Germany by unilateral action at Danzig in any form compelled the Poles to resist, Britain would at once come to their assistance. . . . His Majesty's Government could never be reproached this time, as they had been in 1914, of not having made their position clear beyond all doubt. If Herr Hitler wanted war, he knew exactly how he could bring it about."[10] That was on 15 July. Two weeks later the British Ambassador in Warsaw, Sir Howard Kennard, sent a telegram to Halifax in which he expressed concern that:

> intensive official propaganda is now being conducted in Germany demonstrating the necessity of an isolated war against Poland without any British or French intervention. This, coupled with the notices which have been sent to German reservists who are to be called up during the second fortnight in August, was somewhat ominous. . . . in East Prussia, reservists up to 58 years old were being called up.[11]

That "somewhat" is a wonderful piece of diplomatic *sang froid.*

By the end of July the official Season was over. In its final week there had been four days' racing at Goodwood, held in fine weather which brought out a last display of debs and their mothers in bright summer frocks, a last round of house-parties before people dispersed for their summer holidays. The railways were standing by for record crowds determined to make the most of the brilliant holiday weather that had been forecast. Sailing enthusiasts headed towards Cowes. Meanwhile negotiations with Moscow dragged on, both sides curiously half-hearted. By now the war of nerves had gone on for so long that, instead of being it breaking-point, most people were oddly relaxed. The weather was good, their holidays were booked — some, presumably, in Germany — here was a widespread illusion that events would stand still for the time being while they enjoyed themselves. Hitler was on holiday in Berchtesgarten; Chamberlain was about to leave London for a fishing trip in Scotland. A curious stillness fell, much like the last weeks of that July a quarter of a century previously, when in just the same brilliant weather the country had idled unbelievingly towards the outbreak of War. In 1939, though, there was to be another month of peace.

For the debs, three months of what one of them called "hardly real days" had passed, leaving them much more than three months older and more sophisticated — even those who were reluctant or terrified to start with. Christian Grant's feelings at the outset of her Season were quoted above (p. 135-7). Here is how she looks back on that summer:

> The moment that, for me, crystallizes the state of being eighteen that year was a marvellous moment when I had wandered away from one of those wonderful country-house dances with a young man. We were in a state of happy reciprocal love and we found ourselves in the most beautiful wood and some birds were singing — they must have been nightingales, I suppose, because it was at night — and in the distance we could see the lights of the party and hear the music of the band. We were terribly innocent, and we just sort of kissed each other in a very chaste way and I remember then thinking, this is the most magical thing. One was in this

beautiful wood with the birds and the music in the distance with somebody one loves. It was a very nice time while it lasted.

It is impossible to begrudge happiness like that; and, for Christian in particular, the war was to bring at least as much suffering. Mary Tyser, now Lady Aldenham, speaks for them all when she says:

I can't remember any one thing that stands out from that summer, but maybe the broadcast by Neville Chamberlain of the declaration of war made the most difference to my life. Nothing was ever the same again afterwards.

CHAPTER
EIGHT

The Last Month
of Peace: August

August began with Cowes Week: the last and most picturesque of the summer's events. Sunshine scampered and slid across the waters of the Solent, throwing patterns of light over canvas sails and highly varnished decks. The old men watched, rigid as admirals in their dark-blue reefers (some of them *were* admirals) while the young men showed off their speed and skill in the races, admired by girls with wind-blown hair and tossing skirts. It was a very English image to carry away from the summer of 1939, and a last escapist fling for many of those who sailed all day and danced half the night.

Mollie Acland's father was Commodore of the Yacht Club at Seaview, on the Isle of Wight, and the children had been used to boating all their lives. Her parents had bought a big house at Seaview, to which Mollie invited some of her new friends from the Season.

When we were children, all our friends used to come and stay in July and my parents' friends came in August. Then as we got older *our* friends started to come in August, and in 1939 our house was enlivened by some young men from the Season. We had a lot of servants — the house was bigger than our home in Hertfordshire — so there were plenty of staff to look after us and the guests: in fact we used to have to take on extra people for August. We had the butler, a footman, an extra footman, the cook, a kitchen maid, "a between-maid or two, an under housemaid, two boatmen, two gardeners and an odd-job man called Tom, as well as the nanny and two nursery maids for my younger sisters. (The servants slept two or three to a room, somewhere at the back of the house — I never saw their bedrooms; all except for Cook, who had her own room, and my mother's lady's maid, who did too, and Nanny, who slept in the night nursery.) We had lots of boats there, and a staff boat for when they had time off. There were three rowing boats called Pip, Squeak and Wilfred, and sailing dinghies, and Mermaids. Ninety per cent of our time was spent sailing in August, because after Cowes Week there were the Portsmouth and Bembridge Regattas, the Ryde Regatta — lots of them, so you'd be out all day long. As well as that we swam a lot — somehow we didn't mind the cold in those days — and had a ping-pong table in the old dining-room, where we played if it was really too wet to go out, and there were public tennis-courts.

Apart from Cowes Week, when traditionally it always blows hard — and it did — we had wonderful weather that August. Peter, now my husband, had come to stay for Cowes Week. He was in the RAFVFR by that time, but he managed to come back again at the end of August, and we went to a local place to dance — a sort of nightclub, though not quite — and that's where we fell in love.

On 2 August, a Wednesday, the House of Commons considered how long to adjourn for the summer recess. To the astonishment of many MPS (who had assumed that, in view of the gravity of the international situation, the recess would be brief) Chamberlain insisted that the adjournment should last for the usual two months, until 3 October. It was gestures such as this — whatever may have been said between diplomats at the highest level — that persuaded Germany that Britain was not serious about going to war. The only concession the Prime Minister would make was a promise that Parliament would be recalled should a situation like that of the previous September recur. Winston Churchill opposed him strongly: "In a funny but sad speech [he] said that we must certainly come back early, and gave many reasons including his theme song that the dictators help themselves to a" country whilst we are on holiday! Speech after speech followed along those lines . . . all were against the PM who grinned and bore it."[1]

The divided mood of the House precisely echoed that of the country. A quarter of a century earlier, on 4 August 1914, Britain had entered the First World War after Germany's invasion of Belgium. The parallel was uncomfortably close, and it was not an anniversary that was much celebrated. In 1914 the outbreak of war had been greeted with cheering and hilarity by crowds all over Europe. Then, as now, there had been many who, right up to the last minute, had not believed it could happen. Sir Osbert Sitwell described his father's reaction when he opened his *Times* in 1914 and saw that war had been declared: "What was that? War! War! There would not be a war; how could there be?" In 1939 some people had the same attitude, either hopelessly blinkered by self-delusion and patriotism or simply ignorant of the inexorable march towards a confrontation that could not any longer be side-stepped. Events were now measured in days, not weeks or months, let alone the gathering force of decades. As the *Spectator* analysed it: "A week whose first four days have been marked by no accentuation of crisis is by common consent being described as a period of "lull" in international affairs."[2] Right up to the last weeks there was still optimism — and, in any case, who behaves as though international affairs were more important than packing and getting away for a summer holiday? Who spends as much time reflecting on the balance of probabilities were Germany to invade Poland as they do on deciding which swimsuit will be most becoming, and whether a raincoat is just tempting fate? Certainly not a newly fledged debutante brimming with the social confidence instilled over the last three months, and longing to try it out — and the swimsuit — on the beaches of glamorous Le Touquet, sporty and sophisticated Deauville, chic Eden Roc, slightly passé Biarritz, or — best of all, though mostly for the international moneyed set — Monte Carlo and the casinos of the Riviera.

France was a favourite holiday destination that August: not too far away, "in case", it promised good weather in which to acquire a fashionable tan, and crowds of like-minded people with whom to enjoy the sporting facilities by day and social life by night. Villas were rented all along the Mediterranean coast, and the house-parties of the previous three months simply transferred themselves several hundred miles, to a bluer sky and a more exotic landscape, with little diminution in standards of comfort or service. Sarah Norton's mother, Lady Grantley, was very hospitable:

My mother took a villa in the south of France at St Raphael where my father convalesced after a terrible car accident a few weeks earlier She let me ask a lot of friends out there, and we all had a wonderful time and tried to forget about what was happening elsewhere. A number of people with whom I'd been doing the Season came down to stay — Jane Kenyon-Slaney was one, I remember — and some boys turned up as well. They hadn't been formally invited: they just sort of appeared, and although the villa wasn't grand, we had plenty of room for them.

There was a swimming pool at the villa, where we swam and sunbathed, and we played games, and in the evening we used to take the train to Monte Carlo. It was just like a bus in those days, with little stations right by all the villas, so you could go to the casino for the evening. We didn't gamble, of course: (a) because we hadn't any money, and (b) because it wasn't thought suitable, but we would go along and watch the people who did. Night life was smartish. You'd wear a good cotton frock and sandals, with bare brown arms and legs, but not a cocktail frock, though some of the older people were in evening dress.

Sarah's grandmother used to say, "Darling, the thing is one wouldn't be *seen* in London after 31 July." The general exodus at the beginning of August took a number of people up to Scotland for the grouse shooting. Lady Elizabeth Scott went with her parents, the Duke and Duchess of Buccleuch, to their estate at Wanlockhead, where they entertained a large house-party throughout August.

Helen Vlasto — the deb who had alternated the nights of the Season with days spent nursing at Lambeth Infirmary — was one of many who joined a British Red Cross Society detachment, where she attended lectures in first aid, home nursing and gas warfare. For the family's summer holiday that August her parents did what they had always done, and stayed at Frinton-on-Sea. Helen's grandmother rented a large house there every year, to which she summoned her three children and their families. All the cousins would assemble — many of them seeming exotic and foreign, for they had made their homes in the south of France — and, together with their servants, the extended family would spend a month playing tennis and croquet together, having picnics on the beach, and arguing fiercely over dinner each evening. In 1939, underlying the relaxation of that perfect August, was the unspoken realization that this might be the last such occasion.

France — Scotland — the English seaside resorts: the debs recuperated from the exhaustion of their Season. Few people travelled farther afield, for no one knew whether petrol would be available for private use if war broke out, and people were afraid of finding themselves marooned and unable to get back to England. Indeed, this very nearly happened to Ann Schuster:

Immediately after the Season was over I went to Denmark, because my brother had married a Danish girl when I was about fifteen. I'd been out there to be bridesmaid, and loved it. So I went back in 1939 and stayed with lots of friends for about a month, and it was my Danish host — he was Minister of something — who said, "Look, you've got to get back to England." This was only about four or five days before war broke out, and there was no way by then. The airports were shutting down; my own parents were in Salzburg for a music festival, my brother was on holiday somewhere else. My host managed to get me on to a plane — I think he must have been

Minister of Transport — and said, "Whatever you're going back to, you've got to go, this is the last chance you'll have, otherwise you'll be interned here." It really did hit me then. I'd just been completely unthinking about it before that. We were locked into the aeroplane at Hamburg airport and not allowed to get out and it was all very — when you're seventeen — it was all very exciting. The feeling of elation: good, something's going to be done about it at last!

By mid-August preparations for war were going ahead feverishly. The *Bystander* for 9 August noted:

The August holiday season is upon us, and never before has a peace-time August seen Europe so full of armed men. The camps are crowded in ever country and every road echoes to the tramp of marching men, and ever blast furnace is working overtime, and the British Navy is on the high seas at full strength. It is exactly a quarter of a century almost to the day, since the Navy slipped away into the mists of the North Sea to take up its battle-station at Scapa Flow.

A week later, amid jolly pictures of country shooting-parties or of laughing groups of sun-worshippers beside Mediterranean swimming pools, the same magazine for 16 August recorded:

England's sky last week was filled with more aeroplanes than it has ever known before. 1300 military aeroplanes, four AA divisions, ten BB squadrons and fifteen groups of the observer corps went into action last week in a mock aerial war. For three days, under a low ceiling of rain clouds, the bombers repeatedly attacked and were always observed, though not always intercepted. Civilians cooperated with a midnight-to-dawn black-out.

The newspapers, many of which had hitherto blanketed their readers in a humid fog of jingoistic bluff, finally began to use phrases like "imminent peril of war". Many firms accelerated their air-raid-precaution training. A photograph in the *Bystander* showed a man working in the shadow of the great dome of St Paul's to put up a framework of wire, to catch flying fragments of glass and masonry in case the unimaginable desecration should occur and St Paul's were to be bombed. There was a run on black material with which to make black-out curtains. Shelters were issued to ticket-collectors on the Underground, in case of air-raids: strange little cabins shaped like a diving-bell with scarcely room for a man to sit underneath, which can have offered little more than psychological protection. People's worst fears were unspoken, a terrible mixture of what they knew of the First World War and the science-fiction horrors of a war fought against civilians with gases far more poisonous than the mustard gas that had convulsed the trenches, and planes far more evil than the brave, fragile craft that had jousted gallantly in the last war. One of the young men who escorted many of the debs of 1939 said: "We thought that the Blitzkrieg would take place immediately and everything would be flattened and it would be a question of the survival of the fittest. It was going to be a war fought in the air, and the Army would be the gun fodder, as they were in the First World War. But we never had any doubt that we would win. Never."

Some families were more conscious than others of the need to make urgent preparations for war. Anne Douglas-Scott-Montagu, daughter of Lord Montagu of

Beaulieu (her father had died in 1929 and her mother had married Captain the Hon. Edward Pleydell-Bouverie) recalls that August:

> We were all terribly serious: laying in stores, going to Red Cross things, we were all talking about evacuating, even in August. But I think that we, living on the south coast, were very conscious that we were the front line, and I think we felt — as we did throughout the war — that we might have been invaded. We had pillboxes all over the place and all the boats were laid up. Our garden goes right down to the edge of the river and has massive rhododendrons and my parents organized for all the small boats from the river to come up and be hidden away under the rhododendrons, all round the side of the lawn. We felt that, with Southampton being an important port and Portsmouth a naval base, we were very much in line for invasion: which we were. Yet I don't remember feeling frightened at all. We were very, very patriotic — everyone was patriotic then — none of my friends were pacifists: not one. They all rushed off to join up.

Yet up in Scotland, Madeleine Turnbull was almost wholly unaware how close war was:

> I remember in August '39 — I suppose partly because I was in love — we sort of blinded ourselves and just lived for the moment. We'd taken a farmhouse up at Nethybridge, in Strathspey, and I remember this friend of mine coming to stay with us but he and I never discussed it. Extraordinary, isn't it? Just blind: blind. It came as an awful shock when war was declared. You felt it was the end of your life. We'd been told that if it came the sky would be black with aeroplanes. It was an amazing division in all our lives; you suddenly got this awful sense, for the first time, of the uncertainty of

everything. That you can never rely on anything to be as it appears to be.

One of the very few social events of August was the coming-of-age party held at Chatsworth for the Marquess of Hartington, the son and heir of the Duke of Devonshire. It took place over two days, the 15th and 16th of the month — not so much a party as a whole series of parties: "Thousands of people came over several days of brilliant weather, and by the end of the second day [the Duchess's] right arm was in a sling from too much hand-shaking."[3] In fact Billy Hartington had been twenty-one the previous December, but because of the death of his grandfather, the ninth Duke, his twenty-first birthday celebrations had been postponed; and by mid-August not even the great dark looming clouds of war could persuade his parents to cancel the party again. A photograph in the *Bystander* shows him with his brother Andrew (who became the eleventh Duke eventually), Charles Manners, the Marquess of Granby and the future tenth Duke of Rutland (and another of the great charmers of the Season), and his future brother-in-law. It was the last pre-war gathering of the clan. Shortly afterwards, Ambassador Joe Kennedy, who had never concealed his pessimism about England's chances in a war against Germany, sent his entire family home on the ss *Washington.* Kathleen, whose relationship with Lord Hartington had continued to flourish in spite of opposition from her rigidly Catholic parents, was forced under protest to go too.

The atmosphere in London that August is curiously forecast in an article which Lesley Blanch wrote for *Vogue*. The most curious thing about it is the complete absence of any mention of the impending war. The reason for this apparent *sang froid* was that *Vogue* went to press at least six weeks before the magazine appeared, so copy for the August issue had been written in June. Its blasé tone must have struck its readers as inappropriate at the time; today it seems downright bizarre — but hindsight alters everything:

London in August. Supposedly a dead season, a closed book and an arid waste. When "they" are on holiday; when "their" blinds are drawn; when the town assumes a sullen, brooding air, becalmed between seasons. There is time to think; space to walk; air to breathe. Time to catch up . . . For some, time to try out new joints like the Willoughby, a slap-up, full-dress affair, with swing music and a black band. Or the crazily frescoed Nuthouse in Greek Street with a raffish, bottle party, dress-as-you-please atmosphere, where things hot up about 2 a.m. This month, there is that admirable pianist George Shearing and early in September there will be a new burlesque show.

. . . There are concerts, with the Proms in full blast and new works such as Vaughan Williams' Variations of Dives and Lazarus, Sir Arnold Bax's 7th Symphony, and Arthur Bliss's Piano Concerto. And in London now is the moment to see all those excellent plays which are still running, but which will, by September, give place to others . . . Gielgud at The Globe with *The Cherry Orchard*, *Rebecca* and *Les Parents Terribles*, *Weep for the Spring*; Binnie Hale's *Intimate Revue* . . . plays and more plays, and all eyes focused on Noël Coward's return in his new season at the Phoenix. New films, such as Bette Davis' Carlotta in *Juarez* or Ray Bolger in *The Wizard of Oz*.

Not until November did *Vogue* catch up with the fact that Britain was at war, with an article called glumly, "British Designers Adapt Themselves to War Conditions".

The *Bystander*, on the other hand, began a series called "Women in Uniform" at the end of June, and every week for the next two or three months it highlighted a different branch of women's war work: the Red Cross (showing training, anti-gas lectures and fire-drill), the National Women's Air Reserve, which trained women as ferry and ambulance pilots, ground engineers and wireless operators, the Auxiliary Territorial Service (the ATS), the Women's Land Army, ARP (air-raid precautions), FANY (the First Aid Nursing Yeomanry), and so on. Although the women pictured "doing their stuff" in these various services were largely middle- and more than middle-aged, before very long there would be an influx of debs who, like the rest of their contemporaries, hastened to enlist in whatever branch of war work seemed most useful and congenial.

The *Tatler* was slower to react to the imminence of war, choosing instead to show snazzy pictures of its readers in far-flung holiday resorts with an elegant partner on one hand and a cocktail in the other. The *Tatler* called the international crisis "the current spot of bother" and hoped it would all soon blow over.

Churchill, too, was on holiday. He had gone to France to paint, and was staying with Jacques and Consuelo Balsan at Dreux, together with an artist friend called Paul Maze. Martin Gilbert, Churchill's biographer, recorded:

A telegram reached them, warning that Hitler might invade Poland at any moment. What had been Churchill's reaction? Paul Maze took his pre-war diary from his bookshelf:

"'They are strong, I tell you, they are strong,' Churchill said. Then his jaw clenched his large cigar, and I felt the determination in his will.

'Ah,' he said, 'with it all, we shall have him.'"[4]

The genius of Churchill — who at this stage of late August was still not in the Cabinet; indeed, had not been a Cabinet member since being Chancellor of the Exchequer from 1924 to 1929 — was that he mirrored the attitudes and responses of the English people. Mollie Acland's description of how she and her friends felt about Hitler just before war broke out reflects exactly the determination that Churchill articulated; though in recalling her emotions fifty years later, she unwittingly reverted to the language of teenage years:

By then we were totally and absolutely conscious that war was imminent. We just wondered, is it coming tomorrow or the next day? My uncle said, "The Germans will just wait till the harvest is in and then they'll march on Poland" — and he was absolutely right.

I wasn't a bit frightened — it never *occurred* to us that we could lose. There was a gallant mood among people then. It wasn't a depressing time at all, and I don't remember even thinking of it as "a last fling". *I think we wanted to kill Hitler.* . . . I think it was as simple as that. Obviously we didn't know about the full horrors of the Holocaust, but many of us knew Jewish refugee families and we thought that Hitler was a very bad man and ought to be out of the way before he conquered the world. I think we were totally prepared to die for that.

It's quite important that people who were born after the war should realize what a heck of an awful thing Hitler did. It wasn't only the Jews — it was all of France, and the Low Countries; Czechoslovakia and Poland — he was a megalomaniac, and if he'd got hold of the A-Bomb he'd have destroyed the world.

Since 12 August a British and French military mission had been in Moscow for further protracted talks. By the middle of the month *The Times* reported confidently that the talks "seem to be making good progress, and their work invites the assurance that there will be no big delay in completion of 'the peace front' by the inclusion of Russia." Meanwhile, German-Polish relations had reached a point of nerve-racking tension, with incidents occurring daily right along the frontier, and not just in Danzig.

On 20 August, however, *The Times* carried the astounding news that a German-Soviet non-aggression pact had been agreed, and on 23 August it was formally signed by Ribbentrop and Molotov. Some people remember the announcement of this shattering new development most clearly of all.

The German-Soviet pact destroyed the last frail thread of hope for peace, and from all over Europe people were cobbling together whatever arrangements they could make to get home to England. Even staying in the Balsans' idyllic château near Dreux, Churchill had been conscious of "the deep apprehension brooding over all",[5] and in the end his anxiety led him to cut short his holiday and return to England on 22 August. In the wake of the Nazi-Soviet pact, Chamberlain announced a formal Treaty of Alliance with Poland. It was signed on 25 August, and there was no more talk of "concessions" to Germany. Churchill personally telephoned the Polish Ambassador in London, who told him that he was "completely satisfied with the support he was receiving".

From now on, it could only be a matter of days. One young man from that Season recalls,

> When Ribbentrop's agreement was announced I knew that was a fatal day. By then everyone was doing ARP work and learning things like bandaging, somebody was coming in once a week to teach us about gas — everyone expected there would be a gas attack, though in fact it never came — and first aid, and arrangements were being made to take in evacuees from the London slums. One tried to be calm about the whole thing: that was the form. My mother would have disapproved of anyone getting too excited.

On 24 August Parliament was recalled. Chips Channon's diary recorded the mood of the House:

> I watched the other Members come in and meet one another. They all looked well, many were bronzed. At 2.45 the House met and soon the Prime Minister rose. He spoke in well-modulated phrases and was clear and admirable, but with little passion or emotion ... The House was calm, bored, even irritated, at having its holiday cut short by Hitler.
> ... Certainly tonight London is quiet and almost indifferent to what may happen. There is a frightening calm.[6]

The calm sense of inevitability was not universal. For many debs, this confirmation that the unthinkable was about to happen brought a cold sense of fear. Their brothers and cousins and dancing partners and boyfriends were the ones who would have to lay down their lives to stop Hitler. Dinah Brand (now Mrs Bridge) remembers the moment when realization first hit her:

> I was up in Yorkshire and there was a lot of chat about how this is really it and then I heard over the megaphone at the race meeting people being called up to their regiments and that gave me a tremendous sort of shiver — a shock, that it was happening. And yet, in a sort of way, being so young, you just didn't realize what it would involve. . . . it was exciting and yet terrifying.

Priscilla Brett (now Lady Beckett), was also at York races that August, staying with her future parents-in-law, and she too remembers people being called to their regiments over the tannoy: "There was a great sense of drama: we hadn't the foggiest idea what it would be like. In a way we thought it would be much more dreadful than it was, because of the memories of the last war, and the horrors of that." Ronnie Kershaw was one of the young men called up at that time and, far from being apprehensive, he greeted his call-up with delight — or so, at any rate, it seems to him now:

> I was called up in August, and I was very, very pleased. I didn't like the job I was doing very much, so it was a great relief. I was made a 2nd Lieutenant at about 10/6d a day: so there I was in the Army. At the end of August I went to camp and then after camp I didn't have any more leave. But right up until the end of July I think most people hadn't believed there was going to be a war. They didn't really think that Hitler

would risk it against England. They never thought he would be mad enough — they thought something would happen to prevent it. That was my view as well: but I soon changed it!

Christian Grant had known throughout the summer that war was imminent:

What gave me the greatest clue that something terrible was expected was that the grown-ups — our parents' generation — were so frightfully nice to us; and we sort of knew that they were giving us a particularly wonderful, beautiful summer because they knew more than we knew. It didn't oppress or frighten one, because at that age one has no concept of what a war is. One certainly didn't appreciate that all the young men one was dancing with were going to be killed. Of my men friends, my young men friends, twenty-two of them joined up on the same day, when war started, and at the end of the war only two were alive. And one was a mental wreck and the other was on crutches. And that was the whole of my gang. En bloc, my gang was slaughtered.

In the last few days of August people were hastening back from their holidays. For those who had been abroad, this was often a considerable problem. Sarah Norton's mother packed up their villa at St Raphaël with scarcely an hour's notice:

We'd all been trying to forget what was happening, and had mostly succeeded in having a wonderful time — and then when things really were getting a bit tricky my mother suddenly decided that we had to leave *immediately*. We were in my father's car with my parents and my brother and one other person who wanted a lift and then suddenly lots of other people turned up, begging for lifts, but there was nothing we could do — there was no more room in the car. My mother was quite calm about it all but there was no nonsense: she said, in half an hour we'll leave, and we did. I hadn't even had time to change out of my shorts, so I arrived at the Ritz in Paris still wearing them, but my mother said, "Don't worry. dear, nobody'll notice your shorts." The next problem was getting on to a boat to cross the Channel, but we managed that and my brother Johnnie and I were sent straight up to Scotland.

Now there was nothing to be done except wait. Rosamund Neave said:

People knew it was going to happen yet they couldn't grasp it and couldn't do anything about it, so it was a very static time ... becalmed ... almost like a stillness over the whole country. My mother was beginning to put things away in trunks and to lay in supplies. She bought masses of tea and masses of *vests*, for some reason. People were coming down from Scotland and back from their holidays. It was a very strange time.

August came to an end, and so did twenty-one years of peace.

PART THREE

The War: Real,
Phoney and Aftermath

CHAPTER
NINE

This Country Is at War with Germany

On the very brink of war, events moved with leaden slowness. It was like the nightmare of being chased through a swamp, every footfall sinking deeper, each step slower, being dragged irresistibly down. Right up until the last minute the British Ambassador in Berlin, Sir Neville Henderson, was negotiating with Hitler. Britain offered to tolerate the return of Danzig and the Polish Corridor to Germany, in return for the guarantee of a free port on the Baltic. What was the point — except further to convince Hitler that Britain would not fight?

Reservists were being called up in France, Britain and Germany. Vehicles were being requisitioned; petrol supplies were limited. Stocks of blackout material were exhausted. Country families in England were standing by to receive evacuee children — one-third of all children under five in the areas most at risk were expected. Works of art were removed from the National Gallery and other London museums and stored away in places of safety: some of them hidden in Manod Quarry in the Welsh hills. Stained glass from the windows of

York Minster and Canterbury Cathedral was also removed. Two hundred thousand German troops were massed along the Polish frontier. Hitler cancelled the Nuremberg rally planned for 2 September. In the East End, people were filling sandbags.

The sun shone. The country held its breath.

On 31 August, Hitler gave the order to attack Poland. At 4.45 a.m. on 1 September, German troops marched across the Polish frontier, and at 6 a.m. Warsaw was bombed by German aeroplanes. Churchill was woken by a telephone call early that morning from the Polish Ambassador in London, Count Raczynski, to inform him of the news. He passed it on to the War Office, astonished to find that no one there had yet heard. He then drove up from Chartwell to London, where Chamberlain asked him to join a special War Cabinet as First Lord of the Admiralty. Churchill agreed. A message — but not yet an ultimatum — was sent to Hitler warning that unless German forces were withdrawn from Poland, Great Britain would stand by the Anglo-Polish pact and give its full support and assistance to Poland.

All day the bombing of Polish cities continued, and a million German troops marched in to Poland.

On 2 September it began to rain; first a steady, warm summer rainfall, then a downpour: "terrific, ominous", Churchill recorded.

The British Cabinet was insisting that an ultimatum must be sent to Germany. Chamberlain and Halifax were still trying to prevaricate; still hoping for a miracle. Mussolini was said to be on the point of proposing a conference. France had said that an ultimatum must give a week's grace for the withdrawal of German troops. The French Army needed more time to complete mobilization.

At 7.30 p.m. on 2 September the House of Commons met. Chamberlain's temporizing was heard in silence. Arthur Greenwood, the acting Labour leader, spoke: "Every minute's delay now means the loss of life, imperilling of our national interests and imperilling the very foundations of our national honour." Harold Nicolson's diary describes the reaction:

> He was resoundingly cheered. The tension became acute, since here were the PM's most ardent supporters cheering his opponent with all their lungs. The front bench looked as if they had been struck in the face.
>
> The House adjourns. The lobby is so dark that a match struck flames like a beacon. There is great confusion and indignation. We feel that the German ships and submarines will, owing to this inexplicable delay, elude our grasp. The PM must know by now that the whole House is against him.[1]

In Poland some 1,500 people had already been killed in the bombing of over thirty cities.

The Cabinet met at 11 p.m. that evening, some of its members insisting that an ultimatum must be sent at once. The most Halifax could do by way of compromise was to delay its sending until 9 a.m. the following morning, and this was agreed.

At nine o'clock, therefore, on the morning of 3 September, the German government was asked for an assurance that German forces would suspend their advance upon Poland, otherwise a state of war would exist between the two countries. The two hours given for a reply elapsed without any such assurance being received. Chamberlain broadcast to the nation at 11.15 a.m.

I know to the square yard where I was when war was declared [says Christian Grant]. It's rather like where I was when I heard that Kennedy had been shot. On 3 September 1939, I was standing in my old nursery in our house in Scotland. I happened to be entirely by myself. My old nursery had been turned into a bedroom and I just happened to be there with the radio on. Chamberlain's voice came over the radio. Oh, I remember it very, very well.

Helen Vlasto remembers it too:

On a sunny summer holiday morning my grandmother's family house party began to assemble in the large drawing room of a house called Maryland at Frinton-on-Sea. It was Sunday 3rd September, and we were all to meet at the appointed hour of 11.15 around the wireless set to hear the now inevitable declaration of war. I can still see us all vividly and can remember consciously saying to myself: "This is the most poignant moment of your life to date, and you will never forget it." . . . The drawing room was heavy with the scent of great bowls of roses, cut lavender drying on the wide, sunny window seats, and foreign cigarettes. Here we foregathered, all awaiting confirmation of our worst fears. . . . Now each of us was busy with immediate plans that must be made when those awful words were let loose upon the air for all to hear:

"I am speaking to you from the Cabinet Room at Number Ten, Downing Street . . . and that consequently this country is at war with Germany."

We were at war, but in our garden, nothing had changed. The September sun still shone thoughtlessly down, unmindful of the new and monstrous turn of events. The bees continued to bumble among the roses, and the butterflies to weave their erratic and inconsequential course towards the early Michaelmas daisies and the buddleias.[2]

Elizabeth Lowry-Corry is another whose memory of that moment is sharp: "I do remember, with great intensity, the outbreak of war. On that Sunday we had this wonderful old parson conducting the service, and I remember that service and how we took communion . . . and everyone's faces, and the beautiful day." Ronnie Kershaw remembers that directly after Chamberlain's announcement (by some error) an air-raid siren was heard.

I remember being in London when that air-raid warning went off on the Sunday morning. I was on top of a building somewhere, guarding it; and you could see hundreds of balloons going up — barrage balloons — and it was an awful moment. You thought you were going to be bombed to hell. And nothing happened at all. But in that moment I realized I had a horrible fear of death. If you remember, the average length of life for a serving officer in the First World War was supposed to be very, very low indeed, and so we thought our chances were minimal.

However extraordinary it may seem, there were a number of debs that year for whom the announcement that Britain was at war came as a complete surprise. Lady Elizabeth Scott was one: "I'm afraid the whole summer seemed to be given up to having a good time, and no one of my generation ever thought ahead to the future, or to the possibility of war. *I* certainly never thought it even a remote possibility that there could be a war — until it was announced that morning of 3 September." Lady Cathleen Eliot was another: "Politics were not discussed in my family so it was a complete surprise when war was declared and the atmosphere changed overnight." Rhoda Walker-Heneage-Vivian had little inkling until the last moment and, even when her father tried to warn her of what was coming, she scarcely believed him:

> I had no idea of the approach of war — the only radio at our London house was in the servants' room in the basement — until one day at the very end of the Season, in July, my father suddenly said in a taxi we were sharing, "There is going to be another war." I tried out this statement on various friends, to be met with gasps of surprise.
>
> When war broke we *all* wrote to each other — brave letters wishing each other luck, particularly to every young man — convinced we should all die.

Those who had least idea of what was coming were the girls whose families regarded it as "not done" to discuss politics and the events preceding the outbreak of war. Diana Trafford had been aware that war must be in the offing:

> I did occasionally wonder how many of us would survive the coming war and what would happen if we lost, but it was definitely bad form to discuss such things. I don't know if anyone else thought along those lines. Having listened to First World War stories, especially from the servants, I suppose I more or less expected a continuation from 1918.
>
> I was called up by the ATS a week before war was declared, and my company commander assigned me to the quarter-master's stores. The morning war was declared I was counting

cups when the Q M came in and said, "Well, the balloon's gone up and we are at war." We were all young in the stores and stood silent and rather shocked, and the Q M turned to me and said, "Let's have a look at that cup down there." Blindly and without thinking I pulled it out and brought the whole 128 down in a crashing tangle of broken china, which started us all laughing and broke the tension. The Q M said, "It's all right — your dad will pay for it out of his income tax. Get a broom and sweep it up." I have always thought of him as one of the many, taken for granted, who made winning the war possible.

For a number of people, the first reaction to the announcement that war had been declared was one of relief. Uncertainty is the hardest thing to live with. Now at least the suspense was over. Christian Grant confirms this:

I think a lot of people had a sense of relief. There had been so much coming and going — will they, won't they? will they, won't they? — I think one can cope much more with a given disaster than one can with the threat hanging over one. I don't think either the men or the girls realized at first that people would be killed — not until it started happening. And that didn't happen for the first six months at least.

The uncertainty was soon replaced by a new fear: the fear of the unknown. No one knew what to expect. They — especially the girls, who were less immediately involved — wondered, would it be like the last war, with millions dying in the trenches? Would it be a Blitzkrieg, with death falling on civilians from the skies? Would it be a war of chemical poisons? To begin with people carried their ugly gas-masks everywhere, in case of

317

attack. (*Vogue* in November showed a chic, ingenious little handbag to conceal the unsightly thing.)

Some of the men had a jaunty, careless attitude to death. It was unthinkable that they, personally, might be killed. Lord Cromer — who, as Rowley Errington, had been one of the great charmers of that Season — was just twenty-one when the war began. At that age, and after that sort of summer, it was difficult to take death seriously.

> No, I never expected to get killed . . . no, no. You always thought it was something that would happen to someone else. I think some people were very fatalistic, but it wasn't talked about — it wasn't concentrated on, in the ghastly, macabre way of the 1914-18 war. And yet, at the beginning, I think we visualized it ending up as trench warfare. If you were a footsoldier, which I was at that time, you naturally tended to look at it that way.

Nearly all the men, if not career officers, had been in the Army reserves, the RNVR or the RAFVR for at least the past few weeks. But military training does not, for obvious reasons, harp on the probability of death; rather on the necessity for order, discipline and preparation. Some of the preparations were almost comically inadequate. Lord Cromer again:

> The first few weeks, I remember, the youngsters were all taught to do sword drill, and we all used to go out to parade every morning, on the cricket pitch, having borrowed a sword. Literally, a sword: a real one, an old-fashioned sword — like the Life Guards use for ceremonial occasions. It wasn't a

frightfully useful introduction to combat but it kept us out of mischief.

All the reservists in my particular regiment had been called up when war broke out on 3 September. The reservists were the most extraordinary body of people, because having fought in the First World War they were twenty or thirty years older; and then there was my age group, who were all very young. We were a very motley crew. Nobody knew what to do.

Lord Haig had found the Season, his Finals at Oxford and his polo-playing so immensely tiring that by the end of that summer he was in a state of considerable exhaustion. "You burned your energies out a bit, and I do remember the first year of the war when I went out to join my regiment in Palestine, what a wonderful relief it was, to be absolved from all this hassle." Lord Haig tells an extraordinary story, extraordinary only in the context of its time, for very soon not just Hitler, not just the Nazis, but the entire German race was being portrayed as sub-human, much as they themselves had been presenting the Jews. The story concerns a German friend whom he had met the previous year in Munich:

He wrote to me in July 1939 to say that war was inevitable — it's been marvellous, and let's hope we survive the war and meet again in the future, but for now ... One had of course known quite a number of Germans, especially from the aristocracy, who were against the Nazi way of thinking; my friend refused ever to become an officer. They could force people to join up and fight for the Fatherland, but they couldn't force them to become officers, and so although he took part in battles throughout the war and was seriously wounded three times, he wouldn't become an officer. So in that way he remained true to himself. And when you read the

319

papers screaming propaganda about the German menace, although menace there was, I was able to see it in proportion.

That sense of proportion, particularly on 3 September, would not have been widely shared. Yet, for some, the war brought no sense of relief, but rather a sickening sense of failure. Chamberlain, whose attempts at appeasement sprang not from cowardice but from a deep desire for peace, said in the House of Commons on the morning of 3 September: "Everything that I have worked for, everything that I have hoped for, everything that I have believed during my public life has crashed in ruins."

Unity Mitford's life, too, had crashed in ruins. She had been a total convert both to National Socialism and to Hitler himself. Her ardour was obsessional, but, as her sister Diana wrote, "Her love of Germany was deep, but it was equalled by her love of England. Rather than see these two countries tear each other to pieces she preferred to die."[3] In the Englischer Garten in Munich, at the moment when England declared war on Germany, Unity tried to kill herself. A bullet entered her brain, but she did not die until 1948.

The outbreak of war in 1939 was not greeted with the same universal rejoicing that had rolled jubilantly around the capitals of Europe in 1914. The memory of that last war was too recent. The public-school ethos fostered by the Victorians, which led the sons of the upper classes to dash impatiently into the fray, avid for death or glory, was modified. Patriotism was still there, but war was no longer seen as a rather more dangerous version of cricket. People knew that war could not be avoided and were prepared to fight; but they knew it would be hard and serious. The fun and frivolity, the gaiety and extravagance were over. Britain was confronting the forces of Hitler: superior forces, led by evil men. The *Bystander*, of all papers, summed it up in a column called "The Passing Hour", written by A. G. Macdonell in September 1939:

It seems, then, that there is nothing more to be said. Once again we stand where we stood in the Channel in 1588 when the Armada was approaching, where we stood at Blenheim, at Waterloo, and in 1914, face to face with the powers of darkness. So, good luck to all of us, for we shall certainly need all the good luck there is.

CHAPTER
TEN

An Excellent Introduction
for Life

Suspended between the 1890s and 1980s, the Season of 1939 was far closer in its conventions and the way of life it reflected to the former, yet the young girls who enjoyed or endured it have grown up and lived their lives in the twentieth century, not the nineteenth. Looking back across those fifty years, did the Season have a function: did it work for them?

One deb said, "Society was so that everybody knew each other . . . but, as it was, the war meant that an awful lot of the people you met completely disappeared." Rhoda Walker-Heneage-Vivian hit the nail on the head when she summed it up thus": "Looking back on it now it seems like another world full of empty-headed people — but a happy, carefree world full of colour, beautiful clothes and perfume and, I am sure, an excellent introduction into life *as it was in 1938.*" Others never stopped to think about it: "At eighteen you don't ask yourself questions like what the Season is for. It appealed to me, personally, because I thought it established the fact that I was now grown-up!" And another ex-deb said, "The majority of debs took part in the Season just for fun — and it was a wonderful way of getting to know a great number of other girls of one's own age." It has proved to be successful in its function of introducing eligible young people to one another, even though the prospect for some was not appealing: "The men were *awful*. Deadly dull, no conversation at all, but a handful of debs had such a burning desire to get married that they accepted the first offer. I remember one girl stitching her trousseau and saying glumly, "All this, and John at the end of it!"'

Lady Mary Dunn was already married and a mother by 1939; but she was then and remains now a perceptive observer of the English upper classes. Does she think the Season had a purpose other than as an opportunity to meet a suitable spouse?

The Season was overdone in the 1930s and possibly in the 1920s as well. The amount spent in one night would have kept a whole family out of poverty for a year; so I think it's a good thing that the excesses of 1939 never came back. But, having said that, I think there was more to it than just the narrow wish to make sure that marriages were made among your own class. I can understand that parents wanted to see their daughters taken care of, and wanted them to live a life to which they'd been brought up.

But, in addition to that, these families were very aware of the beauty of their houses and their land: they were aesthetically aware of their heritage, and they felt a great sense of responsibility to see that it was maintained. The house might have been in the family for two or three hundred years; its titles and estates dated back generations. They saw the tenants very much as their responsibility, too; and so they'd

like their son to marry someone who understood all this and
would carry it on.

If that is accepted as the real purpose of the Season —
to keep England's heritage of ancient land and houses
safely within the hands of those who would best
understand how to run them — then that of 1939 was
quite successful. Many of the noblest debs of that year
did indeed marry into the nobility. Lady Elizabeth
Scott, daughter of the Duke of Buccleuch, became the
Duchess of Northumberland. On the other hand, her
great friend, Lady Sarah Churchill, has been married
three times but never to an English aristocrat and has
now reverted to her maiden name. Lady Isabel Milles-
Lade, sister of the fourth Earl Sondes, married the
nineteenth Earl of Derby, but her sister, Lady Diana, is
unmarried. The Hon. Anne Douglas-Scott-Montagu,
daughter of the second Baron Montagu of Beaulieu,
married Sir John Chichester, the eleventh Baronet and
still lives a few miles from her ancestral home. Ursula
Wyndham-Quin, granddaughter of the fifth Earl of
Dunraven and Mount-Earl, married Lord Roderic
Pratt, son of the fourth Marquess Camden, while her
two — equally beautiful sisters married the Marquess of
Salisbury and the first Baron Egremont, thus becoming
mistresses of Hatfield House and Petworth House
respectively.

Returning to the sample of forty-five debutantes
whose families were analysed in Chapter 4 one finds a
high degree of continuity. All but three of those forty-
five debutantes married. Eight of the titled girls
(meaning those whose fathers had titles and a seat in the

House of Lords) married titled husbands. Only one girl married into the aristocracy without having one or other parent titled, and she was exceptionally beautiful. There is in fact a high correlation between good looks and good marriages. All the girls who were frequently named as being among the great beauties of 1939 married "well", as their mothers would have understood the word.

Perhaps the greatest surprise is the number of divorces found among the girls who came out in 1939. Twelve of the forty-five have been divorced, some of them three or four times. This is partly due to the number of hasty marriages contracted soon after the declaration of war and later regretted; while few of the marriages to foreign (usually American or Canadian) servicemen have lasted a lifetime. A divorce rate of over 25 per cent is certainly high, for it was not until the divorce laws were relaxed in 1969 that the number of divorces climbed dramatically. The forty-five women chosen to form this sample are not — it should be stressed — a properly random sample, and it may be that those who divorced are over-represented, and as untypical of their fellow debs as they would be of their whole generation.

Many of those marriages precipitated by the outbreak of war, however, have survived, although others were poignantly short. Sonia Denison married Edgar Heathcoat-Amory in 1940, having met him in the course of the Season, and by 1944 he was dead, leaving her at twenty-three with two young children. The transition, for her, was sudden and gruelling — from the artless fun of the Season into a war during which she worked as a VAD and brought up her two small children alone for the next few years.

Ann Schuster was another girl who married in a rush because of the pressures brought about by the war:

The house had been commandeered; my mother went off on a war job to the Isle of Man, to sort out the people who had been interned there; my father was working in the Ministry of Information; my brother had been called up. The whole family was dispersed, and we had no home. Literally. I got engaged on 5 September, two days after war broke out. I can remember telling my mother, and she was so distracted, poor love, having to get out of the house and everything breaking up around her, and I think she said, "How nice, darling. I'm so glad it's out." But it was a very secondary thing by then. Everything had overwhelmed her, really.

Ann's husband was killed in the war:

I didn't know where he was. I wasn't ever allowed to know until after the war. The General, Colin Gubbins, had to come and tell me that it had happened a few weeks back, but he wasn't allowed to tell me where. I was never allowed to write to Bunny (my husband) or him to me, because in SOE you didn't even have your own name. And so the fact that suddenly something had finished . . . it's rather like having a bad fall: you don't feel it for a while. I was living with my mother at the time, in West Kensington somewhere, and she'd find me writing letters. I used to write every week and send it to the Baker Street headquarters, and in fact I think some of them were parachuted in because one or two of them were found with his things. But I used to go on writing these letters because it hadn't really sunk in. It was happening to everybody. You just went back to work — or whatever you were doing — and then I think the shock of it came later. A little bit like the hurricane of autumn 1987 — you suddenly realized that things could end. Disappear.

It was a considerable shock for a young woman whose world had been largely confined to her close-knit family and the dizzy pleasures of the Season; and — despite a happy second marriage — it left her with a lifelong sense of the impermanence of things.

Death had a universal impact on the girls of 1939. There cannot be one who did not lose a friend — a partner — a brother — or a cousin. Christian Grant, one of the maddest and gayest and wittiest and most original of the 1939 debs, speaks in a very different voice when it comes to the young men who whirled and flirted through the Season with her:

It was of course our dancing partners who were killed: the subaltern generation, the second lieutenants, the flight lieutenants — they were the ones who really got wiped out. They went into the war in 1939 and they had six years of being shot at one way and another, and by jove, they just were killed. And I miss them awfully, even now, I really do. I quite often think back to all the ones I . . . It's something that nobody who wasn't eighteen when the war started ever really understands. And what's more, a particular set of eighteen-year-olds, because the gang I was with were all the boys fresh from Eton who would go and join up the first day. Later in the war, when I worked in an aircraft factory — well, the solid workman is a splendid chap, but he did not volunteer. He waited till he was called up. And I didn't find that the factory workers had nearly the same outlook on this whole question as our group. Ours was a dashing group of young men who had been brought up in a tradition of fighting for their country. And they were just all killed off.

It had been widely anticipated that, as soon as war broke out, a hail of bombs would fall on London and it would be the civilian population that was slaughtered. What happened was mercifully, eerily different. What happened was the phoney war, when for ten months nothing happened. Esme Harmsworth, the beautiful younger daughter of Viscount Rothermere, remembers the strange atmosphere of those months:

> The period from the outbreak of war in September 1939 until Dunkirk in June 1940 was a time of quiet, a time when no one knew what to expect. Therefore people were inclined to continue life much as it had been before. Of course the young men were called up to join one of the armed services and to train for warfare. The young women were not called up so early: in my case, not until mid-1942. During this quiescent autumn of 1939 and the following winter some ex-debutantes went happily skiing in the Alps regardless. No bombing, of course, had taken place in England and the Germans had not commenced their great advance through France.

The strength of the German Luftwaffe had been exaggerated, which increased people's terror of the destruction they were daily expecting. Defence experts had calculated that 100,000 tons of bombs would drop on London in fourteen days. In fact, the total dropped on London throughout the entire war was less than this.[1] Liddell Hart wrote in 1939, "Nearly a quarter of a million casualties might be expected . . . in the first week of a new war."[2] This, a cautious estimate at the time, proved wildly exaggerated. In the event, there were 295,000 civilian casualties from air attack throughout the whole of the war, of whom 60,000 were killed. And while the deaths among the armed forces were high (though far lower, proportionately, than in the First World War) only one of the debs from the 1939 Season was killed as a direct result of the war. Her name was Iris Brooks, and she was in the ATS.

This was not because they were all safely at home. Quite the opposite is true. Almost without exception, as soon as war broke out the young girls did exactly what the young men were doing: they rushed to volunteer for war service. Here for instance, is what Rhoda Walker-Heneage-Vivian did:

> Wartime was a very different kettle of fish. I enlisted with the FANY at the outbreak of war and after a course at Chepstow learning how to drive and maintain heavy vehicles I was sent to Saighton Camp, Chester, which held 500 infantry and 500 gunners. The only females were a Sister and four VADS, and two FANYS to drive the ambulance. My papa nearly died when he heard and I only wish I had kept the letter he wrote about the iniquities of Army Camps etc. etc. From then on I called the camp Satan Camp and settled down to having a whale of a time. Our ambulance was a converted furniture van with "Anytime, Anywhere" written on the door, which made it difficult to be aloof — but I still remained "pure as the driven snow": Papa's influence, no doubt!

Sarah Norton had a fascinating, if secret war: she spent most of it working at Bletchley Park, the centre for code-breaking which monitored and deciphered secret German transmissions.

All the debs did something in the war, even before the call-up in May 1941. Lots went into the wvs but I remember I didn't fancy the idea of having to wear a uniform much, even though many of them were designed by Norman Hartnell and looked very nice. Every day through the war you turned to the casualty lists in *The Times* and thought, oh God, who's it going to be now?

The Hon. Sheila Digby (now the Hon. Mrs Moore) had been a shy and initially reluctant deb, but when the war began she threw herself into it with eager and sometimes excessive enthusiasm:

At the end of my Season, I said I wanted to get a job in London. I was told that my elder sister Pam, afterwards married to Randolph Churchill, was going to be in London and Mummy wouldn't have two daughters in London. So I joined the ATS in August and was helping in the office in Dorchester. I got home one afternoon from the office and was out in a boat on the lake. The butler came to say I was wanted on the telephone, so thinking it was a beau, I ran like mad and out of breath picked up the phone to hear a voice say, "Digby, you have been called up. Report as soon as possible to the Barracks in Dorchester." That was three or four days before the war started.

I arrived to find that I was meant to feed about twenty Tommies in a gym that had been made over into a cookhouse mess, but no food. I was to go into town to get food. Having been used to four or five courses at home even if it was just the family, I went out and got a mass of food and the Tommies seemed delighted. No wonder! A few days later, I was called and was asked what all the bills were! I then discovered that in the evenings they should just have had something like bread, cheese and tea.

Although Minterne, my home, was only ten miles from Dorchester, I wasn't allowed to go home. I was billeted in an attic near the railway station. There was a window in the ceiling which they hadn't been able to blackout, so I wasn't allowed to turn on any lights! Luckily, I was only there ten days before going to Bovingdon Camp.

The sheltered privileged life I had known disappeared with a bang! But because of the strict discipline with which we had been brought up, I didn't find it too difficult to adjust.

Lady Cathleen Eliot worked in a convalescent home, where she had to cook for eighty people. "It was very good experience," she says drily. It was near Sir Archibald McIndoe's East Grinstead Hospital where, in a pioneering unit, he rebuilt the faces of young airmen whose features had melted when their planes crashed or caught fire. His techniques of skin grafting enabled many people to resume normal lives who otherwise would have had to withdraw behind masks and closed curtains. Part of the job of rehabilitating these young men lay in teaching them to confront ordinary people — for although the techniques of plastic surgery were making huge advances, they were very far from perfect. Lady Cathleen used to take these young convalescents with their still-raw faces to the theatre, or to the West End for dinner and dancing. It must have been an ordeal for her, too.

Barbara McNeill, the deb whose dance at Dutton Homestall was one of the very last of the Season, also worked at East Grinstead, nursing in the uniform of the Red Cross. It was while she was there that — by the lottery of billeting — she re-encountered Michael Astor, with whom she had danced and chatted casually during the Season. With the urgency that often characterized such wartime relationships, they married just two months later. Theirs was one of the marriages that was not to last.

One of the hardest things to comprehend about these years is how much *fun* people still managed to have. It was perfectly possible to have a job that was dirty or nasty — like factory work — or harrowing, like nursing, or physically gruelling, like being a Landgirl; and yet at the end of the day to change into what were called "gladrags" and revert to a world of glamour and gaiety. The girls — most of whom were still, after all, under twenty — would drink and dance half the night away before returning at dawn to go back on duty. Anne Douglas-Scott-Montagu — hard at work with the Red Cross — played hard too:

We had a good deal of fun in the war. It's no good pretending we didn't. People would come back on leave and they'd ring up frightfully late in the evening, you might be going to bed, and they'd say, "I've just got back — come out with me." And you'd get dressed again. Get out of bed, put all your make-up on, and off you'd go. Dinner at the Berkeley was one of the places, or sometimes dinner at the 400, dancing through till the early hours of the morning.

And of course eating out was very cheap during the war. Five shillings was the maximum you could pay, and they never allowed a table charge. You were allowed to pay for a roll and butter, I think, extra to the five shillings, and coffee; but otherwise five shillings was the maximum you could spend in a restaurant on any sort of meal. Amazing what they produced for that, too. This went on all through the war, all through the bombing. Oh yes, you got up in the morning; but I didn't have to be in my Red Cross office in Wilton Crescent till half-past nine unless there was some sort of an emergency, and half-past nine is not so early. So I used to go off on my bicycle to work, having been dancing till perhaps four in the morning. It's amazing what you can do when you're only eighteen!

In this respect the Second World War was very like the First. Soldiers home on leave packed a frenzied whirl of West End night life into their brief respite from fighting. The 400 Club and the Embassy were as popular as they had been during the Season; only now the young crowd that thronged there had suddenly grown much older, more independent and worldly-wise. Inevitably, sexual standards were relaxed, and not just because chaperones disappeared as war arrived. People who knew they might never see each other again often saw little point in waiting for a wedding night that might never happen. The young women no longer felt themselves to be children, subject to their parents' discipline and rules. The work they were doing — sometimes paid work — made them separate individuals, people in their own right, and as such they made their own decisions about whether or not to sleep with the men they loved.

A great meeting place in those days for a drink before dinner was the old Berkeley [says Christian Grant]. It's now been pulled down and turned into offices, but it used to be opposite the Ritz, on the corner by a tube station that has also now disappeared but used to be called Down Street. One met in a sort of funny long passage, it wasn't like a proper room but just a long bar where all the before-dinner drinks went on and everyone sat around talking and being jolly. Everyone used to head there at six o'clock and you could be certain of meeting friends there.

Knowing that it was sure to be full of people dizzy with cocktails and laughter and the latest gossip, it was here that Airey Neave — Rosamund's brother —

arrived after his sensational escape from Colditz. Christian Grant remembers:

Suddenly the door from the street burst open and in came Airey Neave. The only way I can describe it is to say that it was like in old pantomimes when the devil used to shoot up through a trap door from underneath the stage in a puff of smoke . . . well, he came in like that. None of us even knew he had escaped, and his arrival had the same sort of explosive quality. You can imagine: he'd just got back to England — and the whole room just erupted in amazement and joy that he'd just sort of walked in.

Ronnie Kershaw remembers the 400 Club as a haven from the war: "We went to the 400 rather a lot, right through to 1942/3. It did very well, the 400 — kept up the feel of the old place. And the girls, too: they managed to look glamorous, in spite of clothing coupons, right through the war." Lord Cromer too was struck by the sudden changes at that time:

In the first year of the war there were no parties as such, but people were looking for amusement and gaiety and so on, but in a different kind of way — by going to nightclubs or what have you. It was a very gay time. And it suddenly became much more sophisticated — particularly the girls, who were no longer sheltered children just out of the schoolroom. They were working with the war effort, in the WRNS or in aircraft factories or whatever.

Working in an aircraft factory is precisely what Christian Grant was doing. Her family home in Scotland had been scheduled as an auxiliary hospital, but after six months during which she sat there and nothing happened, she got bored waiting for patients who never arrived:

So I thought, I must get where the action is, and so I came down to London and got a job in an aircraft factory, making heavy bombers. The factory was on a direct Underground line to Piccadilly, and so one left one's factory bench, still in dungarees, and was instantly in the Ritz bar — well, in half an hour — so it was all very jolly. Until everybody started getting killed.

Marigold Charrington had done some Red Cross training before war began, so she went to nurse at Basingstoke Hospital, near her parents' home.

We had a lot of the casualties from Dunkirk. They were brought straight there with terrific burns, so there I was at eighteen, really flung into it. We coped — how did we cope? — because we had to; and we'd been trained just to carry on. But in any case we were so busy, there wasn't any time to think about how you felt. After all, it was much worse for the men. I remember hearing that my cousin, Christopher Jeffreys, had been killed at Dunkirk, and we were all overwhelmed. A neighbour said, "Marigold, you musn't take things so hard: you must try not to mind so much." But you did. I don't think you talked about it nearly as much as people do nowadays — in fact I don't think I talked at all — but how could you not mind? I always minded.

No wonder that, as Madeleine Turnbull said, "You got a terrific sense of the insecurity of life. The Blitz did that too, because places you'd been dancing in would suddenly disappear."

One of the most traumatic casualties of the Blitz was the Café de Paris, which was bombed on the night of 8 March 1941. It was crowded with people enjoying themselves, confident that no bomb could penetrate 80 feet underground. They were wrong. Just before ten o'clock, when the dance floor was packed and every table was taken, a 50 lb land-mine came through the ceiling and blew up right in front of the rostrum where Snakehips Johnson's band was in full swing. Snakehips was killed, as were thirty-three other people, and over a hundred people were wounded. Helen Vlasto was nursing in Gosport at the time, but she heard news of the bombing:

> There was much said at the time of ghoulish grovelling among the dead and wounded by opportunists looting jewellery and evening bags by candle-light. I can just remember thinking of all those ethereal, perfectly brought up and turned out young people cut down while enjoying a romantic evening out in all their finery. There were touching announcements in the Deaths column in *The Times*: "died in all her glory" and the like.

People can adapt to anything, especially when they are young; and in the Blitz, they even managed to adapt to the threat of bombs: and to find ingenious ways to deal with their worst fears. Anne Douglas-Scott-Montagu had a horror of being disfigured by flying glass:

> I was living in lodgings in somebody's flat in Cadogan Square and I had a very long French window at the end of my bed. So for quite a long time I had an extra mattress on top of the bed,

which I'd propped up on four enormous Monarch polish tins to raise it off the floor; and I put another mattress *under* the bed and slept on that quite happily for a very long time. I wasn't, sort of, I don't think I was frightened of bombs, but I was frightened of the glass.

It is a tribute to the courage of these young women (one cannot any longer call them girls) that they overcame a lifetime's conditioning as creatures of leisure and luxury, for whom a day's hunting was hard work and a night's dancing was exhausting, and threw themselves with efficiency and zest into the real rigours of war work. As we have seen, Lady Cathleen Eliot — who could not boil an egg and would scarcely have known how to make toast without a kitchen maid to cut the bread and Nanny to hand her the toasting fork — cooked for eighty people. Elizabeth Leveson-Gower, whose uncle did not know how many rooms his house had — indeed, who hardly knew how many houses he lived in — worked as a paid laboratory technician (donating all her wages to the hospital at the end of the war). Their upbringings, which had cramped them in so many ways, forcing them into a mould in accordance with their parents'' expectations and the limited role which their class allocated to women, stood them in good stead in one respect. It gave them a clear-cut sense of duty. Armed with little more than this — no practical experience, few ordinary everyday skills, little knowledge of dealing with people outside their own kind — the former debs embarked upon war work with fervour and dedication — and delight.

It was a liberation [says one], it set me free. If it hadn't been for the war I would never have had the chance to find out what I could do — or the satisfaction of doing it. It sounds wicked to say it, but the war was a godsend to me. I never really came alive during the Season, which was a disappointment because it was something I'd wanted to do; but the war made me come alive, all right. Never looked back. I've worked all my life since then, been all over the world and met people, run my own business — I could never have done that without the war. We all lived our own lives terrifically after that.

It comes as the greatest surprise to learn that, despite this evidence that the young women of 1940 were more capable of taking on responsibility than they had ever been credited with, nevertheless the dauntless mothers of the next batch of debutantes managed to organize a Season in the first year of the war. It was not like the last Season of peace — but then, nothing ever was — but it was a Season nevertheless. Perhaps the second greatest surprise is to find Mary Churchill, Churchill's younger daughter, cropping up as one of the debs that year. In spite of the fact that her father was First Lord of the Admiralty, and she herself had been serving in the Red Cross and wvs and was about to join the ATS; in spite of all this, Mary Churchill curtseyed to the cake at Queen Charlotte's Ball that year. Esme Harmsworth (now Lady Cromer) remembers the occasion vividly:

Queen Charlotte's Ball was held in the great room at Grosvenor House as was customary. The debs, all dressed in white, processed down the stairs to curtsey to Lady Hamond-Graeme (Lady Ham n' Eggs) and the cake, then dispersing to their separate dinner-tables to dine. Just after we were all seated, a sudden hush swept through the room. Mary

Churchill rose to her feet and ran to greet her father with a hug; at the same time everyone stood, clapped and cheered: for it was the very evening that Winston Churchill became Prime Minister.

The Season was truncated, of course — though not, apparently, as much as had been expected. Esme Harmsworth again:

Menus for dinners and dances were still no problem. Strawberries were plentiful as was champagne and smoked salmon; cream was still obtainable. Restaurants still produced excellent food, if possibly with less to choose from. By 1941 there was a deterioration, much less on the menus, with ever increasing shortages as war continued. There were some charity dinner dances in London and a few small country dances as well, though nothing as large or as grand as in 1939. Nevertheless, we all wore our best ball dresses. The men, of course, looked far smarter in their "blues" than they ever did in tails. "Blues" was the evening dress for the Household Brigade. Others wore green, dark red or whatever, but they all looked splendid. There were also far more men available as partners, most being stationed in England and in training for the rigours to come, and therefore quite eager for a dance or any form of party or diversion.

After Dunkirk in June 1940, small parties continued. Dinners in private houses or restaurants would be followed by a visit to a nightclub or two ... chiefly the 400 and then the Nuthouse.

The war, which had already begun to affect the freedom allowed to young women, even altered the conditions surrounding debutantes of seventeen or eighteen emerging for their first Season:

Chaperones had become completely outdated and, from the beginning of the war, were suddenly considered unnecessary. As time went on groups became smaller, a foursome, and then just a couple, as a girl would be escorted out alone by an admirer. But there was a new limitation. Petrol was in short supply, so any mileage outside London had to be carefully worked out. Rationing came a little later: five gallons for an eight-horse-power car per month. Later in the war there was none at all for the private motorist.

Even newly emerged, seventeen- or eighteen-year-old debs were not exempt from the desire, and in due course the necessity, to do war work: "For myself, I had two jobs that year. The first was working in the canteen at the Beaver Club (which was a club for Canadian soldiers) as a washer-up; then subsequently as a filing clerk in the prisoner-of-war department at St James's Palace. The latter was vastly preferable, for washing up endless mustard pots after dancing the night away was really no cure for a hangover." Like the debs of 1939, Esme Harmsworth too is nostalgic for her youthful Season: though it must have been a strange, double life she lived, swinging between glamour and drudgery, party-going and danger, the soft lights of the dance floor and the search-lights in the skies:

We still wore long dresses on our evenings out, and sometimes just picked up our skirts and ran in our dancing shoes over broken glass to find a safer refuge like the underground ballroom at the Mayfair Hotel from the perils of the Mirabelle with its glass ceiling, while a nightingale sang in Berkeley Square and the scene was lit by searchlights. We were young and carefree and romance filled the air in spite of all the dangers. There was no seeking greater security in a squalid London tube shelter for us when the bombs fell.

But the war, when it was over, had put an end to the Season in its original form. The young women who grew up in the 1930s had tasted freedom and, while it might be tarter and stronger than champagne and strawberries, they had acquired it and could not forget it.

The post-war years of austerity and rationing changed Society, too. Once again, as had happened after the First World War, families found themselves impoverished by the deaths of their sons, the draining away of money in death duties and taxes, and the gradual decay of great houses whose upkeep many could no longer afford. Equally significant, the Labour governments further undermined the automatic link between ownership of ancestral property and the right to rule. The upper class still existed, but it was no longer a ruling class. This does not mean that its influence and patronage disappeared altogether: it had not then and it has not today. But the process, begun in the 1920s and 1930s in the aftermath of the First World War, whereby the middle class gradually infiltrated and then monopolized the formerly exclusive and controlling Establishment of the upper class, continued after the Second World War, too. This transfer of power from the landed classes to what became known as the new meritocracy meant that, in due course, the Season was little more than a fiction, a stylized aping of the past. When the monarch was no longer a source of patronage, requiring the ambitious to flock to Court to seek his favour, and the aristocracy no longer controlled other great offices, one of the main attractions to the annual gathering in London lost its magnetic pull.

Viewed from the perspective of half a century later, the last Season of peace seems remote and fantastical. Its few months could almost be likened to the jewel-encrusted minuets performed by the denizens of Versailles before the French Revolution. The debutantes of 1939 were the last to inherit a world whose extravagance and luxury were not questioned and needed no justification, a world in which the privilege they were born to was taken for granted.

Court presentations ended in 1958, Queen Charlotte's Ball in 1976 (though plans are under way for it to be revived in 1989). One hundred and seventy-two girls "came out" in 1988; but the words "debutante" and "coming out" no longer have any real meaning. These young women are not being launched into Society, for most of today's eighteen-year-olds have been enjoying a catholic and unsupervised social life since their early teens. There is still a number of girls — a small number — brought up in the country who have gone to boarding school and whose social life has been neglected. Perhaps they are too timid, or their parents too strict, to enjoy the freedom of their contemporaries, and now they need to meet young men in some socially approved forum. One gossip columnist said recently that the Season was still "a very superior dating agency"; and the shy and unsophisticated will always need a bit of a shove into the adult world.

Society — and the word no longer refers exclusively to the upper classes — barely notices the so-called debutantes of the 1980s. No great occasion marks their launching, extravagant parties have become a rarity (there was only one in 1988), and they curtsey neither to the monarch nor even to a cake. Those who do decide to marry will choose their own partners and need pay no more attention to their parents' views and ambitions on the matter than any other girl; though a title still has certain attractions. Whereas the nuances of family and lineage have lost much of their significance, snobbery will always exist. Few except the titled themselves any longer know the difference between one degree of ladyship and another. A fourteenth marchioness and the wife of a loyal Tory back-bencher rewarded with a knighthood are today much of a muchness, if the latter's accent passes scrutiny.

The obsessional curiosity and hero-worship that used to be focused upon the comings and goings of the aristocracy have all but vanished. Even in the gossip columns they now rub shoulders with stars of show business and errant sportsmen or entrepreneurs. Their sexual peccadilloes receive widespread publicity, where once they were sheltered within the bastions of their own kind. Money and celebrity now command the adulation once accorded to rank. When did the public last queue to see a Society bride emerge resplendent from St Margaret's, Westminster, or stand on chairs to catch a glimpse of some well-born beauty?

Instinctive deference to the upper classes has gone; the ability to afford retinues of servants has all but vanished, along with the desire to serve. Many of those who do still keep staff employ Portuguese, Spanish or Filipino couples. If they have English servants, these tend to be aged — sometimes in their seventies or even eighties. Nannies are usually very young girls who expect luxurious perks like a "nursery car", who may call their employers by their Christian names and who often eat with the family. Governesses are extinct.

In half a century the world that the debutantes of 1939 were brought up and brought out to expect has changed — yet *their* world has not changed beyond recognition. They have kept many links with their past, inherited both material and personal attributes from their parents. Most still live in beautiful houses lined with fine old furniture and family portraits. Beyond their walls stretch ordered English gardens edged with herbaceous borders and lawns of that particular lustre which takes decades, if not centuries, to achieve. Now in their late sixties, these women have known grief and experienced problems, but seldom poverty. Their manners remain formal, their courtesy is immaculate and kind, their voices are confident. They still support the Conservative Party, though some may have reservations about Mrs Thatcher's version, and prefer that of Macmillan, or Home, or Butler. They read *The Times* or the *Daily Telegraph,* although a few are thinking of switching to the *Independent.* They sent their children to public schools and have helped, where necessary, to ensure that their grandchildren were educated privately, too. They have learned to cook and make beds — tasks that would have been unthinkable when they were young — but few have to do these jobs daily. Most keep at least one or two staff and the great families still keep great establishments.

The world around them has changed: many believe for the better. In the 1960s when their daughters were growing up, some defied their mothers' hopes by refusing to be presented. They do not disapprove of this. Those who have granddaughters reaching adulthood in the 1980s often spoke proudly of the universities and colleges they were attending or the professions they planned to enter. Not one referred to a granddaughter who would be "coming out". The bitterest regret of many debs of 1939 is that they never went on to higher education — but they were given no choice in the matter, for a clever girl was a "blue-stocking" and who would marry her? Their strongest criticism of today's young is that they have such deplorable manners: no consideration; never write thank-you letters; no deference to their elders; don't lower their voices or their radios or give up a seat. Their greatest worry concerns the widespread use of drugs. They do not necessarily deplore the sexual freedom of today's generation. On the contrary, some expressed relief, almost envy, and more than one had come to the conclusion (based on their own or their contemporaries' experience) that virgin marriages were not a good thing.

Many became nostalgic when recalling their Season but few were sentimental. They are glad they were there, glad they had it, but realistic and hardly even regretful that the world of their parents has gone. Its gradual disappearance over the last fifty years began for them during the war — but that same war that set them free also freed the people upon whose acceptance of a lowly station in life the privileges and comfort of the upper class had depended. J.B.Priestley, in one of his immensely popular wartime broadcasts, said in 1940 that England was fighting, "not so that we can go back to anything: there's nothing that really worked that we can go back to". The aim was for "new and better homes, real homes, a decent chance at last".

The last half-century has seen — said one aristocrat, who did not wish to be quoted by name — nothing less than a social revolution.

The Second World War completely altered our way of life: we've lived very simply since then. Of course I regret it in some ways. In 1939 we lived on a magic carpet. One gave orders then — to staff, people in shops — and people carried them out, for your pleasure and comfort. Now, *we* have to try and fit in with their convenience. In those days before the war there was nothing wrong with being a playboy; it didn't matter if you enjoyed yourself and did little else. Today, one's conscience simply wouldn't allow it. Values were correct then, but standards left a lot to be desired. We had very good servants, totally loyal — yet they weren't pampered. They slept in awful conditions. I have three pairs of hands to look after me today, and they're wonderful; but they expect their own television, telephone, and they live in great comfort.

But I don't think the loss of that old Society has meant the loss of anything very valuable or important. It was very vapid, you know; arrogant and vapid. Now, there's been a levelling down. I have friends today in all walks of life — fifty years ago that would have been impossible. Today we're all classless. There's snobbery, of course; there'll always be snobbery; we're all snobs. But it used to be said that the English loved a lord; today it would be truer to say that the English love a pop star!

It is a warm summer evening. A figure in her late sixties is strolling through a garden ebullient with flowers.

Two large dogs amble after her, flopping down to pant each time she stops. She carries a pair of secateurs with which she deadheads the flowers into a trug, and she bends down occasionally to pull out a weed. A tall old copper beech and spreading cedar throw slanting shadows across the lawn. She wears soft, comfortable clothes and although her bearing is firm and upright she does look, at this moment, as though she might be talking to herself.

Across the wide lawns an old house basks in the last of the sunshine. French windows open on to a stone-flagged terrace, where a group of people sitting on scrolled cast-iron seats is gathered around a tray of drinks. Below them, a wide, shallow flight of steps leads down to the lawn. A young girl, bare-armed and bare-legged, calls out, "Shall I bring you a drink, Granny, or are you going to join us?" Her grandmother beckons, and the girl runs to her across the cool, springy grass.

"You know, Sophie, I expect you're right about us. We *were* ignorant and selfish and spoilt; we saw nothing wrong in idleness. But I tell you this. We did our trivial things in the *most* satisfactory way!"

Appendix: Slang Expressions Current in 1939

Words signifying approval

divine
grand
topping
spiffing
capital
madly
perfectly
frightfully   very
too
too-too

angel — a kind person

Glamour Boy — a good-looking or dashing young man; slightly raffish

gay — frivolous (homosexuals were called "pansies")

absurdly — very (especially as in "absurdly pretty")

chi-chi — a combination of chic and shallow and up-to-the-minute

Words signifying disapproval

tiresome
beastly
poisonous
unnecessary
sick-making

bounder — an unscrupulous man

fast — sexually daring (used only of women)

rum — odd

squify — drunk or tipsy (mild disapproval only)

tommy rot! — nonsense!

perish the thought! — heaven forbid!

beyond the bounds — unacceptable behaviour

up and downer — an argument or row

nobs — working-class word for the upper classes

plebs — upper-class word for the working classes

Expressions

keen on — sexually attracted to

to care for — be fond of

to blow in — to come in unexpectedly

to mob, or mob up — to behave wildly

to rag — fool about

I wouldn't know, I couldn't care less — indifference (these two expressions were disapproved of by the mothers, who thought them "sloppy")

blush-making — embarrassing (thus, very embarrassing — *too-too blush-making*)

in the swim — *au courant*

she could whistle a chap off a branch — she was sexy

fish! — bother!

Select Bibliography

My single greatest debt has been to Robert Kee's chronicle of the year 1939: *The World We Left Behind* (Weidenfeld & Nicolson, 1984). I wrote with it open beside me, and was also lucky in being able to consult him personally. I was very glad of his help.

I also referred constantly to the 1939 HMSO publication, *Documents Concerning Anglo-Polish Relations,* Cmd 6106, which was a further reminder of what the summer of 1939 was really about.

After these two, I relied most frequently upon A.J.P. Taylor's *English History* 1914-1945 (Oxford University Press, 1965), and upon *Who's Who* and Burke's *Peerage,* the edition of 1938 as well as more up-to-date editions.

In alphabetical order of author, I also consulted the following books:

Arts Council, *Thirties: British Art & Design Before the War* (Hayward Gallery exhibition catalogue, 1979)

Michael Astor, *Tribal Feeling* (John Murray, 1963)

Cecil Beaton, *Diaries* 1922-1939: *The Wandering Years* (Weidenfeld & Nicolson, 1961)

Lord David Cecil, *The Young Melbourne* (Constable, 1939)

Chips: The Diaries of Sir Henry Channon, ed. Robert Rhodes James (Penguin, 1970)

Peter Collier and David Horowitz, *The Kennedys: An American Drama* (Pan, 1984)

The Duchess of Devonshire, *The House: A Portrait of Chatsworth* (Macmillan, 1982)

Frances Donaldson, *Child of the Twenties* (Weidenfeld & Nicolson, 1959)
Edward VIII (Weidenfeld & Nicolson, 1974)

Nina Epton, *Love and the English* (Cassel & Co., 1960)

Flora Fraser, *The English Gentlewoman* (Barrie & Jenkins, 1987)

Jonathan Gathorne-Hardy, *The Rise and Fall of the English Nanny* (Weidenfeld & Nicolson, 1972)
The Public School Phenomenon (Penguin edn, 1979)

Christian Miller, *A Childhood in Scotland* (John Murray, 1979)

Shiela Grant Duff, The *Parting of the Ways* (Peter Owen, 1982)

Robert Graves and Alan Hodge, *The Long Weekend* (Hutchinson, 1940)

Rosina Harrison, *Rose: My Life in Service* (Cassell, 1975)

Selina Hastings, *Nancy Mitford* (Hamish Hamilton, 1985)

Christopher Hibbert, The *Court at Windsor* (Allen Lane, 1977*)*

Christopher Hollis (ed.), *Death of a Gentleman* (Burns Oates, 1943)

Roy Lewis and Angus Maude, *The English Middle* Classes (Phoenix House, 1949)

Helen Long, *Change into Uniform* (Terence Dalton, 1978)

Elizabeth Longford, *Victoria R.I.* (Weidenfeld & Nicolson, 1964)

Jessica Mitford, *Hons and Rebels* (Quartet edn, 1978)

Nancy Mitford, *Noblesse Oblige* (Hamish Hamilton, 1956)

Penelope Mortimer, *Queen Elizabeth: A Life of the Queen Mother* (Penguin/Viking, 1986)

Diana Mosley, A *Life of Contrasts* (Hamish Hamilton, 1977)

Nicholas Mosley, *Beyond the Pale* (Secker & Warburg, 1983)

Malcolm Muggeridge, *The Thirties* (Hamish Hamilton, 1940)

Priscilla Napier, *The Sword Dance* (Michael Joseph, 1971)

Harold Nicolson, *Diaries and Letters* 1930-1964 (Penguin edn, 1984)

Lady Mary Pakenham, *Brought Up and Brought Out* (Cobden-Sanderson, 1938)

H. Perkin, *The Origins of Modern English Society* (Routledge & Kegan Paul, 1969) Margaret Pringle, *Dance Little Ladies: The Days of the Debutante* (Orbis, 1977)

Philippa Pullar, *Gilded Butterflies* (Hamish Hamilton, 1978)

John Scott, *The Upper Classes: Property and Privilege in Britain* (Macmillan, 1982)

Ruth Sebag-Montefiore, *A Family Patchwork* (Weidenfeld & Nicolson, 1987)

Godfrey Smith, *The English Season* (Pavilion Books, 1987)

Philip Toynbee, *Friends Apart* (MacGibbon & Kee, 1954)

Lady Troubridge, *The Book of Etiquette* (Kingswood Press, 1987)

The Diaries of Evelyn Waugh, ed. Michael Davie (Penguin edn, 1979)

Loelia, Duchess of Westminster, *Grace and Favour* (Weidenfeld & Nicolson, 1961)

Ursula Wyndham, *Astride the Wall, A Memoir 1939-45* (Lennard Publishing, 1988)

References

Part One: The Girls from the Stately Homes of England

CHAPTER ONE: BECOMING A DEB IS A DIFFICULT MATTER
1. Conor Cruise O'Brien on Evelyn Waugh, *New York Review of Books*, 4 February 1988.
2. Nicholas Mosley, *Beyond the Pale* (Secker & Warburg, 1983), p. 151.
3. Jonathan Gathorne-Hardy, *The Rise and Fall of the English Nanny* (Weidenfeld & Nicolson, 1972), pp. 200 and 24.
4. Jessica Mitford, *Hons and Rebels* (Quartet edn, 1978), pp. 10–11.
5. *London Portrait* magazine, April 1984, Christopher Long: interview with his mother, née Helen Vlasto, a debutante in 1939.
6. H. Perkin, *The Origins of Modem English Society* (Routledge & Kegan Paul, 1969).
7. Nancy Mitford, *Noblesse Oblige* (Hamish Hamilton, 19??), p. 45.

CHAPTER TWO: I'VE BEEN TO LONDON TO LOOK AT THE QUEEN
1. *Diary of Samuel Pepys*, ed. Robert Latham and William Matthews (Bell & Hyman, 1970), vol. 3, 1662, pp. 300–1.

2. ibid., vol. 4, 4 May 1663, pp. 122–3.

3. Historical Manuscripts Commission, *Beaufort,* p. 55 quoted in Ibid., vol. 7 p. 372.

4. Jonathan Swift, *Journal to Stella* (Basil Blackwell, 1974).

5. *Selected Letters of Mary Wortley Montagu,* ed. Robert Halsband (Penguin edn, 1986), p. 66.

6. Lord Hervey, *Memoirs* (Penguin edn, 1984), pp. 4 and 7.

7. Ibid., p. 21.

8. *Correspondence of Horace Walpole* (48 vols), (Yale Univ. Press; Oxford Univ. Press).

9. Ibid.

10. Ibid.

11. Priscilla Napier, *The Sword Dance* (Michael Joseph, 1926), p. 26.

12. Ibid., p. 39.

13. *Correspondence of Horace Walpole.*

14. *Pembroke Papers 1780-94,* ed. Lord Herbert.

15. Queen Victoria's Journal, June 1937 (quoted in Elizabeth Longford, *Victoria R.I.* (Weidenfeld & Nicolson, 1964), p. 74.

16. Ibid. p. 77.

17. Ibid., 27 May 1839, p. 105.

18. Ibid., 29 May 1839, p. 116.

19. Ibid., p. 126.

20. Ibid., p. 125.

21. *The Greville Memoirs 1814-1860,* ed. Lytton Strachey and Roger Fulford.

22. *Mrs Panton: Leaves from a Life* (Eveleigh Nash, 1908).

23. *The Diary of Lady Frederick Cavendish* (John Murray, 1927), vol. I, p. 84.
24. Ibid., pp. 84–7.
25. Ibid., pp. 89–90.
26. Ibid., p. 96.
27. Ibid.
28. Lady Clodagh Anson, *Victorian Days* (The Richards Press, 1957), p. 136.
29. Ibid., p. 131.

CHAPTER THREE: THE CHILDHOOD OF THE DEBS
1. Frances Donaldson, *Child of the Twenties* (Rupert Hart-Davis, 1959), p. 71.
2. Christopher Hollis (ed.), *Death of a Gentleman* (Burns Oates, 1943), p. 188.
3. Helen Long, *Change into Uniform* (Terence Dalton, 1978), pp. 1, 10.
4. Michael Astor, *Tribal Feeling* (John Murray, 1963), p. 73.
5. Ruth Sebag-Montefiore, *A Family Patchwork* (Weidenfeld & Nicolson, 1987), p. 18.
6. John Stevenson, *British Society 1914-45* (Pelican, 1984), pp. 138, 139–40.
7. Seebohm Rowntree, "Poverty and Progress" (details of a study of poverty in York, 1935–6).
8. Herbert Tout, "The Standard of Living in Bristol" (details of a study of poverty in Bristol, 1937).
9. Flora Fraser, *The English Gentlewoman* (Barrie & Jenkins, 1987), p. 212.
10. Jonathan Gathorne-Hardy, *The Public School Phenomenon* (Hodder & Stoughton, 1977), p. 266.
11. Donaldson, *Child of the Twenties*, pp. 50–1.

12. Long, *Change into Uniform*, pp. 17–18.
13. Margaret Pringle, *Dance Little Ladies: The Days of the Debutante* (Orbis, 1977), p. 49.

CHAPTER FOUR: CHANGE YOUR PARTNER, DANCE WHILE YOU CAN
1. Lady Mary Pakenham, *Brought Up and Brought Out* (Cobden-Sanderson, 1938), p. 188.
2. Ibid.
3. *Chips: The Diaries of Sir Henry Channon*, ed. Robert Rhodes James (Penguin edn, 1970), pp. 119–20.
4. Penelope Mortimer, *Queen Elizabeth: A Life of the Queen Mother* (Penguin, 1987), p. 167.
5. *Documents Concerning German-Polish Relations*, Cmnd 6106 (HMSO, 1939), pp. 44–5, 47.
6. *The Times*, 23 June 1939.
7. *Country Life*, 24 June 1939, p. 665.

Part Two: That Unspeakable Summer

PROLOGUE
1. Harold Nicolson, *Diaries and Letters 1930-1964* (Penguin edn, 1984), p. 147.
2. Quoted in Robert Kee, The *World We Left Behind: A Chronicle of the Year 1939* (Weidenfeld & Nicolson, 1984), p. 168.
3. *Chips: The Diaries of Sir Henry Channon*, p. 239.
4. *Documents Concerning German-Polish Relations*, document 21, pp. 50–1.
5. Harold Nicolson, *Diaries and Letters 1930-1964*, pp. 149–50.

CHAPTER FIVE: THE LAST FOUR MONTHS OF PEACE: MAY
1. Kenneth Clark, "The Future of Painting", *Listener*, 2 October 1935.
2. *Country Life*, 13 May 1939, p. 495.
3. *Daily Mail*, 3 May 1939.
4. *Chips: The Diaries of Sir Henry Channon*, p. 254.
5. Loelia, Duchess of Westminster, *Grace and Favour* (Weidenfeld & Nicolson, 1961), p. 189.
6. Christian Miller, *A Childhood in Scotland* (John Murray, 1981).
7. *Daily Mail*, 19 May 1939, Charles Graves column; accompanied by a picture of the nannies.
8. Long *Change into Uniform*, p. 19.

CHAPTER SIX: THE LAST THREE MONTHS OF PEACE: JUNE
1. David Benedictus, *The Fourth of June* (Sphere edn, 1977).
2. Alan Brien, "A Peace of Paper", *Listener*, 12 May 1988, p. 6.
3. Shiela Grant Duff, *The Parting of the Ways* (Peter Owen, 1982).
4. Jessica Mitford, *Hons and Rebels*, p. 71.
5. Ibid., p. 78.
6. Ibid., p. 80.
7. Ibid., p. 143.
8. Sebag-Montefiore, *A Family Patchwork*, p. 108.
9. *The Times*, 9 June 1939.
10. Quoted in Kee, *The World We Left Behind*, p. 208.
11. Nicolson, *Diaries and Letters 1930-1964*, pp. 51-2.
12. Lord Boothby, *I Fight to Live* (Gollancz, 1947).
13. The Duchess of Devonshire, *The House: A Portrait of Chatsworth* (Macmillan, 1982), p. 60.

14. Rosina Harrison, *Rose: My Life in Service* (Cassell, 1975), p. 86.
15. *Documents Concerning German-Polish Relations,* document 25.
16. Quoted in Kee, *The World We Left Behind,* p. 238.
17. Nicolson, *Diaries and Letters 1930-1964,* p. 152.
18. Peter Collier and David Horowitz, *The Kennedys* (Pan Books, 1985), pp. 86–7.
19. Quoted in Jessica Mitford, *Hons and Rebels,* p. 188.
20. Churchill's Carlton Club speech of 28 June, quoted in Kee, *The World We Left Behind,* p.260.
21. Ibid.
22. *Chips: The Diaries of Sir Henry Channon,* p. 251.

CHAPTER SEVEN: THE LAST TWO MONTHS OF PEACE: JULY
1. *The Diaries of Evelyn Waugh,* ed. Michael Davie (Penguin edn, 1979), pp. 431–2.
2. Consuelo Vanderbilt Balsan, *The Glitter and the Gold* (Heinemann, 1955), p. 236.
3. *Chips: The Diaries of Sir Henry Channon,* p. 253.
4. Ibid.
5. Nicholas Mosley, *Beyond the Pale,* p. 153.
6. Diana Mosley, *A Life of Contrasts* (Hamish Hamilton, 1977), p. 97.
7. Jessica Mitford, *Hons and Rebels,* p. 145.
8. Ibid., p. 146.
9. Statement by the Prime Minister in the House of Commons, 10 July 1939, *Documents Concerning German-Polish Relations,* document 35 p. 76.
10. *Documents Concerning German-Polish Relations,* document 36, p. 77.
11. Ibid., p. 82.

CHAPTER EIGHT: THE LAST MONTH OF PEACE: AUGUST
1. *Chips: The Diaries of Sir Henry Channon*, pp. 255–6.
2. *Spectator*, August, 1939.
3. The Duchess of Devonshire, *The House*.
4. *Observer*, 22 May 1988.
5. Martin Gilbert, *Churchill*, vol. 2.
6. *Chips: The Diaries of Sir Henry Channon*, p. 258.

Part Three: The War: Real, Phoney and Aftermath

CHAPTER NINE: THIS COUNTRY IS AT WAR WITH GERMANY
1. Nicolson, *Diaries and Letters 1930-1964*, p. 159.
2. Long, *Change into Uniform*, pp. 15–17.
3. Diana Mosley, *A Life of Contrasts*, p. 155.

CHAPTER TEN: AN EXCELLENT INTRODUCTION FOR LIFE?
1. A.J.P. Taylor, *English History 1914-1945* (Oxford University Press, 1965), p. 437.
2. Ibid.

Index

ISIS

large print and audio books

If you have enjoyed reading this book, you will be pleased to know that many more titles are available.

We have listed a selection on the next few pages. These are available as large print books or unabridged audio books; some are available in both book and audio tape form.

Please write to us at the address below if you require further information or contact your local librarian.

Any suggestions you may have for new large print or audio titles will be very welcome.

ISIS, 55 St Thomas' Street, Oxford OX1 1JG, ENGLAND; tel. (0865) 250333

BIOGRAPHY AND AUTOBIOGRAPHY

Bill Adler	**Fred Astaire**
Charles Allen	**Plain Tales from the Raj**
Chuck Ashman & Pamela Trescott	**Cary Grant**
Hilary Bailey	**Vera Brittain**
Ronnie Barker	**It's Hello From Him**
Trevor Barnes	**Terry Waite**
Winifred Beechey	**The Rich Mrs Robinson**
Christabel Beilenberg	**The Past is Myself**
Cilla Black	**Step Inside**
Sydney Biddle Barrows	**Mayflower Madam**
Piers Brendon	**Winston Churchill** (Audio)
Peter Harry Brown	**Such Devoted Sisters: Those Fabulous Gabors**
Michael Burn	**Mary and Richard**
Patrick Campbell	**Selections from 35 Years on the Job**
Winston S Churchill	**Memories and Adventures**
Joe Collins	**A Touch of Collins**
Bill Cosby	**Time Flies**
George Courtauld	**Odd Noises from the Barn**
Mary Craig	**The Crystal Spirit: Lech Walesa and his Poland**
Peter Cushing	**An Autobiography** (Book and Audio)
Peter Cushing	**'Past Forgetting'**
Roald Dahl	**Going Solo**
Betty Davis	**This 'n' That**
C Day Lewis	**Sagittarius Rising** (Audio)
David Duff	**George and Elizabeth** (Audio)
Jerry Epstein	**Remembering Charlie**
Peter Evans	**Ari: The Life and Times of Aristotle Socrates Onassis**

BIOGRAPHY AND AUTOBIOGRAPHY

Diana Farr	**Five at 10: Prime Ministers' Consorts Since 1957**
David Fingleton	**Kiri**
Angela Fox	**Slightly Foxed**
Michael Freeland	**A Salute to Irving Berlin**
Joyce Fussey	**Cats in the Coffee**
Joyce Fussey	**Cows in the Corn**
Joyce Fussey	**'Milk My Ewes and Weep'**
Eve Garnett	**First Affections**
Ralph Glasser	**Growing Up in the Gorbals** (Audio)
Jon Godden & Rumer Godden	**Two under the Indian Sun**
Joyce Grenfell	**Darling Ma**
Unity Hall	**Philip**
Helen Hayes	**Loving Life**
Bob Hope	**Confessions of a Hooker**
Graham Jenkins	**Richard Burton, My Brother**
Penny Junor	**Charles**
Imran Kahn	**All Round View**
Roger Kahn	**Joe and Marilyn**
Julia Keay	**The Spy Who Never Was**
Laurie Lee	**As I Walked Out One Midsummer Morning** (Audio)
Laurie Lee	**Cider with Rosie** (Audio)

BIOGRAPHY AND AUTOBIOGRAPHY

Laurie Lee	**I Can't Stay Long** (Audio)
Maureen Lipman	**How Was it for You?**
Vincent V Loomis	**Amelia Earhart**
Suzanne Lowry	**Cult of Diana**
Ralph G Martin	**Charles & Diana**
John McCabe	**Mr Laurel and Mr Hardy**
Jeanine McMullen	**Wind in the Ash Tree**
Peter Medawar	**Memoir of a Thinking Radish**
Spike Milligan	**Adolf Hitler: My Part in His Downfall** (Book and Audio)
Spike Milligan	**Mussolini: His Part in My Downfall** (Audio)
Spike Milligan	**Rommel? Gunner Who?** and **Monty: His Part in My Victory** (Audio)
Spike Milligan	**Where Have All the Bullets Gone?** (Audio)
Eugene McCarthy	**Up 'Til Now**
Ray Moore	**Tomorrow is Too Late**
Joe Morella & Edward Z Epstein	**Forever Lucy**
Joe Morella & Edward Z Epstein	**Loretta Young**
Eric Newby	**Love and War in the Apennines** (Book and Audio)
Eric Newby	**Something Wholesale**
Christopher Nolan	**Under the Eye of the Clock** (Book and Audio)
Barry Norman	**The Hollywood Greats**

BIOGRAPHY AND AUTOBIOGRAPHY

Spero Pastos	**Pin-Up**
Carol Lynn Pearson	**Good-bye, I Love You**
Gerald Priestland	**The Unquiet Suitcase**
Siegfried Sassoon	**Memoirs of an Infantry Officer**
Ingrid Seward	**Diana**
Dolly Shepherd	**When the 'Chute Went up**
Isaac Bashevis Singer	**Love and Exile**
John Smith	**The Benny Hill Story**
Daniel Snowman	**The World of Placido Domingo**
Freya Stark	**Dust in the Lion's Paw** (Audio)
Norman Tebbit	**Upwardly Mobile**
Roger Vadim	**Bardot, Deneuve and Fonda**
John Van der Kiste	**Queen Victoria's Children**
Alexander Walker	**Vivien**
Robert Westall	**Children of the Blitz**
Terry Wogan	**Wogan on Wogan**
Ian Woodward	**Glenda Jackson**

SHORT STORIES AND ESSAYS

	Echoes of Laughter
Jorges Louis Borges	**The Book of Sand**
Angela Carter	**Fireworks**
Joseph Conrad	**The Heart of Darkness** (Audio)
A E Coppard	**Selected Stories**
Roald Dahl	**Roald Dahl's Book of Ghost Stories**
Roald Dahl	**Kiss Kiss**
M F K Fisher	**Sister Age**
E M Forster	**The New Collected Short Stories** (Audio)
Jane Gardam	**The Sidmouth Letters**
Leon Garfield	**Shakespeare Stories**
Mrs Gaskell	**Four Short Stories**
William Golding	**The Hot Gates**
Thomas Hardy	**Wessex Tales**
Duff Hart-Davis	**Country Matters**
Henry James	**Daisy Miller**
M R James	**A Warning to the Curious** (Book and Audio)
Bernard Levin	**The Way We Live Now**
Barry Pain	**The Eliza Stories**
Robert J Randisi (editor)	**An Eye for Justice**
Saki	**Beasts and Superbeasts**
E OE Somerville & Martin Ross	**Further Experiences of an Irish RM**
E OE Somerville & Martin Ross	**In Mr Knox's Country**
Edmund Wilson	**Memoirs of Hecate County**
Marguerite Yourcenar	**Oriental Tales**

POETRY AND DRAMA

Lord Birkenhead
   (editor)   **John Betjeman's Early Poems**

Joan Duce   **I Remember, I Remember...**
                          (Book and Audio)

Joan Duce   **Remember, If you will...**

Robert Louis Stevenson **A Child's Garden of Verses**

Leon Garfield   **Shakespeare Stories**

Dan Sutherland   **Six Miniatures**

Andrew Young   **A Prospect of Flowers**

MEDICAL AND SELF HELP

	Longman Medical Dictionary
Christiaan Barnard	**Your Healthy Heart**
William H Bates	**Better Eyesight without Glasses**
Pat Blair	**Know Your Medicines**
Dr Robert Buckman	**I Don't Know What to Say**
Robert N Butler & Myrna I Butler	**Love and Sex After 40**
Margaret Ford	**'In Touch' at Home**
Margaret Hills	**Curing Arthritis**
Tony Lake	**Loneliness: Why it Happens and How To Overcome It**
Tony Lake	**Living with Grief**
Letts Retirement Guides	**Good Health**
Dr Patrick Mckeon	**Coping with Depression and Elation**
Dr Brice Pitt	**Making the Most of Middle Age**
Dr Tom Smith	**Living With High Blood Pressure**
Elaine Stritch	**Am I Blue? Living with Diabetes, and, Dammit, Having Fun**
George Target	**Your Arthritic Hip and You**
Dr Peter Tyrer	**How to Sleep Better**
Lynn Underwood	**One's Company**
Claire Weekes	**More Help for Your Nerves**
Betty Jane Wylie	**Beginnings**
Dr R M Youngson	**Stroke!**

INSPIRATIONAL

Rabbi Lionel Blue	**Kitchen Blues**
Victor Gollancz & Barbara Greene	**God of a Hundred Names**
Christopher Idle	**Famous Hymns and Their Stories**
Christopher Nolan	**Under the Eye of the Clock**
Beverley Parkin	**Say it With Flowers**
Beverley Parkin	**Flowers with Love**
Harry Secombe	**Highway**
	Your Favourite Songs of Praise

POETRY

Lord Birkenhead (editor)	**John Betjeman's Early Poems**
Joan Duce	**I Remember, I Remember...** (Book and Audio)
Joan Duce	**Remember, If You Will...**
Robert Louis Stevenson	**A Child's Garden of Verses**